THE MORAL DIGNITY OF MAN

The
Moral Dignity of Man

An exposition of Catholic moral doctrine with
particular reference to family and medical ethics
in the light of contemporary developments

PETER E. BRISTOW

FOUR COURTS PRESS

This book was typeset by
Koinonia Ltd, Manchester
in 11 on 13 point Times for
FOUR COURTS PRESS
55 Prussia Street, Dublin 7, Ireland
e-mail: fcp@ indigo.ie
and in North America for
FOUR COURTS PRESS
c/o ISBS, 5804 N.E. Hassalo Street, Portland, OR 97213.

First edition 1993
Second edition 1997

A catalogue record for this title
is available from the British Library.

ISBN 1-85182-176-7

Nihil obstat: Stephen J. Greene, censor deputatus
Imprimi potest: Desmond, Archbishop of Dublin
28 May 1996

Printed in Ireland
by ColourBooks Ltd, Dublin

Contents

To my father with gratitude

Preface to the Second Edition

Since this book was first published, two encyclicals, *Veritatis splendor* and *Evangelium vitae*, which cover similar ground, have come out. The first, dealing with the general principles of morals based on the dignity of man, runs parallel to my early chapters; the second has to do with specific matters relating to the rights and duties of life and other questions of medical ethics. Without changing the basic text or structure of the book in any way, I have incorporated relevant references and quotations from these documents and indeed also from the *Catechism of the Catholic Church*.

Veritatis splendor is concerned with the separation between freedom and truth, that is, the truth about the dignity of man, his freedom and rights, natural law, conscience etc. *Evangelium vitae* continues that theme, dealing at some length with the way in which freedom, as understood in western consumer societies, tramples upon fundamental human rights and specifically the right to life of the weakest and most vulnerable, such as the unborn, the handicapped, the terminally ill and the elderly. A State which fails to guarantee equality of rights to all groups cannot be called democratic even if laws, such as those on abortion and embryo research, are passed and favoured by a majority of the citizens. In this sense, we are witnessing nothing less than the struggle of a 'culture of death' against a 'culture of life', and the Pope emphasizes that Christians are obliged to be 'people of life and for life'.

Not only have actions against life ceased to be a crime, but now they are being claimed as 'rights' to be supported by laws of the State. But no majority vote can justify a law which contradicts the eternal laws and the basic rights of some of its members. The fact, furthermore, that some citizens may request euthanasia, for example, lends no justification to it. They are stewards of a life that belongs in its fullness to God, who alone, therefore, has ultimate authority over it. Were the State to give euthanasia legal recognition, it would be lending its authority to a situation of suicide-murder.

The underlying reason for all these developments is the ethical relativism

which permeates western culture. Where absolute principles and values are
lacking, the rights and laws of society become bargaining points between
different parties based largely on self-interest. In such a situation, it is
obvious that the interests of the strong and powerful will prevail against
those of the weak and innocent. It is to this state of affairs that the Church
wishes to draw attention and feels obliged to make her voice heard.[i]

The reasons all this has come about are to be found in the materialism
and hedonism of modern consumer society, past false ideologies about man
and freedom etc. and present-day pressure groups which strive to implement them. This book, as well as addressing similar topics to the encyclicals, also deals with the background and influences which have led to the
present situation.

---

1. On p. 201 below, bibliographical details are given of the main Church documents
referred to in the text.

Introduction

The Second Vatican Council described its purpose very appropriately when it said 'beneath all that changes there is much that is unchanging, much that has its ultimate foundation in Christ . . . that is why the Council proposes to speak to all men in order to unfold the mystery that is man and cooperate in tackling the main problems facing the world today' (*Gaudium et spes*, 1). I, likewise, have sought here to apply the immutable principles of Catholic morality to our evolving times and particularly to the family and sexual matters, on the one hand, and to questions of medical practice on the other. But it was not possible to deal adequately with these issues without first establishing the general principles of moral theology and ethics, which are, in any case, at the eye of the contemporary storm. Hence, consideration has been given initially to the meaning of the human person and his or her rights on which morals turn, to the natural law and conscience, and to a brief historical account of the 'permissive' background to our own times.

A Christian's moral life is not lived in isolation but in the midst of society, so there will always be significant areas where he or she must confront the predominant secular fashions, or conventional morality, in order to spread light and to be a leaven. It is quite insufficient to accept the social moral ethos wholly uncritically. Morals is, above all, about the personal responsibility and accountability for actions which come from a person's grasp of the basic notions of good and evil and the consequences they entail. But, given the sketchiness of this knowledge, this responsibility cannot be properly discharged without adequate and constant formation in which the role of the Church is paramount.

The Church is the guardian and authentic interpreter of the Faith and of a natural morality which is based upon a full understanding of the human person and finds its confirmation in Holy Scripture. Vatican II reiterates the Church's responsibility in the following terms: 'It is her duty to proclaim and teach with authority the truth which is Christ and, at the same time, to declare and confirm by her authority the principles of the moral order which spring from human nature itself' (*Dignitatis humanae*, 14). The unique

7

dignity of the human being takes its origin from the fact that he, or she, is the 'image of God' and is called to the happiness of eternal life. As a being, furthermore, equipped with rationality and freedom, the human person is a subject of rights and duties from which flow the norms and values of the moral order. The latter mark out the path to the fulfilment and perfection of the human vocation. But, equally, all violations of the dignity of the human person are an offence, not only against the individual, but against the Creator himself. This is particularly true of all violations of the fundamental right of man, that is, the right to life itself, and, with it, the right to bodily integrity.

Again the Council speaks as follows: 'Special care should be given to the perfecting of moral theology. Its scientific presentation should draw more fully on the teaching of Holy Scripture and should throw light upon the exalted vocation of the faithful in Christ and their obligation to bring forth fruit in charity for the life of the world' (*Optatum totius*, 16). The Bible speaks to us eloquently, not only about the vocation of the individual, but also about what we may call his or her family vocation, underlining how the sacrament of marriage and family life are central to the vocation of the majority of men and women. Right from the beginning, male and female were destined to live not alone, but in a communion of persons, and the family which thus resulted was, by divine design, to form the first and most basic cell of society. This reality was raised by Christ to the sacramental level and was given the august ideal of mirroring the love and union of Christ with his Church and the communion of Persons which is the Trinity itself.

The renewal of man's moral dignity, therefore, is closely related to the renewal of family life and to a greater awareness of its human and divine origins, in the face of considerable pressure to the contrary. The family is the 'domestic church' and parents are the first educators of the moral life of their children, so it is there that the seeds of virtue are first sown and nourished. As the Pope has written (*Familiaris consortio*, 3), the Church is aware that 'the well-being of society and her own good are intimately tied to the good of the family'. It is for this reason that a right understanding of human sexuality, marriage and family life (so crucial to mankind at the present moment) is the principal focus of this book, together with questions concerning human life and bodily integrity.

Secular and liberal humanism, which pays little or no attention to man's transcendent vocation to eternal life and tends to make moral norms and values relative, has been confronting the Church, in one shape or form, since the Enlightenment of the eighteenth century. Not until this century did it begin to spread to the masses of the people, as a result of wider access to education etc., and thus present a real threat to Christian values. This problem was solved by some after Vatican II by bringing secular morality into the Church herself, uncritically, rather than by endeavouring to lead the world to genuinely Christian principles.

One of the consequences of this attitude of easy compromise is that the fullness of Catholic moral teaching has frequently not been imparted; ignorance is rife among younger generations and confusion widespread among their elders. The Christian moral ethos has been seriously undermined, and very often its principles have become, at best, a matter of debate. Pope John Paul II's response to this predicament is to explain Christian teaching with greater depth and vigour so that it can be appreciated anew and become an important part of his policy of re-christianization. Christianity is centered on the Resurrection, and the Church herself rises from each crisis newly enriched. Her members have always understood the need to be well equipped to defend the truth entrusted to her against hostile currents, but it must be admitted that, in the past, apologetics has been associated primarily with defending the Faith and only secondarily with morals. Today, the rational defence of the latter, though always dependent on faith, is of the utmost importance.

The challenge facing the Church and society should not be under-estimated. During this century, certain ideologies of social engineering and conditioning—originally promoted by a few writers and propagandists—have gradually come to be accepted by a majority of the population. A particular attitude to human sexuality has, and is, being used as a means of social control, through abortion and contraceptive practice, as well as *in vitro* fertilization and embryo research. Some results of this are the destabilizing of the nuclear family, extensive permissive behaviour and the threat of genetic manipulation which already exists in the form of selective abortion.

The social revolution has been accompanied by a technological one in matters to do with human life. The discovery of DNA in 1953 has opened up our knowledge of human genetics and led to the diagnosis of certain hereditary diseases and the development of genetic therapy to treat them. The technique of *in vitro* fertilization, first carried out in 1978, and the activities associated with it, such as the cloning of embryos, surrogate motherhood, and the sex determination of the child, are matters requiring moral judgement. Moreover, the *Human Genome Project* (a coordinated world-wide enterprise to trace all the genes of the human cell and study their bearing on human personality) has enormous moral implications.

However, the principal purpose of Christian moral teaching is not simply the apologetic one of defending it against secular currents. Morality is concerned with giving guidance and presenting an ideal to imperfect human beings. It may be described generically as the norms and values governing the behaviour of man in his present state, striving to be what he ought to become, according to his true end in God. Consequently, it is intimately tied to a proper understanding of the human person and his unique dignity. John Paul II has written: 'To rediscover and make others rediscover the inviolable dignity of every human person is an essential task, in a certain sense, the central and unifying task, of the service which the Church, and the lay faithful in her, are called to render to the human family' (*Christifideles laici*, 37). It is concerned, above all today, with threats to the human person and human life itself, and the domination of human life by advancing technology. Christian teaching seeks to harness the latter in such a way that it be for the good of man and not for his doom. But the Church's teaching is also about man attaining his true end and happiness in the blessedness of Heaven. Morality properly lived should lead to contentment and fulfilment in this life, but can only reach its full realization in the next one.

Our standpoint, then, is the Christian one that a normative science cannot be developed without a teleological understanding of the human being and his or her actions. Take sexuality itself, which is based on the masculinity and femininity of the human being: these characteristics are not accidental but pertain to the nature of the human person and will endure after the resurrection of the body. Then, the earthly purpose of sexuality, that is, procreation, will have ceased, but the male/female sexual difference will remain and will be a feature of the human being's praise and glory of God. Consequently, a consideration of the purpose of human sexuality tells us that it is not something to be used at will. It should be employed according to its true finality in conformity with the dignity of the human person; and as with sexuality, so with human behaviour as a whole.

The temporal and eternal consequences of man's behaviour, whether of human virtue or wickedness, are amply described both in the Old and New Testaments. Shortly before the Israelites entered the Promised Land, Moses spoke to them for the last time, reminding them of the Commandments and observances of the Law. He said: 'See, I set before you this day life and good, death and evil. If you obey the commandments of the Lord . . . , then you shall live and multiply, and the Lord your God will bless you in the land you are entering to take possession of it . . . ; therefore choose life' (Deut 30:15-16, 19). St Paul went on to echo the same idea when he wrote to the Romans: 'there will be tribulation and distress for every human being who does evil, the Jew first and also the Greek, but glory and honour and peace for everyone who does good, the Jew first and also the Greek' (Rom 2:9-11).

This book arose as a response to the challenge issued by Pope John Paul II in his homily at Wembley, London, in 1982 when, after referring to the decline in fundamental moral values, he concluded: 'Underlying all this there is often a false concept of man and his unique dignity. . .'.[1] These words can be taken together with others from *Gaudium et spes*, 41, which point out that 'the Church is entrusted with the task of opening up to man, the mystery of God who is the last end of man'. Getting morals right includes getting man himself right, and this is given a sure answer in Christ, who 'reveals man to himself' (*Gaudium et spes*, 22).

Much of the material had its origin in the author's talks and discussions with students in London, especially at Netherhall House, and also with the Catholic Doctors of Southwark on the prominent ethical issues of the 1980s. To all of them, a debt of gratitude is owed. Apart from medical ethics, there was the continuing task of explaining *Humanae vitae* in line with the Pope's appeal to theologians 'to illustrate ever more clearly the biblical foundations, the ethical grounds and the personalistic reasons behind this doctrine' (*Familiaris consortio*, 31).

Special thanks are due to the Revd Dr John Berry of the Linacre Centre, who read the whole manuscript and made many valuable suggestions. Gratitude also to the many who read parts of it and made their contributions. The last chapter began as a paper at an environment conference and first appeared in print in *Scepter Bulletin*, London; I am grateful to the editor for permission to reprint it.

1. *The Pope in Britain*, CTS, London, 1982.

PART I

The Insufficiency of Today's Morality

Today, Christian morality is challenged in various ways, but especially by the twin forces of permissiveness and the anti-life mentality. The permissive attitude summarily sets aside fundamental norms and values which in the past have been almost universally accepted, including the inviolable value of human life itself. This mentality has been growing for decades and has its roots much further back, but things have come to something of a head with permissive trends being enshrined in legislative systems, supported by State benefits, furthered by the mass media and, in general, becoming part of the ethos of our western society.

The moral debate about human life issues covers a host of matters—both old ones known to our ancestors, such as contraception, sterilization, abortion and euthanasia, and wholly new ones resulting from the scientific progress of recent decades, such as *in vitro* fertilization, embryo research, genetic therapy and engineering, and the related field of eugenics. All are agreed that moral guidelines are necessary—that we should not necessarily do all that technology permits, nor should science alone dictate the norms in matters so intimately concerned with human life. However, the fragmentary and conflictive nature of the ethical response underlines the present state of morals and does not augur well for the interests of man himself.

The consequence is that the family unit, and hence the social and moral fabric of society, as well as weak and innocent life, whether of the unborn, the handicapped or the aged, are under grave threat. It is, indeed, a paradox that a society which has developed a reputation for defending fundamental human rights should in a subtle way overthrow the rights of some of its weakest members. Behind this lies a utilitarian philosophy which calculates that some lives will be useful and others won't, some will be capable of reaching a minimum level of happiness and others not, etc. And where permissivism is concerned, it is prepared to use the human body as an instrument of pleasure rather than as a means of self-giving and commitment to a spouse and family. The permissive preoccupation with pleasure and the satisfaction of desires has led, among other things, to alcohol and drug abuse and addiction which afflict an increasing number of the West's population, especially young people.

There are a number of factors at work here. A dominant one is the wave of permissive legislation that has spread through western countries in recent decades. Spearheading this, in Britain, was the legalization of abortion in 1967 and the introduction of no-fault divorce two years later, making the termination of marriage a much easier and quicker process. In the period since then, legal backing has been given for the distribution of contraceptives to girls under 16 years old *without* their parents' consent and (in 1990) for research and experimentation on human embryos. It is argued that personal morality is not primarily a matter for the law and that, where possible, the two should be kept apart. It was further contended, at the time, that such legislation was simply permitting, in an ordered fashion, what was already happening and was thereby protecting the lives of mothers who attempted back-street abortions or assisting marriages that had already broken down. But, in fact, the numbers of abortions and divorces have multiplied many times over since the laws were enacted; promiscuity has increased enormously among the young, leading to the now widespread phenomenon of living together; and homosexuality has actually been promoted in some places.

The argument that the State has no business enforcing personal morality fails to take account of the fact that the law has a pedagogical value, especially for the man in the street who is guided in his morality by it. Furthermore, man is weak and needs the support of his peers and society to live up to his moral ideals. Besides, the State is responsible for the 'common good' of society and must, therefore, provide the sum total of means available to help people to fulfil their all-round well-being, which includes their moral good. This means upholding by law all basic human values and rights. While there is a distinction between law and morality, there is also a connection, in that law must be guided by morality.

Behind the exaggerated separation of these two realities there is a deeper reason, namely, the lack of a common or shared morality. A society is only as good as its members. The conventional wisdom tells us that each member of society must be allowed to pursue the behaviour and activity he thinks best, without restriction on his freedom from civil law and provided his activity does not inhibit the freedom and rights of others. There is, however, here no notion of a moral truth to which all human behaviour is subject; hence, ethics becomes totally relative. The result is that it is very difficult in the atmosphere of the times to say that anything is absolutely good or bad. Goodness simply becomes relative to your choices and impossible to define.

G.E. Moore called it 'a non-natural indefinable quality'.[1] It has to be assessed and re-assessed according to changing circumstances. The true good of the human person is thus obscured.

SECULAR MORALITY

The rationale of permissivism and anti-life practices has only become possible as a result of a moral tradition that is antithetical to Christian ethics. This is why it is necessary to understand some of the background and assumptions of that thinking. The secular liberal tradition does not admit that there is a universal morality for all mankind, or a common end; instead, there is a variety of overlapping moral values based on choice. That is to say, according to this view no system is capable of giving objective moral truth. While some liberals say that such a thing is not possible, others maintain that one system complements another and together they contribute to the building up of moral truth.

The most influential moral philosophies within secular liberalism which characterize our age are 'autonomous morality' and utilitarianism. The former is a typical product of the Enlightenment which was originally intended to be an ethic that depended on reason alone and not on authority or Revelation. In Kant—one of its main exponents—it also meant a reason considered independently of empirical experience and thus universally applicable to all mankind. But it came to mean reason independent of an external moral law; and so, instead of reflecting this law, reason becomes the creator of it. Morals, rather than being what the law dictates to each one, become what each one dictates to himself. The result is that ethics become subjective and relative and unable to furnish man with any absolute and universal norms. Perhaps here we can see the origin of the fact that today duties and rights are frequently decided autonomously by the individual and yield such gratuitous statements and claims as 'a woman has a right to choose'; 'my body is my own to do with as I wish', 'homosexual rights' and so on.

Utilitarianism is the doctrine which identifies good and bad actions by the degree of benefit or harm accruing from them, whether for individuals, groups or society in general. Since it is also hedonist, by 'benefit' it understands happiness or pleasure and even material pleasure, although this latter point is disputed in the different versions of it. Nevertheless, it can be said that the name derives from the usefulness of actions to produce pleasure and

1. *Principia Ethica*, Cambridge, 1903.

avoid pain, and thus maximize the happiness of human beings, following the famous dictum of 'the greatest happiness of the greatest number'. There are many difficulties with the theory of utilitarianism, even for its adherents, which I shall refer to later on, but its influence on private and public morality in this century is indisputable.

The manner in which situation ethics and utilitarianism form the background to our time is well brought out by the Warnock Report's characterization of morality: 'Moral questions, such as those with which we have been concerned here are, by definition, questions not only that involve a calculation of consequences, but also strong sentiments with regard to the nature of the proposed activities themselves.'[2] By 'calculation of consequences' is meant a calculation of benefits over harm which is a development of the utilitarian principle. 'Strong sentiments' on the other hand, refers to emotive arguments and subjective feelings about moral questions. On these premises there can be no absolute moral laws, such as, for instance, 'It is always wrong to take innocent human life' or 'It is always wrong to commit adultery,' such as Christianity has always defended.

This view has also supplanted one of the longest held and most sacrosanct traditions within the medical field, namely, the Hippocratic Oath. The 1948 Declaration of Geneva demanded of doctors the following commitment: 'I will maintain the utmost respect for human life from the time of *conception*'; in October 1983 the Assembly of the World Medical Association changed the Declaration to read: 'I will maintain the utmost respect for human life from the time of *commencement*' (my italics). It has been argued that 'precisely when and where life begins is an open question, because embryos are not only being aborted, they are also being grown *in vitro* . . .'.[3] This revision is a clear indication of a fundamental shifting of the moral ground.

In specific statistical terms, permissive morality and anti-life policies have given us the following situation. In England, illegitimate births now account for a quarter of all children born, and 18% of all conceptions are terminated by abortion. While 10% of all marriages end in divorce, today there are 43% as many divorces as there are marriages contracted in any one year.[4] One consequence of this is that a quarter of all children live with one parent only at some time before they are sixteen. In the United States this figure has reached 50%. Some children are conceived *in vitro* in a laboratory, and there is legal backing in England for experimentation on human embryos up to

2. *The Warnock Report on Human Fertilization and Embryology*, London, 1983.
3. *The Lancet*, 10 December 1983.
4. *Social Trends*, HMSO, London, 1990.

14 days followed by mandatory destruction if they are not inserted into the womb.

It goes without saying that all of this is contrary to the Christian and natural law concepts of the sanctity and dignity of each human life, the fundamental equality of each individual, the sanctity of family life and the inviolability of the matrimonial bond. While it is true that society cannot change unless the individual changes, it is not just a matter of individual morality but of social morality as well, and a matter for serious reflection on the part of the community of mankind.

And yet, from another angle, nobody who seriously considers these matters really wants to do away altogether with absolute moral principles, because it is certainly not in the interests of man to do so. Who doesn't want to say that the extermination of the Jews and the handicapped in the Nazi concentration camps was *absolutely* evil? Who doesn't want to say the same about child abuse? And yet for those who subscribe to a relativist morality or situation ethics this *cannot* be said on their premises—which points to a contradiction at the very heart of their position.

Furthermore, both permissive ethics and the anti-life mentality rest on a false notion of man and his true purpose and happiness. So, for example, permissivism is based on a partial, and therefore incorrect, concept of human freedom. It tends to regard freedom as the unrestricted exercise of one's self-interest and the satisfaction of one's desires limited only by the proviso that it doesn't infringe the same freedom in others. This derives from old-fashioned liberalism with its 'live and let live' mentality, and the ever-present utilitarianism which sees man's good in terms of what is most pleasurable. It is thus a recipe for licence rather than true liberty and tends to lead to further enslavement as is shown, for example, by the unrestricted use of drugs or alcohol or sexuality.

The Catholic Church, however, points out that freedom is subject to the full truth about man and an important part of that is that 'man fulfils himself by a sincere gift of himself' (*Gaudium et spes*, 24). Consequently, when he conceives his life in terms of service to others and realises the altruistic nature of his vocation, he is closer to true freedom. It may be noted here that the massively influential Freudian theory of the libido, which insists on sexual gratification if repression is to be avoided, assumes an understanding of man that is more or less the opposite of the Christian one. The restrictions of the moral law facilitate rather than limit his freedom, liberating him from his own selfishness. Hence, true liberty is in many ways opposed to the satisfaction of one's own desires and to the pursuit of self-interest.

THE QUALITY-OF-LIFE MENTALITY

During most of this century, a quiet revolution has been taking place centered on the question of human life and man's control over it. The inherited philosophies of autonomous morality and utilitarianism have been translated into the practical politics and pressure groups of the twentieth century and have given society a concern for what is called the quality of life at the expense of the sanctity of life. The original motivation of the family planning campaign was to liberate the lower classes of society from oppression and squalor, but this had changed by the sixties to a concern for a worthwhile and useful life for all. There are different reasons behind the contraceptive and anti-life arguments. Some want to increase the so-called 'quality of life' by raising the standard of living and eliminating handicap and inherited disease as far as possible; others dwell on population fears; while still others want to promote women's right to choose. In all of them we can detect a tendency to treat man for his 'usefulness' rather than according to his intrinsic value.

The predominance of quality-of-life arguments and their hold over the population has not come about altogether by accident. They have been skilfully advanced in Britain by bodies such as the Eugenics Society (founded 1913), the Family Planning Association (previously the Birth Control Association, founded 1920), and the Abortion Law Reform Association (founded 1935). Their overwhelming success, however, has come mainly since the sixties with the legislation that has put many of their objectives on the statute book. The above-mentioned bodies have achieved their aims, by skilful use of the media and moulding public opinion, by feeding on the philosophical vacuum inherited from the last century, by an incoherent anthropology and, above all, perhaps by the 'medicalization' of their campaign.

The eugenic preoccupation with the health and well-being, not only of the individual, but also of the race and society, is a feature of this century. Eugenics played a predominant part in the early birth control campaign, only to be discredited in the popular mind by the Nazi experiments in pursuit of the super-race. Nevertheless, the Eugenics Society in Great Britain never ceased to exist, and the emphasis was switched from positive to negative eugenics, that is to say, to the elimination of genetic handicap, abnormality and disease. Social considerations have entered into the notion of health, as is demonstrated by the World Health Organization's definition of it as 'a state of complete physical, mental and social well-being'. The proponents of the abortion law in Britain insisted, successfully, that it be allowed not simply for therapeutic but also for social reasons. The majority of abortions have always been done on these latter grounds, giving us, in practice, a *de facto* situation of abortion on demand. Such is the reverence which the conventional wisdom reserves for the quality of life, and the scant regard in which it holds its sanctity and inviolability, that foetal screening is routinely used for the detection of abnormality, and selective abortion is recommended should abnormality be found, as it is also sometimes at the initiation of *in vitro* fertilization. Apart from ideological reasons, this is often due to the gynaecologist's fear of legal action against him should a pregnancy not reach normal term and the cost-benefit justification of technological intervention. It is also reported that abortions are carried out for such minor conditions as cleft palate, which can be treated by performing a fairly routine operation on the child while it is still in the womb.[5]

The advance of medicine and people's belief in its effectiveness to alleviate suffering and improve the quality of our life has given rise to what has been called the 'medicalization' of life. Margaret Sanger, the first birth control campaigner in America, had already realized that winning over doctors to her side would give respectability and plausibility to what was a controversial matter. An important element in the achievement of the family planning campaign goals, therefore, has been the medicalization of their case. Hence, its proponents succeeded in arguing that contraception was a health need, and as early as 1966 the Ministry of Health in Britain was saying that family planning education was 'a most important part of health education'. The campaigners gradually brought round to their viewpoint the representative bodies, such as the British Medical Association, the General Medical Council and the Royal Colleges, which were anti-birth control until well into the century. By 1969, the Family Planning Association had trained 90% of general practitioners in contraceptive techniques, which they were soon to be paid to put into practice.

There is a clear link between the campaign for family planning and permissive morality. The trend in the 1960s moved away from linking contraception with the downtrodden and hard-worked wife to winning over young couples in order to 'protect future generations'. Sex education in schools was seen as vital, and family planning and the quality of life were at the heart of it. By 1973 the subjects of population, sex education and environmental studies were increasingly being included in the syllabus of schools and adult education centres.[6] Hence, today's children are taught

5. *Sunday Times*, 4 February 1990.
6. Cf. Audrey Leathard, *The Fight for Family Planning*, London, 1980, p. 155.

about parenthood as human biology and reproductive science in a wholly
amoral way without taking account of the full spiritual reality of man, the
natural law, or the fidelity and commitment of married life. When sexuality
is disconnected from the responsibility of personal love within a life-long
commitment of marriage, the door is open to widespread permissiveness,
because it empties sexuality both of its finality and its sacred character.
What is more, by putting sex educaiion in the hands of schools and the
State, it takes it away from the parents and family to whom it properly
belongs.

It is by such means that the autonomous morality and utilitarianism of a
past age have turned into the permissiveness and anti-life mentality of our
own time. What could be more indicative of autonomous morality than the
notion of an 'unwanted pregnancy'! And one of the founders of utilitarianism, J.S. Mill, in his essay *On Liberty* in 1859, wrote that 'to bestow a life
which may be either a curse or a blessing, unless the being on whom it is to
be bestowed will have at least the ordinary chances of a desirable existence,
is a crime against that being.' The Church's tradition of natural law morality
mixes with these relativist ethical traditions like oil and water. The all-
pervasiveness of the latter also makes the comprehension of the former
even more difficult to grasp.

Those who have carried out the quality-of-life revolution believe that it
has widened personal freedom and individual choice. Their critics point out
that it eliminates the freedom of the unborn, the handicapped and, increasingly, the aged, to the most fundamental of all rights, that of life. It is true
that the standard of living and the quality of life of the majority of men and
women have increased immeasurably in comparison with previous centuries,
but what is an advance for some is a sentence of death for others; and this is
unacceptable. It has rightly been called 'social Darwinism'—a type of civil
survival of the fittest.

The Church is in no way against increasing the quality of our life or
scientific progress, as long as these are in conformity with moral norms and
man's dignity. But it defies logic to turn quality of life and technological
advance into moral principles, branding those who oppose them reaction-
ary and unenlightened. The Church does not put forward absolute, immutable moral values simply because they are traditional but because they
correspond to the unchangeable truth about man and his true interests.
When screening and selective abortion become so widespread, and with
such things as sex-determination of infants and cloning the embryo to
produce twins not far away, if there are no moral restrictions and guidelines,
it is only a short step to babies made to order. When babies are seen as

artefacts, they will inevitably be routinely eliminated if they don't measure up to expectations.

Such a situation was conceivable in the early part of the century only in the intellectual imagination of the devotees of a 'Brave New World'. Even the early birth control campaigners were against sterilization and abortion. And yet we can see in the birth control movement and the contraceptive mentality the parent principle of most, if not all, of the anti-life practices we now experience. In response the Church maintains that the right to life, the procreative finality of sexuality, and the inviolability of the marriage bond are unchangeable values. In doing so, she upholds the dignity of man and his *true* quality of life.

AN AGREED MORALITY

The question then arises as to what chance there is of a return to an agreed morality, at least as regards fundamental values and basic principles and rights. There are two ways of working towards this; one is by the right use of reason and reflection, and the other, which is complementary to it, is by a renewed faith and acceptance of Christianity. With regard to the first, the source of morality is the human person, his or her dignity and acts. When we reflect on man and his needs, a series of basic values which must be always and everywhere affirmed becomes self-evident to all of us. These values include life, truth, friendship, rationality etc., and from them can be deduced the various precepts of the moral law. The working out of this natural law will be discussed in chapter three.

With regard to the second, Catholic morality is taught by Revelation and the Magisterium of the Church. This is necessary, not because it is inaccessible to reason, but because of the fallibility and scepticism of the human mind. In the present state of fallen nature, man can grasp the essentials of morality but not the whole of it. Consequently, Christian Revelation and Church guidance ensure that morals are grasped in their entirety and with certainty. Equally, they can only be fully practised by means of grace. Revelation is not opposed to reason; it simply goes beyond it and complements it. As Newman says, 'the sense of right and wrong, which is the first element in religion is so delicate, so fitful, so easily puzzled, obscured, perverted, so subtle in its argumentative methods, so impressible by education, so biassed by pride and passion, so unsteady in its course, that, in the struggle for existence amid the various exercises and triumphs of the human intellect, this sense is at once the highest of all teachers, yet the least luminous; and the Church, the Pope, the hierarchy are, in the Divine purpose, the supply of an urgent demand.'[7]

The Enlightenment concept of an 'autonomous morality' goes a long way to explaining the modern conventional and secularized ethics. The writers of that period endeavoured to base morals on reason alone, that is, on reason emancipated from the shackles (as they saw it) of Revelation, theology and indeed previous tradition in general. Nevertheless, such an enterprise is doomed to failure, both theoretically and practically, because it takes insufficient account of reason's innate tendency to fallibility and scepticism; thus, in endeavouring to exalt reason, it in fact diminishes it. Far from destroying it, Revelation confirms and protects reason. Consequently, the 'emancipated reason' not only fails to grasp the norms of the natural law, but it also misunderstands the flawed nature of man himself, which is the underlying cause of all moral deviations.

The mistake of those who pursue autonomous morality is to put subjective certainty in the place of the natural moral law or, even in its extreme form, in the place of God himself. As a consequence, they demote reason and condemn it to error because it is being made the arbiter instead of an instrument of truth. In other words, in the effort to upgrade reason they actually debase it. In this scenario, the end of man becomes those ends which reason fabricates, such as freedom, pleasure, utility, duty etc. From here derives the fact that today, for many, there are no such things as permanent, absolute or objective values which go beyond personal opinions; such people want to reserve the right to move the goal-posts on each occasion and judge morality by attending only to the particular circumstances of each occurrence.

What happens when freedom loses its essential link with the truth and ignores the evidence for a universal and objective law is well brought out by *Evangelium vitae*, 20 :

> If the promotion of the self is understood in terms of absolute autonomy, people inevitably reach the point of rejecting one another. Everyone else is considered an enemy from whom one has to defend oneself. Thus society becomes a mass of individuals placed side by side but without any mutual bonds. Each one wishes to assert himself independently of the other and in fact tends to make his interests prevail. Still, in the face of other people's analogous interests, some kind of compromise must be found, if one wants a society in which the

7. J. H. Newman, *Letter to the Duke of Norfolk*, London, 1876.

maximum possible freedom is guaranteed to each individual. In this way any reference to common values and to a truth absolutely binding on everybody is lost, and social life ventures on the shifting sands of complete relativism. At that point, everything is negotiable, everything is open to bargaining—even the first of the fundamental rights, the right to life.

The Church, in contrast to secular thinking, teaches a morality based on the unity of mankind: 'All men are endowed with a rational soul and are created in God's image; they have the same nature and origin and being redeemed by Christ, they enjoy the same divine calling and destiny; there is here a basic equality between all men and it must be given greater recognition' (*Gaudium et spes*, 29). Or again: 'All men in fact, are destined to the very same end, namely God himself, since they have been created in the likeness of God . . .' (ibid., 24). Speaking in the context of the savagery of nuclear war and terrorism, Vatican II says: 'the Council wishes to remind men that the natural law of peoples and its universal principles still retain their binding force. The conscience of mankind firmly and ever more emphatically proclaims these principles' (ibid., 79).

The Commandments of the Judeo-Christian tradition are held by Christians to be universally applicable to all men and as incorporating absolute norms and values. Hence, they are predicated upon the essential unity of all men and are not simply given to a determinate people at a particular time, but are for all time. Christ said that he came to fulfil the law and not abolish it. As Vatican II says, 'there is a growing awareness of the sublime dignity of the human person, who stands above all things and whose rights and duties are universal and inviolable' (*Gaudium et spes*, 26). It thus re-affirms such absolute values as truthfulness, the sanctity of life and fidelity in marriage, as against the claims of permissiveness and the anti-life mentality, declaring that lying, killing and adultery, for example, are always wrong.

The natural moral law is therefore accessible to reason, albeit not without some mistakes and gaps, and can thus be supported by rational argument. It is based on an understanding of the human good, which in turn depends on 'the full truth about man' (*Humanae vitae*, 7). Referring to the morality of the transmission of life *Gaudium et spes*, 51, says that 'objective criteria must be used, criteria drawn from the human person and human action'. Hence, man and his actions are the subject matter of morals. But morals is not just about man as he is; it is more about what he should become; and therefore the truth about man includes his destiny, or end. However, if reason is considered to be so weak that it cannot know the essential nature of man and his purpose, then it will be unable to discover the universal principles of morals. As MacIntyre says, morals is about man as he is striving to be what he ought to be according to his *telos*, or end. He has rightly shown that history teaches us that morals requires three things—an understanding of man as he is in his present state, an appreciation of him as he should be if he fulfils his end and destiny, and a set of moral precepts to show him how to get there.[8] These latter are furnished by the natural law which, in its basic precepts, is self-evident to human reason.

The observance of the moral law, though primarily for the glory of God, is also in the interests of man. This is why it is proposed by the Church to all men and is an important way in which the Church serves the world: 'Hence the norm of human activity is this: that in accord with the divine plan and will, it should harmonize with the genuine good of the human race, and allow men as individuals and as members of society to pursue their total vocation and fulfil it' (*Gaudium et spes*, 35). There need be no clash, then, between man's interests and laws and God's law, anymore than there is between faith and reason, because they both proceed from the same source.

If, on the other hand, man insists on stepping outside the natural law, even partially, to make of himself what he pleases, which is the *de facto* programme of autonomous morality, then, as C.S. Lewis has shown, this leads 'to the power of some men to make other men what they please'.[9] And the same writer warned five decades ago that if advancing technology were not subject to an objective morality, especially in regard to contraception and eugenics etc., far from leading to man's dominion over nature, it would result in his subjection to it, because he, and the future of mankind, would be at the mercy of the irrational impulses of a few.[10]

Thus today, fifty years later, the Pope, writing of the contemporary situation in *Evangelium vitae*, bears out the accuracy of this insight. He says:

> the original and inalienable right to life is questioned or denied on the basis of a parliamentary vote or the will of one part of the people— even if it is the majority. This is the sinister result of a relativism which reigns unopposed: the 'right' ceases to be such, because it is no longer firmly founded on the inviolable dignity of the person, but is made subject to the will of the stronger part. In this way democracy, contradicting its own principles, effectively moves towards a form of

8. Alasdair MacIntyre, *After Virtue*, London, 1981, p. 52.
9. C. S. Lewis, *The Abolition of Man*, London, 1978 ed., p. 37.
10. Ibid., p. 41

totalitarianism. The State is no longer the 'common home' where all can live together on the basis of principles of fundamental equality, but is transformed into a *tyrant State*, which arrogates to itself the right to dispose of the life of its weakest and most defenceless members. from the unborn child to the elderly, in the name of a public interest which is really nothing but the interest of one part.

2

The Dignity and Purpose
of the Human Person

Many of the contemporary issues discussed in sexual and medical ethics turn on what we consider the human person to be. Specifically they depend on how we understand human life, as distinct from animal and plant life, and the degree of man's dominion over it. There is a distinct tendency, for example, to treat the human body as an object of pleasure or to manipulate and instrumentalize it in the laboratory and the operating room. In reality, however, the body is an integral part of the human person, and our authority over it is restricted. Understanding man as a substantial unity within the duality of body and soul enables us to appreciate the restricted nature of his dominion.

There is general, if not universal, agreement on the dignity of man and his pre-eminence in the world. As Vatican II puts it, in *Gaudium et spes*, 12: 'Believers and unbelievers agree almost unanimously that all things on earth should be ordained to man as their centre and summit.' Not all agree, however, on the nature of this dignity or, most importantly, on the end and purpose of man. Some, content with a materialist and biological concept, tend to treat man as an advanced animal, or a complicated machine. This entails the conclusion that the difference between a man and a monkey is simply a difference of degree rather than of kind. On this view, there would be a similar difference between a man and a tiger as there is between a tiger and a fly.

Man is not to be explained simply as a material and biological whole. Like other living beings, he has a life principle, or soul, but in his case it is spiritual. Nor, however, is he a consciousness imprisoned in a body. Rather, he is a person composed of a body and soul, both of which are integral parts of his person-hood. Boethius' time-honoured expression puts it very adequately, by defin-ing the human person as 'an individual substance of rational nature'.

Others say that man's dominant characteristic is freedom, and it is up to him to choose his end and make of himself what he will. This, however, overlooks the fact that man's ultimate end is given to him, not selected by him, as we shall see, and his freedom is limited to accepting or rejecting it.

Still others deny that man is free, claiming that he is conditioned to make the choices he does. Most agree, however, that man has an autonomy and freedom of his own, but within certain limits. These limits are set by the truth about man and human life. Consequently, we must define freedom in terms of man, and not man in terms of a supposed absolute freedom.

Perhaps the biggest single obstacle to agreement among moralists about the good of man is that they base it on human nature as it is found today, without any consideration of the Fall and the change brought about by original sin. Too many have overlooked the fact that morals is about man, not simply as he is now but as he ought to be according to his end and purpose. This can be glimpsed in the vaguest way by reason alone, but it can only be fully and certainly known by Christian Revelation. Only there do we get an account of the pre-history of man 'in the beginning' as he was created in the state of original innocence according to the divine plan and in his reconstituted form after the Incarnation and Redemption. Only by contrasting historical man with his original state can we attain to the full truth about him and, indeed, properly understand the significance of the Redemption. As *Gaudium et spes*, 22, says, 'In reality, it is only in the mystery of the Word made flesh that the mystery of man truly becomes clear. Adam was the type of man who was to come, and Christ, the new Adam . . . fully reveals man to himself and brings to light his high calling.'

There are different sides to the complex reality of the human being and, hence, he has different needs and goods which fulfil him. But just as the different parts of his nature form one substantial unity, so the different goods of man are ultimately orientated to a supreme good. This last end of man is the guiding light of ethics which can be defined in the words of Alasdair MacIntyre as, 'man-as-he-is seeking to be what he should be according to his *telos* (last end)'.[1] But this supreme good itself follows from a correct understanding of man to which we must now devote a more thorough investigation.

TOWARDS A FULL UNDERSTANDING OF MAN

The dignity of man and his pre-eminent position in the universe are due above all to his rationality and freedom. It is in virtue of these characteristics that he is like God and at the same time is distinguished from the rest of the animal world. In the first chapter of Genesis (1:26) we read, 'Then God

1. Alasdair MacIntyre, *After Virtue*, London, 1981, p. 53.

said, "Let us make man in our image, after our likeness; and let them have dominion over the fish of the sea, and over the birds of the air, and over the cattle and over all the earth, and over every creeping thing that creeps upon the earth.'" Like all living beings, he possesses a soul which is the source of his life and movement, but in his case it is a rational soul—a fact borne out by its capabilities.

Man, therefore, is quite different from other forms of life on earth. This is made clear when we are told that he was 'alone' and did not have a helper fit for him until the creation of woman. It is also brought out by the fact that Adam is asked to give a name to all the creatures God had created. Hence, he was able to use language, which means he had reason. It is man's rationality, exhibited in language and in abstract and universal knowledge, which sets him apart from animals. He is able, not only to know individual things by sensation as do animals, but to know what kind of things they are and to give them common names. Furthermore, he is capable of knowing other universals, such as good and evil, and of making choices.

The human person, therefore, transcends and dominates the material world of experience in a way that animals do not. The latter enjoy a rich sense life and, based on this, a form of cognition or instinct and desire or striving, which only warrants a materially based animal soul or life principle. Some animals are capable of sophisticated technical activities, such as the underground 'cities' of ants or the chimpanzee's ability to join two sticks together to gather in a banana from outside the cage. But these feats are explicable in terms of instinct and routine, in the case of the first, and hit and miss instinct in the case of the second. The characteristic acts of a rational intellect such as the use of language and self-reflection are conspicuously lacking in animals. It is a commonplace in Thomistic philosophy that the highest in one species approximates to the lowest in the next. Thus, the highest simians approach man, yet the gap between them and man is obvious in that a) animals take a long, long time to 'learn' the simplest manoeuvres, whereas children learn exponentially, and b) one generation of animals does not pass on such acquired knowledge to the next.

Furthermore, animals haven't advanced through the centuries in the way that mankind has. Man's material and technological progress is part of his domination of the world about him. The human person enjoys an interior subjective life which, when taken as a whole, is called his biography, a fact that cannot be said of animals. As far as machines are concerned, all they can do is done in virtue of being instruments of man.

Subsequently, when he receives a command from God regarding his moral behaviour, the limits of man's autonomy and freedom are laid down.

'You may freely eat of every tree of the garden, but of the tree of the knowledge of good and evil you shall not eat, for the day that you eat of it you shall die' (Gen 2:16-17). Here it is apparent that man has free choice. He can determine his own behaviour and own ends by choosing between good and evil. As the Book of Sirach (17:5-6) says, 'He made for them tongue and eyes; he gave them ears and a mind for thinking. He filled them with knowledge and understanding and showed them good and evil.' His freedom, however, is subject to the truth about himself and the truth about God, who is his last end. He cannot change this truth and end. If he tries to, he succumbs to the temptation 'you will be like God' and puts himself in the place of God, and suffers death and the deterioration of his nature.

Man has dominion over the visible world of animal and plant life, but this dominion does not extend to human life, which he should respect both in himself and in others. Authority over man's life remains in God's hands from whom it comes. This is confirmed later in chapter four of Genesis, which records Cain's killing of his brother Abel and his subsequent punishment.

Is man truly free? Since man is the highest value in the visible world, no temporal value totally satisfies him and, therefore, none fully determines him. As regards spiritual values, since these are known to him only by way of sense knowledge and, therefore, indirectly rather than directly, the full force of their attractiveness is not apparent to man in such a way as to pre-determine him. Thus, we argue man is free. He may choose among the goods and values of the world, but we must make an exception of his destiny. There is only one destiny of man, as we shall see, and he can only accept it or reject it. He can choose the means or intermediate ends, such as his wife, his job, his leisure, but the end is only one. A man seeking to win an Olympic gold medal may select different methods of training and tactics for running the race, but ultimately he can only win it or lose it; he cannot half win it. By the use of his freedom, man makes of himself what he becomes and, therefore, he has a responsibility for what he does and is accountable for his actions.

THE HUMAN SOUL AND THE UNITY OF MAN

In Scripture, the soul is initially spoken of as the 'breath of life'. Thus, Genesis 2:7 describes the creation of man in the following way: 'the Lord formed man of dust from the ground, and breathed into his nostrils the breath of life; and man became a living being.' Hence the soul is the principle of life and unity of being. The human person is a unity, but containing the duality of body and soul. It is often said that the Bible refers to man using the term 'body' to designate the whole man and stress his personal unity (cf. e.g., Ps 144:2; Is 66:23). This is true, but the duality of man is equally emphasized in biblical tradition, as, for example, 'Do not fear those who deprive the body of life but cannot destroy the soul' (Mt 10:28).

The Church defines man's soul as 'the substantial form of the body'.[2] The form here does not refer to the shape, precisely because the soul is spiritual, but rather to that which gives unity, as well as life and movement, to the person. This principle cannot be material, since the matter of the body changes completely every few years, and hence the person would have no continuing unity; so it must be immaterial. In the case of the person, the soul is intrinsically independent of matter in the sense that it is capable of actions, such as rational knowledge and self-reflection, which do not have their origin in a material organ and, hence, are what we call 'spiritual'. Being spiritual, the soul is not made of parts and, therefore, cannot corrupt. This allows us to affirm its immortality. As the Book of Wisdom (2:23) says, 'man was made for incorruptibility.' And Vatican II (in *Gaudium et spes*, 24) said: 'man is the only creature on earth whom God has wanted for himself', that is, he is the product of eternal love.

The twin faculties of the human soul, intellect and will, work through material organs usually, though they can transcend them. All knowledge begins in the senses, though human knowledge subsequently surpasses empirical knowledge. Man is a finely balanced unity; his body and soul are separable, but not separate in this life, when they form one substance. The separation of the two is what constitutes death. From this point on, the soul, which has the capacity to subsist in itself, continues to exist as a disembodied soul. Nevertheless, even after death, the soul does not cease to 'aspire' to be reunited to the body, in view of the previous substantial unity between the two. The glorified body will be so dominated by the soul after the final resurrection that it too, then, will be immune from corruption.

The unity of man has always been threatened by the dualism of the Platonic and Cartesian schools. The drawbacks of this view are considerable and dangerous. To say, as Descartes does, that man is two substances—body and soul—makes a satisfactory connection between them impossible, because a substance correctly understood is always an individual. Such a position has been held up to ridicule, notably by Gilbert Ryle, who describes the dualistic concept of man as 'the ghost in the machine'.[3] To

---

2. Council of Vienne, 1312 (Dz. 902).
3. Gilbert Ryle, *The Concept of Mind*, London, 1949.

characterize the soul as a ghost is to play into the hands of materialists who can properly say, 'If we cannot know the soul, then what use do we have for it?' And to call the body a quantified extension is to subject it to the same laws as a machine. From here derives the predominant contemporary view of the body as an instrument or a tool with which we can do as we please. Cartesian dualism, which sees man as a consciousness who possesses a body, is foreign to Christian tradition, which understands the human body as an integral part of the person and as something to be treated with the respect and responsibility which is owed to the person as a whole.

This dualism has arisen again in our own time with all those who see a tension between freedom and nature. For them, this tension is resolved by positing a division within man himself. The goods of the body are simply physical and pre-moral, and the moral goods must be determined by reference to the whole person (by which they understand the self-conscious and reasoning subject). This is the standpoint of proportionalists and other moral revisionists. In reply it must be emphasized that the body is part of the whole person, and, consequently, the goods of the body are goods of the whole man.

Veritatis splendor, 48 is very explicit on the point. Speaking of the above-mentioned revisionist position it says: 'This moral theory does not correspond to the truth about man and his freedom. It contradicts the *Church's teaching on the unity of the human person* whose rational soul is *per se et essentialiter* the form of his body. The spiritual and immortal soul is the principle of unity of the human being whereby it exists as a whole—*corpore et anima unus*—as a person . . . it is in the unity of body and soul that the person is the subject of his own moral acts. . . . It is in the light of the dignity of the human person—a dignity that must be affirmed for its own sake that reason grasps the specific moral value of certain goods towards which the person is naturally inclined.'

As a consequence of man's substantial and organic unity, the parts of the body all work towards the good of the whole, not for themselves. Equally, the many different historical episodes in the life of each individual form part of the biography of a single person. Though, like Shakespeare, we might distinguish the seven ages of man, 'the mewling and puking infant', the whining schoolboy 'creeping like snail unwilling to school', and the soldier 'full of strange oaths', etc.,[4] they all form part of the life of one human individual. His personal identity is continuous from the cradle to the grave. It is, of course, the human soul which is the ultimate explanation of the unity of a human life.

This unity of life entails many consequences. The various parts or aspects

4. *As You Like It*, II, vii.

of a man's nature mean that there are various basic goods which correspond to them, such as life, knowledge, play and friendship. But, if the human person is a unity, then, equally, these basic goods will form part of an overall supreme good of the person as a whole. Furthermore, since men enjoy a common nature, it will be the same for all men. The unity of the human person also means that his actions are not isolated events but form part of a continuum which makes him the sort of person he is. They are part of his biography. They are all moral acts, if done consciously and freely, in the sense that they lead him nearer to his last end and supreme good, or further away from it. Insofar as they lead to it, they enhance his human dignity. Moral life for man consists, then, in the right ordering of all his activities to a unified end.

Man is thus a spiritual and material being at one and the same time, in virtue of which he rises above the rest of the visible world and has a transcendent vocation. Herein lies his dignity, and on this dignity, rising as it does above cultural and other differences, the universality and immutability of the moral law is based.

Human life has an absolute value within the world, and man should act as the steward of it and never as lord over it. Furthermore, man should never be treated as a means to an end, but as a quasi-end in himself. This is known as the 'personalistic norm'. It may well be asked here, of course, whether this norm is observed in many areas of human activity. Does an employer not use his workers, an officer his soldiers, and parents their children? This may be true, to some extent, but we must always allow for the personhood of other human beings, their rational and free natures. We can exhort them to have good ends, because the pursuit of evil is not rational, but we cannot impose our ends on them. And, therefore, we may formulate the following principle: 'Whenever a person is the object of your activity, remember that you may not treat that person as only a means to an end, as an instrument, but must allow for the fact that, he or she too has, or at least should have, distinct personal ends.'[5]

THE ULTIMATE GOOD OF MAN

If man is the end and summit of the visible world, we are entitled to ask what the end of man is. Someone might object with regard to our exposition so far: 'You are assuming that the Christian explanation of man's

5. K. Wojtyla, *Love and Responsibility*, London, 1981, pp. 26-28.

destiny is also the true one, but how do you justify this? How do you show that God is the end of man; could it not equally be work, or culture, or power, or honours, as people often consider it to be today?' In our response we will take it for granted that man's last end is also his good; we must ensure that it is truly ultimate (that is, that it is not a means to a further end) and responds to a definition of the whole man.

Alternatively we can approach the question by asking what man is for? What is his function? Things are usually called 'good' in the measure in which they fulfil their function well. We all know what it is to have a good accountant or dentist. Wartime pilots knew what it was to have a good navigator. To ask, then, what man is for or what his function is, is the same as asking what his ultimate good is or what his destiny consists in. Since we are going to deal with ethical questions concerning human life (the procreation of it, sickness and death), the pivotal and fundamental importance of knowing just what human life is will be obvious.

In seeking the ultimate good of man, St Thomas Aquinas asks himself successively whether this consists in the goods connected with the different parts of the human person until he arrives at that which is truly ultimate.[6] He thus discusses whether it consists in the goods of the body summed up in sense pleasure, or in external temporal goods, or in the goods of the intellect, and, if so, whether in the practical intellect or the speculative.

As to bodily pleasures, these are connected in the main with the actions of eating and sex, which are not ends in themselves, but are directed to health and procreation. Hence, neither the action nor the pleasure is the last end since they serve as a means to a further end. Could it consist in the acquisition of temporal goods, such as honours, wealth or power? These, however, can be used by evil men for evil purposes, as well as by good men, and so cannot be absolutely and ultimately good. As often as not, they lead to man's downfall and not his fulfilment. It seems evident that any ultimate destiny man has will be related to a good of man's soul or intellect, such as knowledge, rather than to any bodily good.

This brings us to the goods and values of the intellect and, in the first place, the practical intellect. This is the territory of man's behaviour and action; it covers the fields of the moral virtues and also prudence and the making of things. These last two come in here because St Thomas defined prudence as the 'right way of acting' and art or skilful work as the 'right way of making things'. He notes that the last end of man must have to do with the most perfect of objects, but the practical intellect has to do with

6. *Summa contra Gentiles*, Bk. 3, pt. 1.

contingent, pragmatic matters, which are of a lower order than necessary ones. Consequently, the last end of man does not consist in the exercise of prudence or any of the moral virtues. This becomes clear when we realize each of the moral virtues is directed to some further end. Fortitude, for example, becomes a means in time of war to obtain victory and peace, or it consists in the arduous and difficult acquisition of what is worthwhile. Deeds of justice are directed to keeping peace among men through each one possessing his own peace. Furthermore, moral virtues enable man to observe the mean and moderate his passions. But it is impossible for the moderation of man's passions to be his ultimate end, since the passions, like external things, can be directed to something less than man.

For similar reasons, no manufactured thing, or consumer product, can be man's last end, for he in fact is *their* end. The fruits of industry and technology are for the service of man and his use, and not he for them. In general, since man himself is the highest value in the visible creation and he transcends it by his spirituality and immortality, nothing in it will satisfy him in an ultimate sense.

Consequently, man will only find complete satisfaction in the good of the speculative intellect, which is ordered to the contemplation of truth. This activity is an end in itself. What is more, it is proper to man and angels, but it is not found in animals. Man's last end, therefore, consists in the fullness of truth, which, as St Thomas would say, all men know to be God. Truth unites man to what is above him and fulfils the demand of his nature; as we have said so often, his supreme good transcends the purely temporal order.

Moreover, *all* human actions should be directed to this as their last end, that is to say, all the basic values participate in, and form part of, the ultimate good. So the body must be healthy and free to achieve it, and it is the products of the manufacturing industry, and material goods and services, which make this possible. Attainment of the last end requires freedom from the disturbance of the passions, which must be controlled by the moral virtues and prudence. It equally requires freedom from external disturbance, which is the purpose of civil law. All things are ordained to man, therefore, and man is ordered to God.

St Thomas wrote that 'it is consequently apparent that all things are ordered to one good, as to their ultimate end . . . and this is God.'[7] It is in the search for, and pursuit of, communion with God that man achieves his fulfilment and happiness. This is the way in which Christianity completed Aristotle's notion that man's final end, his *eudaimonia* (weakly translated

7. Ibid., ch. 17, 1 & 2.

as fulfilment or happiness, but which really refers to the all-round flourishing of human activity), is brought about by the contemplation of truth. Happiness, then, contrary to much modern thinking, is not so much pursued for itself in isolation as something which ensues when man truly seeks his final end.

In the vast majority of everyday moral decisions, of course, we are concerned, not with the final end, but with intermediate ends. We ask, 'Is this a fair and honest thing to do?, a true thing to say?' etc. However, the 'good' that is sought in each particular act, if it is truly a good, will be a participation in the ultimate good, and, if not, it will be a contradiction of it. The goods of life, truth, friendship, rationality etc., which we have partially identified, are in fact fundamental participations in the supreme good.[8] But here we must guard against a misunderstanding, because this does not mean for a moment that the last end is the only criterion of judgement. The view that the 'fundamental option' of the person determines the morality of his actions is only part of the truth.[9] It is a necessary condition but not a

---

8. See the next chapter for a full account of the goods referred to.
9. For fundamental option see also p. 88 and *Veritatis splendor*, 65-9, especially: '[65.] The heightened concern for freedom in our own day has led many students of the behavioural and the theological sciences to develop a more penetrating analysis of its nature and of its dynamics. It has been rightly pointed out that freedom is not only the choice for one or another particular action; it is also, within that choice, *a decision about oneself* and a setting of one's own life for or against the Good, for or against the Truth, and ultimately for or against God. Emphasis has rightly been placed on the importance of certain choices which "shape" a person's entire moral life, and which serve as bounds within which other particular everyday choices can be situated and allowed to develop.

'Some authors, however, have proposed an even more radical revision of the *relationship between person and acts*. They speak of a "fundamental freedom", deeper than and different from freedom of choice, which needs to be considered if human actions are to be correctly understood and evaluated. According to these authors, the *key role in the moral life* is to be attributed to a "fundamental option", brought about by that fundamental freedom whereby the person makes an overall self-determination, not through a specific and conscious decision on the level of reflection, but in a "transcendental" and "athematic" way. *Particular acts* which flow from this option would constitute only partial and never definitive attempts to give it expression; they would only be its "signs" or symptoms. The immediate object of such acts would not be absolute Good (before which the freedom of the person would be expressed on a transcendental level), but particular (also termed "categorical") goods. In the opinion of some theologians, none of these goods, which by their nature are partial, could determine the freedom of man as a person in his totality, even though it is only by bringing them about or refusing to do so that man is able to express his own fundamental option.

'A *distinction* thus comes to be introduced between *the fundamental option and deliberate choices of a concrete kind of behaviour*. In some authors this division tends to become a *separation*, when they expressly limit moral "good" and "evil" to the transcendental dimension proper to the fundamental option, and describe as "right" or "wrong" the choices of particular "innerworldly" kinds of behaviour: those, in other words, concerning man's

sufficient one. The aforesaid theory overlooks the fact that it is the individual act which is right or wrong, and this is ascertained by judging the
intention of the person and the end and purpose of the action, namely, the
moral object. One may have a correct orientation to the last end but carry
out acts which are at variance with that very orientation.

To evaluate human behaviour, therefore, one must look at the intentions
and structure of actions. In any action there are many possible intentions. If
one signs a cheque one may intend to pay a bill, or make a donation and
create goodwill, or show how much money one has, or give a bribe to
secure a contract.[10] (This is traditionally known as the *finis operantis*, the
intention of the subject.) Equally, the structure and purpose of the action,
that is to say, the object chosen (known as *finis operis*), must be evaluated.
One might decide to act in conformity with the usual rules for the action or
against them, so one must sign one's own name and not someone else's, one
must have money in the bank account etc. For the action to be upright both

---

relationship with himself, with others and with the material world. There thus appears to be
established within human acting a clear disjunction between two levels of morality: on the
one hand, the order of good and evil, which is dependent on the will, and, on the other hand,
specific kinds of behaviour, which are judged to be morally right or wrong only on the basis
of a technical calculation of the proportion between the "premoral" or "physical" goods and
evils which actually result from the action. This is pushed to the point where a concrete kind
of behaviour, even one freely chosen, comes to be considered as a merely physical process,
and not according to the criteria proper to a human act. The conclusion to which this
eventually leads is that the properly moral assessment of the person is reserved to his
fundamental option, prescinding in whole or in part from his choice of particular actions, of
concrete kinds of behaviour.

[The text now goes on, in no. 66, to discuss what the Bible says about radical commitment
and points out that, if freedom is not properly used, the result is slavery. 'This is precisely the
case when an act of faith—in the sense of a fundamental option—becomes separated from
the choice of particular acts, as in the tendencies mentioned above.' And then it continues, at
no. 67:]

'These tendencies are therefore contrary to the teaching of Scripture itself, which sees the
fundamental option as a genuine choice of freedom and links that choice profoundly to
particular acts. By his fundamental choice, man is capable of giving his life direction and of
progressing, with the help of grace, towards his end, following God's call. But this capacity
is actually exercised in the particular choices of specific actions, through which man
deliberately conforms himself to God's will, wisdom and law. It thus needs to be stated that
the so-called fundamental option, to the extent that it is distinct from a generic intention and
hence one not yet determined in such a way that freedom is obligated, *is always brought into
play through conscious and free decisions*. Precisely for this reason, *it is revoked when man
engages his freedom in conscious decisions to the contrary, with regard to morally grave
matter*.'

10. This example is given by G. E. M. Anscombe, 'On *Humanae vitae*', in *Human love and
Human life*, ed. J. N. Santamaría & J. Billings, Melbourne, 1979.

the intention of the subject and the moral object of the action must be good. A defect in either of these aspects will issue in a morally bad action.

The sources of morality, therefore, are threefold, namely, the moral object, the intention and the circumstances. But, as *Veritatis splendor* clearly teaches, some actions are always wrong, regardless of circumstances and consequences. Hence, the circumstances are not truly a determinant of the morality of an action on their own but only insofar as they change the moral object. What they can do is increase, or diminish, the goodness or the gravity of the action. Of the other two elements, the moral object is the most important. In the words of the above-mentioned encyclical (at no. 79): 'The primary and decisive element for moral judgement is the object of the human act, which establishes whether it is *capable of being ordered to the good and to the ultimate end, which is God*' (italics not ours).

This said, however, it is the last end of man, founded on the unity of the human person and a common human nature, which, in turn, gives unity and objectivity to the moral law. While freedom dictates that there will be pluralism among human beings, in the sense that different people will pursue different human goods in varying degrees, according to personal choice and inclination, none of the basic human goods may be dispensed with or overridden. To do so would be anti-rational and would, therefore, militate against the true good of the human person. This is because the basic goods are all fundamental participations in the ultimate good of man and respond to the truth about him. They mark the true limits of human freedom, such that outside of them freedom becomes licence, and they point to the objectivity of the moral law. Genuine pluralism and freedom, therefore, do not mean that there are different and equally valid ends and goods, for different persons or groups, which are contradictory among themselves and dependent only on personal choice. Such a view ignores the fact that man's true good, his ultimate good, is given to him, not selected by him, and it is for him to recognize it and accept it. Conscience cannot create what is good or moral; it merely discerns or recognizes it. Man's moral growth and dignity consists in following his conscience.

[3]

The Natural Law and Human Rights

Ethics and morality demand that we have a clear criterion for determining what right and wrong consist in, and thus for distinguishing between good and evil actions. We are aware that this must be based on the whole truth about man, take into account his destiny and be applicable to all human beings. It must also be able to give us some fixed and exceptionless norms which enable us to say that some things are intrinsically good or bad; otherwise we won't be able to maintain that such things as the Nazi extermination camps or holding prisoners of war as a human shield are absolutely evil. It cannot be a so-called consequentialist ethic, based on a calculation of benefits over harm, because this yields the useful, or pleasurable, good but not the moral good.*

* *Veritatis splendor*, 75, discusses this ethic as follows: 'But as part of the effort to work out such a rational morality (for this reason it is sometimes called an "autonomous morality") there exist *false solutions, linked in particular to an inadequate understanding of the object of moral action. Some authors* do not take into sufficient consideration the fact that the will is involved in the concrete choices which it makes: these choices are a condition of its moral goodness and its being ordered to the ultimate end of the person. *Others* are inspired by a notion of freedom which prescinds from the actual conditons of its exercise, from its objective reference to the truth about the good, and from its determination through choices of concrete kinds of behaviour. According to these theories, free will would neither be morally subjected to specific obligations nor shaped by its choices, while nonetheless still remaining responsible for its own acts and for their consequences. This *"teleologism"*, as a method for discovering the moral norm, can thus be called—according to terminology and approaches imported from different currents of thought—*"consequentialism"* or *"proportionalism"*. The former claims to draw the criteria of the rightness of a given way of acting solely from a calculation of foreseeable consequences deriving from a given choice. The latter, by weighing the various values and goods being sought, focuses rather on the proportion acknowledged between the good and bad effects of that choice, with a view to the "greater good" or "lesser evil" actually possible in a particular situation.

'*The teleological ethical theories (proportionalism, consequentialism)*, while acknowledging that moral values are indicated by reason and by Revelation, maintain that it is never possible to formulate an absolute prohibition of particular kinds of behaviour which would be in conflict, in every circumstance and in every culture, with those values. The acting subject would indeed be responsible for attaining the values pursued, but in two ways: the values or goods involved in a human act would be, from one viewpoint, *of the moral order* (in relation to properly moral values, such as love of God and neighbour, justice, etc.)

In a word, we want an objective standard to distinguish right from wrong. In its most basic manifestations goodness is self-evident to all of us. We all know that it is wrong to tell lies, or practise injustice, or do harm to our neighbour, or kill the innocent etc. These things are written on our mind and heart, on what we call our conscience, and thus they form part of an unwritten law.

The notion of a natural morality, or law, which applies universally is not only found in Christian writers, such as St Paul, St Augustine and St Thomas. We also come across references to it in the Greek poets such as Sophocles, as well as in Plato and Aristotle, and Cicero and the Stoics. Plato's ideas, or forms, were the ideals which human activity was supposed to aim at, and to act in conformity with them was to act 'according to nature'. He thus worked out a natural morality around the four cardinal virtues of prudence, justice, fortitude and temperance. Aristotle, too, discerned an ethics and law which were objective and universal, and which he referred to as 'natural'. He wrote: 'Now of justice. There are two forms of it, the natural and the conventional. It is natural when it has the same validity everywhere.'[1]

According to the Stoics, nature is not a matter of blind chance but has a divine purpose to it which is rationally discernible. Hence, the law of nature is one and immutable, applying to all men and discernible by all. Cicero (106-43 BC) was to give classic expression to this. He wrote:

> There is in fact a true law, namely right reason, which is in accordance with nature, applies to all men and is unchangeable and eternal. By its commands this law summons men to their duties; by its prohibitions it restrains them from doing wrong . . . . It will not lay down one rule in Rome and another in Athens . . . but there will be one law, eternal and unchangeable, binding at all times upon all peoples. There will be, as it were, one common master and ruler of men, namely God, who is the author of this law, its interpreter and its sponsor. The man who will not obey it will abandon his better self.[2]

---

and, from another viewpoint, *of the pre-moral order*, which some term non-moral, physical or ontic (in relation to the advantages and disadvantages accruing both to the agent and to all other persons possibly involved, such as, for example, health or its endangerment, physical integrity, life, death, loss of material goods, etc.). In a world where goodness is always mixed with evil, and every good effect linked to other evil effects, the morality of an act would be judged in two different ways: its moral "goodness" would be judged on the basis of the subject's intention in reference to moral goods, and its "rightness" on the basis of a consideration of its foreseeable effects or consequences and of their proportion.'

1. *Nicomachean Ethics*, 5.7.   2. *De Republica*, 3.22.

EXISTENCE AND DESCRIPTION OF NATURAL LAW

Because man's nature is received, so is the law of his nature. Natural law is, in fact, already there at the creation; it is written into the created order. Creation is a calling into being, and goodness is being from the point of view of desirability. By the same token, evil is either a privation of being, or it arises from a disordered desire for the good, as in the case of envy. That which apprehends the order of being and goodness is reason; speculative reason in the first case and practical in the second. The way we usually express this is by saying that the natural law which is laid upon us is apprehended in the conscience of the individual.

St Thomas defines natural law as 'the participation of the eternal law in the rational creature'.[3] The eternal law is that by which God creates and conserves all things in being and orders them towards their end by his Providence. Insofar as it applies to man, and is reflected in human reason, it is called the natural law. By natural, then, we mean rationally grasped. *Dignitatis humanae*, 3, of Vatican II, states that 'the highest norm of human life is the divine law itself—eternal, objective and universal by which God orders, directs and governs the whole world and the ways of the human community according to a plan conceived in his wisdom and love.'

Although God, or the *summum bonum*, is essential to the natural law, we don't have to know God, or Revelation, in order to be acquainted with that law. It may be known, as it were, upwards from reason as well as downwards from Revelation. It is discerned by reason from the inclinations and goods of man. In its fundamentals, it is self-evident to all, as we shall see, although from there on people vary in their grasp of it. St Paul says that it is inscribed on the minds and hearts of the Gentiles (cf. Rom 2:14-15).

However, to know the natural law more fully, one needs to have a sincere desire to seek the truth and live in accordance with it when one comes to know it (cf. *Dignitatis humanae, 2)*. Like truth itself, the moral law is not just an instinct, or a convention, but an objective standard which is obligatory for the human being if he is to fulfil his potential. It is reflected in man's conscience and, like a light, guides him and points the way; but conscience does not create this law. It is already there. It enables man to discern for himself, by the light of natural reason, the difference between good and evil; and this light is nothing more than the imprint of the divine light in us. By this 'light', man is a true partaker in divine Providence, in a more excellent way than other creatures in that he provides for himself and

3. *Summa theologiae*, I-II, q. 91 art. 2

others; and by reason and freedom he is able to recognize the unchanging truth according to which he must live, and in the measure in which he lacks it he is obliged to seek it.

When the word 'law' is mentioned, most people will think instinctively of the law courts and the law of the land. It is in this sense that law may be defined, paraphrasing Aquinas, as a 'rule of reason, promulgated by one who has care of the community for the common good'.[4] It may be either prescriptive (having the force of a command) or permissive (giving the legal power to do something). Such law is written down, either in code or statute form, or by way of precedent as in the common law system. Natural law is also a rule of reason, though it is unwritten, since it is inscribed on the mind and heart of man. Critics sometimes maintain that natural law is 'static', that it fails to take account of man's historicity. It is true it is unchangeable in its fundamental precepts, but, taken as a whole, it possesses the flexibility of all law, growing with human progress to cover fields previously unheard of, such as transplant surgery and human genetics, etc.

Consequently, we find a remarkable degree of similarity in the moral systems of the past and among diverse peoples, despite occasional differences. C. S. Lewis writes:

> If anyone will take the trouble to compare the moral teaching of, say, the ancient Egyptians, Babylonians, Hindus, Chinese, Greeks and Romans, what will really strike him will be how very like they are to each other and to our own. . . . Think of a country where people were admired for running away in battle, where a man felt proud of double-crossing all the people who had been kindest to him. You might as well try to imagine a country where two and two made five.[5]

OBJECTIVITY OF NATURAL LAW AND THE *IUS GENTIUM*

Yes, it will be said, but how can there be an objective standard of behaviour if disagreement about it is so widespread? My point is that, when, by reflection, we get back to the most basic principles on which all our practical judgements are founded, we will see that every reasonable person agrees with them. There will be a good measure of disagreement about the detailed conclusions from the basic values and more specific commands of

4. *Summa theologiae*, I-II, q. 90 art. 2 and 3.
5. *Mere Christianity*, London, 1952, p. 17.

the moral law, but this is because it is imperfectly known. The fact that people disagree at times, even about the basic values, and that we can all transgress them on occasions, doesn't put the moral law in doubt. It simply shows that, while they have the same origin, the natural law differs from the law of nature in that it is not fulfilled automatically, because we are dealing with free and fallible human beings. But it has this similarity with the law of nature—that it is there, whether people know it in its fullness and practise it or not. To deny it is like saying the law of gravitation did not exist until we discovered it. The moral law, in common with the law of nature, is discovered and not invented.

Where there is most agreement is on the so-called first principles of practical reason, that is, that one should do good and avoid evil. Of course, it may be argued that some people seek to further their aims by deliberately doing evil. However, even if someone advocates anarchism as a way of life (overturning the established system of law and order), or terrorism, or drug abuse, he does so because he sees some merit or good in it. This occurs because he has a wrong idea of the human person and his destiny, but nevertheless he seeks the good as he sees it.

The anarchist, and the terrorist, may claim that they do not accept your system of justice because it favours the rich, or is prejudiced against certain groups of people. They will argue, one way or another, that it is not fair; but by the very act of making such an appeal, they are betraying a belief that there is such a thing as fairness, or justice, which deep down we all hold. Very reasonable people may disagree about moral systems and will argue that one system is better than another, but if this is so they are assuming an objective standard by which to judge between better and worse.

Over the centuries, there has also been a broad measure of agreement about unwritten law in general, not only in its basic values, but also in its everyday practicalities. The *ius gentium* (law of peoples) is such a system of unwritten law which comes somewhere between natural law and positive (or statute) law. It is based on the traditions and customs of the people, in that it expresses what the average man or the custom of the ages considers to be the 'right thing' or the 'fair thing' in a given situation. It is to be found in Roman law and is the basis of English common law. The *ius gentium*, in fact, developed as an extension of the law for Roman citizens to encompass alien peoples and nations. It was the manifestation of a natural justice which applied everywhere and to everyone.

The self-evident goods and values known to human beings and generally agreed upon also form the basis of human or natural rights. If there is no natural law, then there are no natural rights either, because they have the same foundation. And natural rights and the *ius gentium* form the basis of international law, which grows increasingly as the world moves into the era of larger political and trading blocks and ever-advancing communication technology.

Nevertheless, natural law is not a well understood concept in our own time. This is due to the rise of liberalism and the fact that we have inherited an impoverished explanation of it. Once again the main culprit is the Enlightenment. We must press for the proper establishment of the moral law on the conditions that have been established and especially on a correct notion of the human person. The Encyclopedists, however, passed on a false account of how natural rights and natural law originate. Hobbes, Locke and Rousseau, for example, liked to assume a state of pure nature in which man is shorn both of his supernatural dimension and of the sophisticated accretions he has acquired through progress. The state of nature is a purely imaginary concept, and each of these three writers presents a different version of it. So, for example, they disagree as to whether man is hostile or friendly to his neighbour in the state of nature, but they agree in saying that, to overcome any hostility or to protect personal rights and cooperate better, men drew up a social contract. Hence, society becomes an artificial construct, rather than a natural phenomenon, as it had been for their more orthodox predecessors.

However, this is the notion we have inherited, and many tend to think that, because we have progressed beyond the state of primitive nature, we have superseded the natural law. But the latter is in no way based on a supposed state of nature (a very imprecise concept, to be sure), but on reason. By 'natural' we mean that it is rational, the product of reason—the characteristic proper to the human animal and common to all men of all time.

CONTENT AND STRUCTURE: BASIC VALUES AND PRECEPTS

Since morals is directed to action, it is based on practical reason, which works with first principles, argumentation and conclusions in a parallel fashion to that of speculative reason. In ordinary thinking, 'being' is the most fundamental notion we apprehend, since the understanding of it is included in whatever a man knows. Hence, the first indemonstrable principle of speculative reason is that a thing cannot be and not be at the same time (the principle of contradiction on which all other principles are based).

Now, St Thomas explains that the first thing that the practical reason knows is the 'good', since 'every agent acts for an end which is sought under the aspect of good'. Being, insofar as it is sought by practical reason and desired by the will, is in fact what we mean by the good. Hence, the first principle of practical reason is founded on the notion of good, namely, 'The good is that which all things desire',[6] or at which they aim. If this is so, then man understands that he must 'do what is good and avoid what is evil' even if he misunderstands what goodness consists in. All other precepts of the natural law depend on this.

What we need to know are those basic goods and values which together go to make up the overall well-being of man. These follow from the natural inclinations and ends of the human being. Whatever flows from the human person as such—his faculties and the activities directed to his end as a man—forms the basis of the natural law and natural rights. These basic goods and values are not known immediately in the way that we know the data of the senses; however, on reflection, we realize that all men consider them to be self-evident. They are not the result of a process of argumentation; they are a matter of simple apprehension.

The combination of human inclinations which can be rationally grasped by man and which form the basic substratum of the natural law can be summarized as follows:

- the inclination to self-preservation and hence to the value of life and its physical and moral integrity;

- the inclination to conjugal union by which man and woman form the first communion of persons, with the purpose of procreating and educating children;

- the inclination to truth and knowledge, and hence culture and art etc.;

- the tendency to a relationship with God as a manifestation of the awareness of one's creaturely condition;

- the tendency to work as an expression of the human being's power of dominion and development of the earth and, hence, also to leisure and relaxation;

- the inclination to practical reasonableness according to which men organize their lives in a rational way and freely make their own choices;

- the tendency to friendship, love and harmony with one's fellow man, such that each person be treated as a value in themselves and with charity and never as an object or thing;

6. *Summa theologiae*, I-II, q. 94 art. 2.

- the inclination to political and other forms of association for the achievement of common ends and, thus, to justice.

Together with these we should add two basic rules for the proper development of these tendencies. They are:

- *the law of solidarity* among men according to which men and groups of men are co-responsible for the achievement of man's ends, and

- *the law of perfection and development*: man is a perfectible being and thus he and society as a whole are called to a continual material, moral and spiritual improvement.

The values resulting from these fundamental inclinations of man constitute the basic manifestations of the goodness itself to which man tends and which he desires. Consequently, we can speak of a series of primary goods and values of the human person such as the following: life, conjugal union, truth and knowledge, culture and art, religion, work and leisure, practical reasonableness and freedom, friendship and justice. These, in their turn, can be translated into the basic specific manifestations of the first principles of practical reason, namely, that good is to be done and evil avoided. Hence, these values yield primary practical precepts such as 'One must not take innocent life', 'Truth should be told', 'One should be kind to one's neighbour', 'Respect another's property', 'Conjugal life should be respected' and so on. From their dependence on the first principle of practical reason, they already have obligatory force; they are not simply descriptive. Furthermore, it is wrong to consider the precepts of natural law as abstract. This may be true of the scientific enunciation of them, but in human behaviour each one is a dictate of practical reason given in historical circumstances and thus is specific and concrete.

It may, of course, be objected that the basic values and goods are simply natural instincts we have, like self-preservation, the sexual instinct and the desire for food. But this would be to overlook the fact that they are rationally grasped. Of course, we share the instincts of self-preservation and sex with the animals, but it is stretching the meaning of words to call the desire of truth or the capacity for friendship 'instincts'. However, even those instincts which are shared with animals are grasped by human beings as goods and values on the rational level. Hence, reflecting on self-preservation, man comprehends the inviolable value of a human life, just as in contemplating human sexuality he understands its finality in procreation and the formation of offspring. The difference is that any instinct can be used for good or ill, but a rationally grasped basic human value is always and intrinsically good.

Someone may further question whether these values are not simply social conventions which we have inherited. This line of thought, however, represents a fundamental misunderstanding which needs to be clarified. While we have learnt these values from our parents and teachers, they are not true because we were taught them; rather, we were taught them because they are true. To say that the moral law is a social convention that could be otherwise is like saying that the laws of mathematics could be other than they are.

ORIGINAL AND SUBSEQUENT PRECEPTS

Those norms which follow directly from an understanding of the human person as such are 'original' or basic precepts, while those which follow via some intervention of man's will and presuppose a degree of social development are called 'subsequent' precepts. It will be noticed that the original precepts include what we know from Revelation to be the Ten Commandments, each of which, therefore, is a basic precept of the natural law (including the third one designating a day to be kept holy for the worship of God, though it is not a matter of natural law which day that should be). We also make a distinction between principles and precepts. The precepts depend on the first principles of practical reason, which may also be expressed in precept form. The basic precepts are the specific manifestations of those first principles and precepts in mandatory form. (We include under the title of original precepts, then, what St Thomas calls primary principles and proximate conclusions. According to this classification the Ten Commandments coincide with the proximate conclusions.)

In addition to these original precepts of natural law we may also speak of subsequent ones which are dictated by human reason but require the intervention of man and some measure of human development. So, for example, it is a matter of natural law that man receive an education, but such a precept would only be operable up to secondary level in those countries which have reached a sufficient degree of material advancement. Or, there are laws concerning organ transplants, but these have only appeared since the technique was developed and can only apply in those places where it is practised. Again, the law providing for self-defence is a subsequent precept, because it depends on the decision of one man, or State, to attack another. The importance of this distinction between basic precepts and subsequent ones is considerable because, while the original ones are universal, that is, they are always and everywhere valid, the subsequent ones vary according to historical circumstances of time and place. An example of a natural law which has varied because of a change of historical and social circumstances is usury. When money was used as a mere means of exchange, there was no right to interest on a loan, but when it took on the nature of capital, the lender could demand a return on his capital, since by lending to another he was depriving himself of its capacity to earn for him. In all these cases, the norm has not changed, but rather another norm has taken its place due to changed historical circumstances.

The basic precepts, unlike their derivatives, cannot be obliterated from the human mind. They can, of course, be opposed on particular occasions, as when someone takes another's life or refuses to admit the obvious truth; but the general principle will return to consciousness, and, in many cases, the wrongness of the action will be admitted, however tentatively. St Thomas made a distinction between propositions which are self-evident in themselves and those which are self-evident to us. Consequently, even self-evident statements will not be accepted by everybody all the time. This may be due to passion, self-interest or, more likely, an incorrect understanding of the terms used. So, for example, somebody who wrongly conceives marriage to be a 'union for the sake of sensual love and self-gratification' will not grasp the wrongness of adultery. As we proceed further away from the basic precepts to the subsequent ones and the more specific manifestations of the natural law, so there will be more disagreement. The fact that the Commandments are not known in their entirety and by everybody does not take away from their obligatory nature or, indeed, their objectively self-evident character. Julius Caesar comments in *De bello gallico* that the Germans did not recognize theft to be evil,[7] but that in no way lessens the wrongness of theft. What is expected of those who have gaps in their basic moral knowledge is that they, at least, make a sincere search for the truth in the hope that they will come to recognize that moral certainty and completeness is to be found in the revealed Decalogue.

UNIVERSALITY AND IMMUTABILITY

Veritatis splendor confirms that the primary principles of the natural law are universally valid and immutable because they are based on those

---

7. Quoted in ibid., I-II, q. 94 art. 4.

unchanging elements of human nature which transcend cultural conditions. 'The negative precepts of the natural law are universally valid. They oblige each and every individual, always and in every circumstance. It is a matter of prohibitions which forbid a given action *semper et pro semper*, without exception, because the choice of this kind of behaviour is in no case compatible with the goodness of the will of the acting person, with his vocation to life with God and to communion with his neighbour. It is prohibited—to everyone and in every case—to violate these precepts. They oblige everyone regardless of the cost, never to offend in anyone, beginning with oneself, the personal dignity common to all' (no. 52).

It is true that cultures change and vary, but the very fact that they can progress shows there is something in man which transcends them, namely, human nature. The encyclical goes on: 'to call into question the permanent structural elements of man which are connected with his own bodily dimension would not only conflict with common experience, but would render meaningless *Jesus' reference to the "beginning"*, precisely where the social and cultural context of the time had distorted the primordial meaning and the role of certain moral norms (cf. Mt 19:1-9)' (no. 53).

SOME INDISPENSABLE MORAL RULES

To pass from the most general principles to more specific conclusions we must act in accordance with certain rules. These are basic moral requirements, which most of us are familiar with but which we must observe in our ethical reasoning if we are not to go astray.

The first is that each basic value must be respected in every act. All the above-listed goods are basic manifestations of the total good of the individual. Since each is, therefore, an intrinsic good, it cannot be directly transgressed without doing evil. Thus, one's attitude to these goods gives rise to the good and bad actions found in a moral system. This doesn't mean, however, that these goods are all of equal importance but simply that each is inviolable. Clearly, religion is more important than intellectual knowledge, but the latter must be preferred to sport. And so, while the martyr may die for religious truth and the soldier in defence of a just cause and his country, he must not throw away his life or lose it unnecessarily, for example, as a suicide pilot. Neither of these people is directly choosing death: the martyr is opting for his conscience and the soldier for justice. Again, a parent may desire a child's examination success, but not at the expense of his or her mental and physical well-being.

It is a well-known moral rule that 'the end doesn't justify the means'. You should not carry out an action because of the benefits which are supposed to accrue if that action transgresses a basic good. You should not take a life deliberately in order to save another life or in order to save a person from suffering. A dictator may not tell his people lies with the excuse of controlling them and keeping law and order. An army may not torture its prisoners of war to extract useful intelligence information. If any of these things were allowed in one case, how could we stop proponents of mass killing from claiming they were doing it for beneficial purposes?

Our criterion of good and bad, then, is not simply a calculation of relative benefit and harm; it is based on self-evident basic human goods which may never be opposed. This gives us a criterion to judge between good and evil and also, where necessary, between good and good. But perhaps the most difficult moral cases are those between competing evils, that is, where evil results whichever action you choose. These are the so-called 'hard cases' particularly beloved of proponents of a relativist morality. Such cases remind us of the need to bear in mind the principle that one may 'never do evil that good may come of it' (cf. Rom 3:8). Thus, one may never directly do or desire an evil which would come about by going against a basic good or a norm of the moral law. However, there are good actions which bring about evil effects not directly willed or intended; some of these actions are permissible in certain circumstances. We will now turn our attention to this question.

RULES FOR THE RESOLUTION OF HARD CASES

More and more in moral debate about conflict situations, the hard case is brought up. What does one do, when a pregnant mother with a cancerous uterus must have an operation to survive although, as a result, she will lose the child? What happens when the foetus gets stuck in the wall of the womb or in the fallopian tube, and an ectopic pregnancy results? What does a Catholic assistant working in a pharmacy do, when his contract requires him to sell contraceptives, and his livelihood depends on the job? What does one do with a patient who is brain dead but living in a persistent 'vegetative' state on a ventilator? In other words, one is sometimes faced in moral questions with situations where both courses of action either seem to be wrong or bring with them evil consequences.

• *The Principle of Double Effect*   Some of these issues can be resolved by a well-known principle in moral theology, that of double effect. Clearly, one may never do evil even if a good effect is foreseen coming from it, but, on the other hand, one *may* carry out a good action, under certain conditions, despite the fact that one foresees a serious evil resulting from it. We must, however, pay careful attention to the conditions, because while this principle authorizes a series of actions it also excludes many others.

The four conditions are as follows:

1   the act done must be good in itself;

2   the agent must have a right intention, that is, he or she must desire the good effect and not the evil one;

3   the first effect must be good or at least equal first with the evil effect (this prevents a good effect resulting from an evil one);

4   there must be a proportionately grave reason to justify the act.

The application of these principles means that surgeons may justifiably operate on a pregnant woman whose cancerous uterus will lead to her death if she is not operated on during her pregnancy, even though they know the action will bring with it the undesired death of the child. The reason is that the act itself is good (to remove cancer from an organ); the first effect is good, that is, the restored health of the mother (this is also the intention); and the reason is proportionately grave (to save the mother's life). But there is all the difference in the world between this and the abortion of a child because the mother is suffering kidney failure or hypertension or some other health hazard. In these cases, the first action (abortion) is not good, and one is doing evil that good may come of it. One may only proceed when one is directly treating the mother's ailment itself and for a just reason. The fact that the mother's life is endangered (a point often exaggerated) is not a justification if the therapeutic method is not itself good.

With regard to other forms of cooperation in evil, such as, working in a pharmacy that dispenses contraceptives, or a bookstore that sells pornography, or with a lawyer who deals with divorce legislation, or voting in immoral legislation, the principle of double effect may sometimes apply. But these are complex matters and a whole section will be devoted to them later.

• *The Principle of Totality*   This is the principle underlying all surgical operations, which are justified on the understanding that they benefit the total physical well-being of the person.[8] It is an extension of the principle of

8. Pope Pius XII to Roman Guild of St Luke, 12 November 1944.

self-preservation. The mutilation of a physical organ for no good reason is not allowed. However, a diseased organ may clearly be extracted for the good of the whole. In these days of transplant surgery, this principle is extended to cover the donation of an organ from a live owner to benefit the life of a third party. This may be done (for example, the donation of a kidney) provided it does not gravely endanger the life of the donor or prejudice his total physical well-being. The action must also accord with the conditions for the indirectly voluntary as described above. The ethics of transplant surgery will be given fuller treatment later.

THE DIGNITY AND RIGHTS OF THE HUMAN PERSON

The most fundamental human rights flow from the ends and tendencies of man, in the same way and at the same time as the precepts of the natural law. They belong to human beings because they are persons, rather than under any other title, and take for granted the radical equality of every person. This leaves no room for discrimination on grounds of handicap, age, race, colour etc. In the last analysis, man's dignity comes from the fact that he is made in the image of God. If the human being is master of creation, and of his own acts, it is only as a secondary cause dependent on the primary causality of God. Just as all authority derives from the first Being and Wisdom, and all law from the eternal law, so all rights come from the rights possessed by God himself, some of which he shares with man.

If man has the duty to attain certain ends, then he must have the rights to do so. If he is destined to fulfil and develop himself spiritually, intellectually and physically, then he must have a correlative capacity to do this. Hence, a right may be defined as a moral power to do, or have, something. So, Suarez called it 'a kind of moral power which every man has, either over his own property, or with respect to that which is due to him'.[9] There is a difference between a law and a right, although they are related as the foundation to the founded. A law is a norm of action (*norma agendi*), whereas a right is a capacity or power of acting (*facultas agendi*). Rights are of different importance just as natural laws are, some being prior to others.

The human person is part of the material world and the State, yet at the same time he transcends them due to his spiritual dimension. His perfection, however, consists above all in the fulfilment of his moral and spiritual potential. This fact orders and conditions his rights, all of which should be

9. *De Legibus*, I, ii, 5.

compatible with his spiritual well-being. Since he reaches this well-being by means of the natural law, and his dignity depends on following it, no rights can exist outside of it.

This Christian basis of human rights is at odds with the rationalist and positivist interpretation given to them. This latter claims that man is subject to no law other than that of his own will, and freedom is emancipated from a transcendent Being and Law, such that he creates the law for himself. He confers on himself the 'right of self-will', as Newman described it, or he must 'obey only himself' in the words of Rousseau.[10] It is from this source that people lay claim to many of the moral deviations and contradictory 'rights' of the present time. From it comes a wrong idea of dominion over human life, as a consequence of which man arrogates to himself the 'right' to manipulate human life at its beginning in the laboratory by embryo research, or take it away at its end by euthanasia. From here also comes the feminist claim that a woman has an *absolute* right over her own body and the consequent 'right' to choose in the matter of abortion.

Maritain has said: 'The French Declaration of the Rights of Man framed these rights in the altogether rationalist point of view of the Enlightenment and the Encyclopedists, and to that extent enveloped them in ambiguity.'[11] By this he meant that a document such as this, based only on positive law, created contradictory rights. The result has sometimes been, historically, that a reaction sets in from those who maintain the bankruptcy of all human rights. Neither extreme is tenable, but the dilemma only points to the necessity of founding rights on the true dignity of man, which in turn is based on his being made in the 'image and likeness of God.'

The State exists to foster the common good, that is to say, the creation of conditions necessary for individuals in society to fulfil their own ends and achieve fulfilment and perfection. Though there is a situation of mutual service between the individual and the State, the latter is predominantly at the service of the person and the family, rather than the other way round. Logically and naturally, the State is made up of the amalgam of families whose purpose is to facilitate the fulfilment and all round well-being of the individual persons who comprise them. The person, therefore, transcends the State, and, in fact, the whole natural order is directed towards the good of the person.

Consequently, the State or community must respect the goods of man. It must respect the moral law and the rights and duties of conscience to know

10. Cf. J. Maritain, *The Rights of Man*, London, 1944, p. 38, and J. H. Newman, *Letter to the Duke of Norfolk*.
11. Maritain, ibid., p. 45.

the law of God and tend towards him. It must also respect the universe of truths to which the intellect tends, that is to say, the truths of science, wisdom, literature, history etc. Within the State or society of man, there follow from the rights of the person his civic (or political) rights and his social rights, which have to do mainly with work and employment. Hence, rights such as those of universal suffrage or the right to strike are based on positive law but are dependent on the natural rights to freedom and to employment. We will not be concerned here with these, for we want only to establish the fundamental rights of the human person as a basis for the matters to be discussed in future chapters.

Because of the dignity and transcendent vocation of the human person, and because of the State's subordination to man, every human being enjoys a series of fundamental rights which must be observed if he is to fulfil his destiny. The most basic one is that of life and existence, for it is presupposed to all others. This is true from the moment of conception and includes the right to procreate and multiply the human race. There then follows the right to personal freedom, that is, to be master of one's own acts and answerable and, therefore, responsible for them. This includes the right to choose one's state in life, and marry the person of one's choice, and enjoy sufficient protection for one's family. Man's intellect gives him the right to seek knowledge and be told the truth in the media, education, preaching etc. Linked to this is the right to seek the truth about God and the free exercise of religious worship. On the level of practical reason, there is the right to the perfection of a moral and rational human life in which happiness essentially consists and, on the physical level, the right to bodily integrity, health and leisure.

These rights, however, all include duties, and since they affect basic goods none of them can be opposed to other basic goods (according to the rules we set out above). So, for example, the right to life is the right to the preservation of one's life, and so there can be no right to take it away; indeed, there is a duty to preserve it. The same holds true for bodily integrity, which must be maintained, except in the case of a diseased organ which may be extracted in the interests of the physical whole. There can be no right to dispose of one's life at will: dominion of it belongs to God; we only possess stewardship of it. Again, because no right can go against a basic good, there can be no 'right' to choose in the matter of abortion or to destructive embryo research. Such a view contravenes the fundamental right of the most innocent human being—the foetus in the womb.

It is manifest that rights may be abused in various ways. Some 'rights' are claimed by individuals, or groups, who simply desire something, or believe they have need of something, or want to establish a position with respect to an opposing group. If such claims do not fulfil other conditions, these criteria are quite insufficient. Claims to rights for homosexuals and women's right to choose in abortion are cases in point. A clear distinction, however, must be made between the so-called homosexual, or pro-choice rights etc. and the rights which homosexuals, or supporters of abortion, enjoy as persons and which they share with all other people.

Rights are limited by other peoples' rights as well as by responsibility to the natural law. Free speech, for example, is conditioned by the right of others not to be libelled or slandered, and by the need to maintain public order as well as by the natural duty to tell the truth. Property rights allow one to extend one's house as long as it doesn't obscure one's neighbours' view, or cause them unreasonable inconvenience. Rights such as these, as we have seen, are *established* by positive law but *founded* on some prior natural law. The idea that all rights are based on positive law is, in Maritain's words, 'a destructive illusion', because it is impossible to achieve without contravening other basic rights, as the abortion issue dramatically demonstrates. As we know, on the other hand, the natural law tradition teaches us that *no* basic value can be used to override another basic value, and the same applies to the corresponding rights.

Pope John Paul states in *Evangelium vitae*, 20, that: 'to claim the right to abortion, infanticide and euthanasia, and to recognize that right in law, means to attribute to human freedom *a perverse and evil significance*: that of an *absolute power over others and against others*. This is the death of true freedom: "Truly, truly I say to you, everyone who commits sin is a slave to sin" (Jn 8:34).' And he adds elsewhere in the same encyclical (at no. 96) that 'when freedom is detached from objective truth it becomes impossible to establish personal rights on a firm rational basis; and the ground is laid for society to be at the mercy of the unrestrained will of individuals or the oppressive totalitarianism of public authority.'

Though limited by natural law, rights are not necessarily limited by positive law if this conflicts with the natural law, because a law which is not based on natural law is not a law at all. Citizens of a State are, therefore, not acting illegally when they oppose laws favouring abortion and embryo research. It must be remembered that, while the human person from one point of view is a part of the whole (the national community), from another point of view he himself is a spiritual whole and therefore transcends it. This means, firstly, that rights of conscience should be respected when this does not endanger the common good and, secondly, that all rights should be ordered to the spiritual good and last end of man.

[4]

The Light and Truth of Conscience

Where morality most affects the ordinary person is in his or her day-to-day decisions, and it is this act of moral judgement which, in the first instance, we call conscience. In this sense, conscience may be described as an act of the mind telling one what is right and wrong and which approves or disapproves of one's actions either by peace of mind or by remorse. This common experience of disapproval was often noted by Shakespeare, as when Richard III says:

> My conscience hath a thousand several tongues,
> And every tongue brings in a several tale,
> And every tale condemns me for a villain.[1]

This gives us a description of what may be called 'particular conscience', but it must be completed by an understanding of 'general conscience'. Rightness and wrongness come from the natural law, which is imprinted on the mind and heart of the individual. Consequently, conscience is the apprehension of the natural law, which is the impression of the eternal law within us. By this we simply mean that the first principles of morality are self-evident to everybody, and it is impossible to obliterate them from the mind. The intellect is able to deduce further moral norms from these premises; in this it is ably assisted by the traditions and customs of its upbringing and, in the case of Christians, by the teaching of the Church. A degree of moral knowledge and the virtue of prudence are called for, but again this is not simply a specialist matter; it is available to everybody.

A true conscience reflects the natural moral law faithfully. In other words, it is one in which there is a link between the particular and general moral conscience. Vatican II lays stress on conscience being a reflection of the eternal law within us. 'Deep within his conscience, man discovers a law which he has not laid upon himself, but which he must obey. Its voice, ever

---

1. *Richard III*, V, iii.

calling him to do what is good and to avoid evil, tells him inwardly at the right moment: do this, shun that. For man has in his heart a law inscribed by God. His dignity lies in observing this law, and by it he will be judged' (*Gaudium et spes*, 16). In another document we read: 'It is through his conscience that man sees and recognizes the demands of the divine law' (*Dignitatis humanae*, 3).

Conscience is the application of the law to specific situations. It is not itself a faculty but is rather a judgement of the practical intellect. *Veritatis splendor*, 59, tells us: 'The judgement of conscience states "in an ultimate way" whether a certain particular kind of behaviour is in conformity with the law; it formulates the proximate norm of morality of a voluntary act, "applying the objective law to a particular case".'

In some European languages the word for 'conscience' and that for 'consciousness' are the same, pointing to the fact that conscience is an awareness of a natural law, that is to say, of the fundamental values and principles of human behaviour. Such is the traditional teaching of Christianity handed on through the Fathers and based firmly on Scripture. St Paul tells us: 'As for the Gentiles, though they have no law to guide them, there are times when they carry out the precepts of the law unbidden, finding in their own natures a rule to guide them . . . their conscience utters its testimony, and when they dispute with one another they find themselves condemning this, approving that' (Rom 2:14-15).

The dignity of man is closely connected with his conscience, because it is a spark of the divinity within him. It is the voice of God in us and not the creation of man. Thus, again *Gaudium et spes*: 'His conscience is man's most secret core and his sanctuary. There he is alone with God, whose voice echoes in his depths' (no. 16). This is the reason why conscience must be followed—because it manifests the will of God to the individual. As we shall see, conscience can err, of course, but nevertheless its light is never completely extinguished. The intellect is naturally orientated towards the truth. With goodwill (which is essential) and by understanding conscience correctly as explained here, it need not go wrong. Man's dignity grows when he follows a conscience based on the dictates of the natural law and goodwill. As long as any ignorance is not blameworthy, his dignity is not impaired.

Over the last two hundred years, however, the conventional wisdom has tended to break the link between the eternal law and conscience, and ignore the fact that the latter is a reflection of the former. The Enlightenment and Kant gave rise to the idea of 'autonomous conscience', which dictates norms to itself. Judgements of conscience from then to our own day have become, for many, simply subjective decisions based on feelings, utilitarian principles, self-interest etc. Indeed, some are prejudices cloaked with an appeal to conscience. It is for this reason that two groups of people can come to diametrically opposed conclusions on important subjects, such as abortion and embryo research, and both appeal to conscience for their decision.

Newman foresaw this trend in the latter half of the last century: 'When men advocate the rights of conscience they in no sense mean the rights of the Creator, nor the duty to Him, in thought and deed, of the creature; but the right of thinking, speaking, writing and acting according to their judgement or their humour without any thought of God at all. They do not even pretend to go by any moral rule, but they demand what they think is an Englishman's prerogative, for each to be his own master in all things, and to profess what he pleases, asking no one's leave and accounting priest or preacher, speaker or writer, unutterably impertinent who dares to say a word against his going to perdition, if he likes, in his own way. Conscience has rights because it has duties, but in this age with a large portion of the public it is the very right and freedom of conscience to dispense with conscience, to ignore a Lawgiver and Judge, to be independent of unseen obligations . . . . It is the right of self-will.'[2]

Pope John Paul II has this to say in *Veritatis splendor*, 32:

> Certain currents of modern thought have gone so far as to *exalt freedom to such an extent that it becomes an absolute, which would then be the souce of values*. This is the direction taken by doctrines which have lost the sense of the transcendent or which are explictly atheist. The individual conscience is accorded the status of a supreme tribunal of moral judgment which hands down categorical and infallible decisions about good and evil. To the affirmation that one has a duty to follow one's conscience is unduly added the affirmation that one's moral judgment is true merely by the fact that it has its origin in the conscience. But in this way the inescapable claims of truth disappear, yielding their place to a criterion of sincerity, authenticity and "being at peace with oneself", so much so that some have come to adopt a radically subjectivistic conception of moral judgment.
>
> As is immediately evident, *the crisis of truth* is not unconnected with this development. Once the idea of a universal truth about the good, knowable by human reason, is lost, inevitably the notion of

2. J. H. Newman, *Letter to the Duke of Norfolk*, op. cit.

conscience also changes. Conscience is no longer considered in its primordial reality as an act of a person's intelligence, the function of which is to apply the universal knowledge of the good in a specific situation and thus to express a judgment about the right conduct to be chosen here and now. Instead, there is a tendency to grant to the individual conscience the prerogative of independently determining the criteria of good and evil and then acting accordingly. Such an outlook is quite congenial to an individualist ethic, wherein each individual is faced with his own truth, different from the truth of others. Taken to its extreme consequences, this individualism leads to a denial of the very idea of human nature.

These different notions are at the origin of currents of thought which posit a radical opposition between moral law and conscience, and between nature and freedom.

The idea that man can dictate his own moral norms is a perennial temptation. By it he pretends to *create* his own moral values. 'You will be like God knowing good and evil' (Gen 3:5), says the devil to Adam and Eve. Such a notion is very widespread among those, for example, who believe we may use contraceptives, abort babies, get divorced and practise sex before marriage 'as long as our conscience doesn't accuse us'. In such a case, goes the argument, we can act with impunity in spite of the fact that Christian Tradition and the Magisterium have consistently declared these things to be immoral. This is justified by saying that man must re-interpret the general norms in his own cultural, social and historical circumstances. To this one must reply that conscience is not a feeling, or an intuition, but an act of judgement based on reason. Furthermore, it is a reason which mirrors the eternal law, which is immutable throughout the centuries.

In all this we may notice a subtle attempt to change the norm of morality. Where it was once the eternal law which dictated, through conscience, moral norms, it is now autonomous conscience itself, or the principle of benefit over harm, or the greatest happiness of the greatest number, or simply self-interest which does so. Hence the need to re-affirm that moral principles are the reflection of the eternal law in the human intellect. *Veritatis splendor*, 60, states that the dignity and authority of conscience

derive from the truth about moral good and evil, which it is called to listen to and express. This truth is indicated by the 'divine law', *the universal and objective norm of morality*. The judgement of con-science does not establish the law; rather, it bears witness to the authority of the natural law and of the practical reason with reference to the supreme good, whose attractiveness the human person perceives and whose commandments he accepts.

It is true that some of the particular moral conclusions from the eternal law require a degree of moral knowledge and training that most people do not have, especially in the circumstances of today; but for that very reason Revelation and the Magisterium are at the service of conscience and not at odds with it. The moral norms which these authorities proportion to us are not contrary to man's freedom, or an arbitrary expression of the will of God. They are, rather, moral and salvific truths, which reveal the truth about the good of the human person.

FREEDOM OF CONSCIENCE

The Church defends the right and the duty of the person to follow his or her conscience, even when invincibly in error; hence, Newman's phrase that it is the 'aboriginal Vicar of Christ'. But, at the same time, she demands that conscience be formed and educated so that nobody acts with culpable or vincible ignorance. If someone could and should have come to know the law or the facts of the case and did not do so, that person is morally answerable for his or her actions. This is 'vincible' ignorance and so does not excuse as a cause of morally bad actions. Consequently, one errs in following such a conscience. If, however, that ignorance could not reasonably have been overcome (that it to say, is 'invincible'), then a fault is not committed and conscience does not lose its dignity.

Conscience is the core of the individual's personality; it is where one is alone with God and one's responsibilities, and, according to the Church's teaching, its dictates or judgements must be tolerated even if wrong. Vatican II is justly famous for its declarations on religious freedom, and freedom of conscience, properly understood. What it has to say is based on the fact that no violence may be used to force a right judgement, since an action has moral worth only when it is done freely. This is not to say that error has rights but that *persons* do. Nor do we know, in a particular case, to what extent a person is responsible for his judgements, the pressures on him, the information available to him etc. All the Church says is that if he were able to overcome his ignorance, and has not chosen to do so, he is guilty of culpable ignorance. If he has avoided finding out the moral law, or has purposely not checked, for example, if such and such a financial transaction is fraudulent, he is guilty of vincible ignorance and is, therefore, culpable.

Vatican II (*Dignitatis humanae*, 3) puts it in the following way:

> It is through his conscience that man sees and recognizes the demands of the divine law. He is bound to follow this conscience faithfully in all his activity so that he may come to God, who is his last end. Therefore, he must not be forced to act contrary to his conscience, nor must he be prevented from acting according to his conscience, especially in religious matters. The reason is because the practice of religion of its very nature consists primarily of those voluntary and free internal acts by which a man directs himself to God. Acts of this kind cannot be commanded or forbidden by any purely human authority.

At the same time, what the Church consistently condemns is freedom of conscience where this means mere licence to form the moral views that one likes. This is not freedom but licence (moral free-for-all). It is in this sense that the Popes of the last century condemned the expression, and the Church continues to condemn it today. *Dignitatis humanae* makes clear that man is bound to accept a commitment to seek the truth. Therefore, to acquiesce in a so-called free-thinking role is not permitted. The same document says: 'all men are both impelled by their nature and bound by a moral obligation to seek the truth.' And, having found it, 'They are bound to adhere to the truth . . . and direct their whole lives in accordance with the demands of the truth' (no. 2). What the Church rejects is the supposed freedom of the self-appointed conscience which prescinds from God.

Freedom must be subject to the truth, which is why Blessed Josemaría Escrivá wrote as follows:

> The only freedom that can assail the faith is a misinterpreted freedom, an aimless freedom, one without objective principles, one that is lawless and irresponsible, in a word, licence. Unfortunately, this is what some people are advocating, and their claim does indeed constitute a threat to the faith. This is why it is inaccurate to speak of 'freedom of conscience' thereby implying that it may be morally right for someone to reject God. We have already seen that it is in our power to oppose God's plans for our salvation. It is in our power but we should not do so. If someone adopted this attitude deliberately, he would be sinning,

by breaking the first and most important of the commandments, 'Thou shalt love the Lord thy God with thy whole heart.'[3]

Or again, Newman insists that the natural or divine law must be the standard of truth or the backdrop of conscience which is, at least, sought after:

> The rule and measure of duty is not utility, nor expedience, nor the happiness of the greatest number, nor State convenience, nor fitness, order and the 'pulchrum'. Conscience is not a long-sighted selfishness, nor a desire to be consistent with oneself; but it is a messenger from Him, who, both in nature and grace, speaks to us behind a veil, and teaches and rules us by His representatives. Conscience is the aboriginal Vicar of Christ, a prophet in its informations, a monarch in its peremptoriness, a priest in its blessings and anathemas, and even though the eternal priesthood throughout the Church could cease to be, in it the sacerdotal principle would remain and have a sway.[4]

Freedom of conscience is really a paradigm case for an understanding of all freedom. It must be administered with responsibility and be subject to the truth, or to an honest search for the truth. The duty to follow one's conscience is paralleled by the duty to seek the truth and the freedom to do so. Indeed, Vatican II teaches that real freedom comes from obeying a true conscience. By following it when it is true and correct, one becomes more and more human; by disobeying it, one offends against human dignity. Moral life invites man to effect a dominion over self, which is a demand of his nature and which the kingly character of baptism additionally confers on him. Thus, the Shakespearean dictum 'Conscience doth make cowards of us all'[5] expresses only part of the truth, namely that our conscience, at times, causes remorse, but its main purpose is to make dignified and whole persons of us.

TRUE AND FALSE CONSCIENCE

There is a clear difference between a *certain* conscience and a *true* one. Certainty applies to the psychological conviction with which one holds a

3. *Friends of God*, Dublin, 1981, p. 25.
4. *Letter to the Duke of Norfolk*, op. cit.
5. *Hamlet*, III, i.

view. As noted, a conscience is true or false according to whether it is in conformity with the natural law or not. Error in a conscience may be culpable or inculpable depending on whether the ignorance which causes it could be overcome or not. Vincible ignorance occurs when someone neglects to seek the truth, either of the law or the facts, whether in a singular case or in general.

The foundation of the distinction between vincible and invincible ignorance lies in the disposition of the will with regard to the search for the true good. When the will is upright, generally man can reach the truth. If he has used the means to reach it, even though without success, his conscience authorizes him to go ahead. There is an obligation to follow one's conscience provided it is true or invincibly ignorant. The possibility of the latter can be seen in our Lord's treatment of the Pharisees, who were blamed not for suffering from true blindness, but for not *wanting* to see, for 'if you were *really* blind, you would be without sin' (Jn 9:41; italics added). St Paul says that he who erroneously judges that eating sacrificial food is wrong cannot eat it without sinning (cf. Rom 14:1-23). The reason for the obligatoriness of the invincibly ignorant conscience is that its command is taken in good faith as the expression of the will of God.

One should not, on the other hand, follow a vincibly erroneous conscience. Doubt and lack of security in judgement point to such a conscience. Where serious and practical doubt are experienced, a person should refrain from acting. Dissatisfaction and uneasiness with a proposed line of action indicate the need for further enquiry before acting. An absence of doubt and unease point to an absence of vincible ignorance.

In order to overcome the doubt, all available means must be used. What do these consist in? They involve acquiring the necessary knowledge of the moral law and maintaining vigilance and an interior struggle (particularly through the frequent reception of the sacraments) so as to avoid allowing conscience to become deformed by the disordered desires of the will (cf. Heb 13:8). The light of conscience comes from the light God grants to each one, by nature and by grace. Everybody is responsible for keeping that light alight and not letting it go out. False advice and the pressures and fashions of the environment can influence one's decision, but they never take away the basic ability to distinguish between good and evil (cf. Rom 14:12 and Gal 6:4).

A deformed conscience usually comes about through a practical neglect of moral truths, followed by the tendency to justify oneself, and hence attenuate and change those truths. It is truly said: 'If you don't act as you believe, you end up believing as you act.' Since it is not easy to reject the evidence of the first principles, what usually happens is that one begins by obscuring them, provoking doubt and finding difficulties for their practical application. This is done by habitually seeking out the hard cases, for example, wife-beating to justify divorce, the mentally retarded woman as an argument for sterilization, social deprivation or handicap for abortion etc., in order to justify a general moral principle. This deformation is increased by the moral and doctrinal confusion of society, by bad reading etc. In the last analysis, conscience formation depends on one's personal responsibility. People may sometimes be deceived inculpably, but it is difficult for that to happen without some internal complicity.

Typically deformed consciences are the lax, the perplexed and the scrupulous. By a lax conscience we mean one that, for insufficient reasons, judges something not to be a sin, or not to be a serious sin, when in fact it is—for example, people who give little importance to defrauding a person of his salary, consenting to impure thoughts, attending or watching immoral shows etc. As time goes on, a lax conscience becomes hardened and scarcely adverts to the fact that sins are being committed. Judgements made with a lax conscience are, by and large, vincibly ignorant and, thus, culpable.

Contrary to the above, a man with a scrupulous or perplexed conscience fears sinning yet has no grounds for his fear. The scrupulous person, for futile reasons, believes something is a sin which isn't, so he becomes very anxious about having a bad thought, or treating somebody unkindly etc. Scrupulosity often comes from the need to feel security, and has its roots in pride and self-love due to forgetfulness of others and an inordinate concern for one's own well-being. It can also come from pathological dispositions such as nervousness, psychical weakness and so on (in such cases, psychiatric help may be needed). Exceptionally, scrupulosity can be permitted as a means of purification, but in this case it is transitory and gradually disappears.

Only a certain conscience may be followed, that is, one that is free from reasonable doubt. That doesn't mean that there may not be reasons for not following a particular form of action, but only that there aren't *grave* reasons. It is never licit, however, to act with positive practical doubts of conscience where the doubt is based, not on facile reasons, but on serious ones and is of a practical, not a speculative, nature. In such cases, one is first of all obliged to employ the necessary means to reach certainty before acting. This is done by studying the moral law and the case in question, and asking advice from somebody who is competent and sound. Once this has been done, one may use what are known as 'reflex principles' in all cases except the very gravest, such as those concerning the validity of the sacra-ments, where there is a risk of losing eternal life, or when a matter involves an established right of a third party. The more important reflex principles are: (a) in doubt one must stand by presumption; and, (b) possession is nine tenths of the law. In the case of presumption, a person of normally well formed and upright conscience may presume to be in the right in case of doubt, whereas one with a normally lax conscience should presume the opposite.

EDUCATING CONSCIENCE

The fact that we are fallible human beings who frequently make mistakes and experience doubt in making conscientious decisions points to the ongo-ing need for the formation of conscience. Bishop del Portillo writes:

> The problem of conscience is fundamentally a problem of truth, 'to practise the truth in love' (Eph 4:5) . . . . This love of truth is the starting point for the formation of conscience. Today, this love must conquer and cure a widespread and dangerous illness, namely, indif-ference to truth. This attitude stems from the idea that possessing truth is not a primary value for man. Frequently it arises from the prejudice that truth causes division among men and is, therefore, harmful for peace and harmony in society.[6]

This task of education involves, for everybody, the effort to acquire the necessary moral knowledge, the cultivation of the virtues, especially humil-ity and sincerity, and, for the Christian, repentance, sacramental confession and spiritual direction. With regard to the first of these, a vague goodwill and desire for authenticity is not enough. A knowledge of natural law and, for Christians, of divine positive law or the Commandments is required. This should be on a par with the general education and formation of each person, enabling him or her to apply the right criteria to matters that arise.

Since the Church is the guardian of Revelation and the authentic inter-preter of divine law, to have moral knowledge a person needs to have an adequate knowledge of what the Magisterium teaches. For this knowledge to be practical, one frequently needs to seek advice. To be able to judge the

6. *Position Paper 202*, Dublin, October 1990.

morality of an individual act in light of general principles, one needs the help of experience. A person without much experience should take counsel, hence the importance to a Christian of spiritual direction with a learned, discerning and holy person.

Since errors are unavoidable in our behaviour, humility and sincerity in recognizing them are indispensable for the formation of conscience. The pride of man, who is tempted 'to become like gods' and dictate norms to himself all too easily, justifies actions like abortion, sterilization and euthanasia when they become widespread in the society. Without an examination of conscience and sincerity of life, the light of conscience too readily becomes dimmed. When this happens, the sacrament of penance is a necessary source of rectification, because it confers grace and heals human weakness and the waywardness of the will.

CONSCIENCE, THE MAGISTERIUM AND *HUMANAE VITAE*

The light of conscience and the first principles of morality, together with their more detailed conclusions, are made firm and certain by Revelation and the Magisterium of the Church. It is impossible for man to know the whole moral law without making a mistake due to his fallen human nature and weakness of will. The most general principles are known, although even these can be obscured for long periods of time, as is the case with the self-evidence of the procreative good in marriage. However, as the principles and deductions become more particular, it is more difficult for us to grasp their morality accurately, as for example in the case of *in vitro* fertilization, or in cases where, whatever the course of action, some evil effect seems to follow.

For a Catholic who believes it to be based on divine authority, the Church's teaching is not something separate from his conscience, or opposed to it, but rather an essential part of the formation of it. A Catholic draws light from Scripture and Christian Tradition. As a modern treatment of the subject puts it:

> If a Catholic finds a measure of conflict between some of his or her convictions and the Teaching of the Church, this conflict will be *within* the person's conscience, and not a conflict *between* the person's conscience and an alien authority. This is true because the teachings of the Church—as far as the believing Catholic is concerned—are teachings of a faith he, or she, freely accepted and made

his, or her, own. They enter into the formation of the believing Catholic's conscience (italics added).[7]

In the past three decades considerable debate has been generated over the Church's authority to teach on morals. Those who have taken up a position of dissent and challenged the Church's traditional teaching on moral and sexual matters claim that she does not teach these truths infallibly; for example, in the case of the prohibition on artificial birth control. To this it must be said that the moral teaching of the Church must be covered by the certainty that has always been claimed for it, because, without a reliable knowledge of these matters, people would be left without the means to attain their salvation (cf. *Humanae vitae*, 4).

The Church's and the Pope's infallibility may be expressed either by the solemn or extraordinary Magisterium, or by the ordinary. To use his solemn Magisterium the Pope must speak *ex cathedra*, that is to say, in his office as supreme Pastor with the intention of binding all the faithful on a matter of faith or morals. An Ecumenical Council may do likewise. But, it must be borne in mind that what is communicated by the ordinary Magisterium may also be infallible teaching if it meets certain conditions. By 'ordinary Magisterium' we understand the authentic day to day teaching of the Pope on his own, or that of the Pope and the bishops together. The conditions may certainly be said to exist in the case of *Humanae vitae*. Thus we may say the doctrine it contains is *taught* infallibly even though it is not *defined* infallibly. For this reason, the present Pope has said that the ordinary Magisterium must be considered as the *usual* source of the Church's infallibility.[8]

This was clearly and providentially stated at Vatican II in *Lumen gentium*, 25. It says

> Although the bishops taken individually do not enjoy the privilege of infallibility, they do, however, proclaim infallibly the doctrine of Christ on the following conditions: namely, when even though dispersed throughout the world but preserving for all that amongst themselves and with Peter's successor the bond of communion, in their authoritative teaching concerning matters of faith and morals, they are in agreement that a particular teaching is to be held definitively and absolutely.

7. Lawler, Boyle & May, *Catholic Sexual Ethics*, Huntingdon, Indiana, 1985, pp. 110-11.
8. John Paul II, General Audience, October 1987.

More specifically, therefore, the conditions are:

1   The bishops should be in communion with each other and with the Pope (such communion is integral to being a Catholic bishop).

2   It should be on a matter of faith and morals, into which latter category *Humanae vitae* clearly fits.

3   The bishops dispersed throughout the world must agree on a particular teaching. This refers to moral (rather than mathematical) unanimity of judgement and also to the whole of Christian tradition rather than just one period of time (such as the contemporary one). Nevertheless, it is evident that if at one point a doctrine is taught infallibly, then it is infallible for all time even if at some time in the future there is a falling away of bishops who believe in it. Nobody doubts that, up to 1962, no bishop in any way dissented from the traditional teaching on the immorality of contraception.

4   There should be agreement in proposing that the judgement be held definitively. This doesn't refer to the manner of the formulation of the teaching, i.e., whether it is solemn Magisterium or ordinary; it concerns the Church's intention that it should be accepted as definitive.

This infallibility is 'co-extensive with the deposit of revelation which must be religiously guarded and loyally and courageously expounded' (*Lumen gentium*, 25). This raises two questions: 1) whether the immorality of contraception can be said to be taught in Revelation and 2) what the limits of that deposit are. The most explicit reference to contraception in Scripture is probably the story of Onan (see p. 101f). In the New Testament various forms of impurity are prohibited and, it can be said, the underlying reason for this is that they contradict the procreative purpose of the marriage act. Clearly, if this is the case, contraception can be said to be condemned implicitly under the same heading.

Even if it were considered that the doctrine on contraception were *not* directly revealed in divine Revelation, it would still come within the scope of the infallible Magisterium. A truth which is necessarily linked to a doctrine which *is* directly revealed can also be taught infallibly by the Church. As Newman put it, using the analogy of national sovereignty, a country needs to have control over its territorial waters in order to defend its own territory. But the teaching on contraception is so closely allied to the directly revealed doctrine on marriage, that the Church faithfully upholds her teaching on marriage by firmly maintaining the immorality of contraceptive conjugal acts. Thus, the phrase quoted at the beginning of the previous paragraph was publicly confirmed at the Council to mean that: 'matters which do not directly belong to the revealed deposit but are necessary to guard and expound it are within the scope of infallibility'.[9] The way in which the dissent over *Humanae vitae* has led to support for sex outside marriage, homosexual behaviour etc. demonstrates, beyond reasonable doubt, how essential the teaching of the encyclical is to the Church's doctrine on marriage and sexuality as a whole.

Hence, the ordinary Magisterium may present a particular teaching in a new formulation; it may increase its depth and profundity; but in no way, and on no occasion, can it be said to mislead the faithful. If, as in the case of *Humanae vitae*, it teaches infallibly and definitively, it does not make sense to talk about future changes in the Church's teaching. Vatican II speaks clearly about the type of assent that should be given to the ordinary Magisterium, whether of the Pope or of the bishops collectively. It says of the Pope's teaching:

> The offering of a religious allegiance of mind and will is owed in a special way to the authentic magisterium of the Roman Pontiff, even when he is not speaking *ex cathedra*; it must be offered in such a way that his supreme magisterium receives respectful acknowledgement. The result should be a sincere adherence to the judgements which he has delivered, that complies with his manifest meaning and intention.[10]

Thus, whether proposed by the solemn or the ordinary Magisterium, infallibility and irreformability attach to those moral teachings of the Church which are taught in a definitive manner and fulfil the other conditions referred to above. The reason why fundamental moral laws are irreformable is because of the nature of such statements. The most basic principles of morality are absolute norms and hence immutable by definition. Declarations about the wrongness of killing the innocent, adultery, or the contraceptive act are unchangeable truths because these acts are 'intrinsically evil'. They have occasionally been taught by the solemn Magisterium, but we should normally expect to find them communicated by the Church's ordinary teaching.

9. John Finnis, 'Infallibility', in *Human Love and Human Life*, ed. J. Santamaría & J. Billings, Melbourne, 1979.
10. *Lumen gentium*, 25; see also Pope Pius XII, *Humani generis*, 15.

[5]

The Roots of Permissiveness:
Some Previous Views of Ethics

At this point it may be asked why the principles of a natural law morality are not more widely accepted and adhered to. The question is closely related to a further one which enquires how the opposite system of permissive morality has come about. Intellectual reasons account for part of the answer.

The subjective and relative nature of much modern morality is simply a reflection of the same characteristics prevalent in modern thought as a whole. Two tendencies have dominated the latter; one is the restriction of the range of reason, and the other is the immanent character given to knowledge. Both find their roots in the seventeenth-century French philosopher, Descartes. His search for indubitable knowledge, which reason alone can give, led him to take mathematics as a model of certainty and his own clear and distinct ideas as a criterion of truth. His empiricist successors expanded this to include only those propositions which can be verified by the senses.

Descartes marks the beginning of a system of thought known as rationalism, because it endeavours to unleash the power of reason alone to give knowledge, independently of theology, past tradition etc. This approach gives rise (together with empiricism) to the peculiarly modern and scientific view that knowledge is confined to two kinds of truths—truths of fact (that can be tested either by Descartes' criterion or by the rule of empirical verifiability) and truths of reason, namely, those of mathematics and logic. Pascal, for example, limits rational knowledge to these two last-mentioned areas, adding that after this our beliefs are founded on nature, custom and habit (a position which was later to influence Hume).[1]

The objection to rationalism is not that it values reason but that it undervalues it. What began as an attempt to increase the power of reason ends up by diminishing it. This demotion of reason is at variance with the teaching of Christianity and common sense. St Paul and the Magisterium

1. A. MacIntyre, *After Virtue*, London, 1982, p. 52.

71

make it clear that the natural truths of religion (the existence of God, the soul, freedom) and those of morality (knowledge of right and wrong) can be known without the aid of Revelation (cf. Rom 2:9). Common sense tells us that there are many things the mind can know which are not susceptible of scientific proof. Most obviously a man can know his wife loves him; he can be certain of it but not in the way that rationalists want.[2]

An even more crippling blow to the power and range of reason was given by Descartes' insistence on starting philosophy with his own thought and making his own thinking self the first and most indubitable proposition. This was his famous 'Cogito ergo sum' ('I think, therefore I am'). This had the result, though it was unintended by Descartes, of identifying reality with thought, so that, in effect, 'to be' is 'to be thought'. If you start off with the notion that the only thing you know with certainty is the contents of your own mind, you end up being unable to establish the existence of anything outside of it. Hence, the existence of the external world is always a problem for this system of thought (which is known as idealism). Nobody is an idealist, of course, when it comes to catching a train or digging the garden!

Both these tendencies—of rationalism and immanent idealism—incline man's knowledge to be subjective. Truth, instead of being the correspondence of the mind with external reality, becomes one's own thought. Rather than objective truth, what these philosophies offer is subjective certainty and, furthermore, on these premises that is all one will *ever* have. Moral truth follows the same pattern. Thus, Kant's categorical imperative is a 'universal' norm which the mind dictates to itself without any reference to an external law, or lawgiver. Catholic thought, on the contrary, is realist and objective, in the sense that what is known immediately is things themselves and not the content of one's own mind.

All this resulted from the anti-Aristotelian/anti-Scholastic tempo of the age. Suddenly the human mind was unable to know the essential nature of man and his destiny, or even his substantial unity, or the transition from potency to act. Moral values, too, were to fall outside the sphere of reason and the certain knowledge of 'facts', especially in a thinker like Hume. For him, what moves man to action in practical life is not reason but the passions. The former plays a subservient role in rationalizing man's passions, according to his own self-interest and pleasure (and the avoidance of pain). However, it should be noted that Hume was not entirely subjective inasmuch as morals also took account of one's particular social tradition.

2. See Philip Trower, 'Experience and Revealed Truth', *Position Paper*, Dublin, June 1992.

THE IS/OUGHT CONTROVERSY

One of the consequences of the demotion of reason is that knowledge is divided up and compartmentalized into facts, beliefs, traditions, customs etc., according to a hierarchy of certainty. Only the first category—facts— yields really sure knowledge. What is more, there is no legitimate movement between the compartments, because they are different kinds of knowledge. For this reason, we meet the much heralded modern objection that you cannot derive 'values' from 'facts'; you cannot get an 'is' from an 'ought'.

This criticism was first made by David Hume. He says: 'in every system of morality, which I have hitherto met with, I have always remarked that the author proceeds for some time in the ordinary way of reasoning, and establishes the being of a God, or makes observations concerning human affairs; when, all of a sudden, I am surprised to find, that instead of the usual copulations of propositions, "is" and "is not", I meet with no proposition that is not connected with an "ought" or an "ought not".'[3] He goes on to say that a reason should be given for this 'inconceivable' deduction. But, of course, he has already pre-determined the invalidity of this transition from 'is' to 'ought' by putting moral judgements outside the sphere of reason anyway. It is not necessarily an invalid step; but on the premises of his questionable epistemology, it is always illegitimate.

There are cases in which the transition from description to obligation can be made. For example, from the premise 'He is a doctor' it may be validly inferred that 'He ought to do whatever a doctor ought to do'.[4] At least, then, when one is talking about function words and functional descriptions, one can validly infer evaluative conclusions. If the human being can be defined according to his true end and destiny, such that we know his function and the meaning of his existence, then morally obligatory conclusions about his life will legitimately follow. The full truth about man, then, leads to obligation and responsibility. The Church makes not only this claim but the further one that man is under an obligation to seek the fullness of truth about himself and the meaning of his life.

Outside of these cases, it remains true that one cannot derive normative conclusions from descriptive premises except under certain conditions. From the fact that a company has halved its profits, it does not follow that the chairman ought to resign. St Thomas does not derive obligatory precepts directly from the nature of man but rather via the first principles of practical reason, which say that good shall be done and evil avoided. The values

3. David Hume, *A Treatise of Human Nature*, III,1, i.   4. A. MacIntyre, op. cit., pp. 54 ff.

which constitute the basic participations in goodness, such as life, truth, friendship etc., are already value-laden and take on an obligatory character when formulated as basic precepts. The is/ought dilemma proceeds from an insufficient notion of practical reason and of its relation with its speculative counterpart.

THE AUTONOMOUS ETHICS OF KANT

Hume's demotion of reason's power alarmed Kant and 'woke him from his dogmatic slumbers' but, in attempting to strengthen the role of reason, he only confirmed its weakness by his acceptance of some of his predecessor's presuppositions and conclusions. The citadel of reason had been breached and, instead of repairing the foundations, Kant papered over the cracks, albeit very ambitiously. For him moral obligation, variously referred to as 'the moral law', 'conscience', or 'the categorical imperative', was an elementary, self-evident demand of reason. It was 'an undeniable fact' and 'belonged to man's essence'. In order to avoid the Humean objection that morality could not be deduced from empirical facts, Kant maintained that moral obligation was *a priori* (that is, self-evident) and independent of experience. It is expressed as a universal law or categorical imperative: 'Act always in such a way that the intention of your will can always stand as a principle of universal legislation.'[5]

This principle has the peculiarity of being purely formal and does not tell us what the content of the good is. No values are expressed or suggested at this stage. Indeed, as Kant explains in a celebrated phrase, 'It is not possible to think of anything in the world which can be taken as good without qualification—except a good will.' And 'a will is good, not because of what it does, or because of its ability to reach any particular good, but because of its intention.'[6] The intention is good when it is pure, that is, when it is dictated by reason alone, and not by some extraneous motive such as happiness or reward. One should follow the moral law out of duty alone.

This duty ethics does not take away freedom; indeed it necessitates it, because without it there cannot be true obligation and responsibility to act correctly. Freedom is a demand of reason and obligation. Happiness is the result of acting in this way, but one does not act in this way in order to be happy. Kant is correct to see in man's moral reason, or conscience, a spark

5. I. Kant, *Critique of Practical Reason*. The quotations are taken from J. Hirschberger, *A Short History of Western Philosophy*, London, 1976.
6. Ibid.

of the divine. Consequently, he is able to defend in the most explicit terms the dignity and importance of man. Another formulation of the categorical imperative is: 'Act in such a way that you always use humanity, whether in yourself or in any other person, as an end and never as a means.'[7] Whether his system warranted these conclusions is another matter.

Kant tried to justify them by an ingenious piece of argument which endeavoured to show that they were demanded by practical reason, and so were presuppositions or, as he called them, 'postulates of practical thought'. He believed that practical reason, or ethics, could establish truths, or facts, that pure reason could not. In his critique of metaphysics, Kant had denied that God's existence, the immortality of the soul, or freedom could be demonstrated by reason, largely because of the objections of the preceding empiricists. In matters of behaviour, however, it was otherwise. Immortality was a pre-requisite of moral life since the moral ideal could never be reached in the present worldly existence, and God has to be postulated if we are to be rewarded. There must be a supreme reason, which is the foundation of the moral law and also powerful enough to reward us with happiness.

In sum, Kant, is justifiably regarded as the greatest exponent of autonomous morality, that is, one which relies on reason alone in the sense that it does not have its source in an external law or experience, but rather in the mind of the subject. The individual dictates laws to himself albeit believing them to be universal. As a contemporary Thomist, Joseph de Torre, has written: 'In a morality based on reality rather than on the human mind, norms are universal, valid for every person, because they reflect unchangeable realities, namely God as last end and the constants of human nature. On the other hand, according to Kantian doctrine any action can be good; it is enough to "think of it" as universal.'[8] In orthodox Catholic morality, conscience reflects an objective moral law and does not create it in the way Kant suggests. We see here one of the principal origins of the man-centred and subjective morals which are so much a hallmark of contemporary life.

Thus, the moral problem of modernity is first and foremost an epistemological one. MacIntyre has summed it up in the following way:

> reason for him [Kant], as much as for Hume, discerns no essential natures and no teleological features in the objective universe available for study by physics. Thus their disagreements on human nature coexist with striking and important agreements and what is true of them is true also of Diderot, of Smith, and of Kierkegaard. All reject

7. Ibid.   8. J. M. de Torre, *The Humanism of Modern Philosophy*, Manila, 1989.

any teleological view of human nature, any view of man having an essence which defines his true end. But to understand this is to understand why their project of finding a basis for morality had to fail.[9]

UTILITARIANISM

Utilitarianism is the most influential ethical doctrine of our time in one or other of its various forms and so deserves closer examination. It was initiated by Jeremy Bentham (1748–1832) and popularized by John Stuart Mill (1806–73) and is so called because it is concerned with the usefulness of human actions to produce pleasure, which is, in turn, equated with goodness or happiness. Bentham writes: 'utility is any property in any object whereby it tends to produce benefit, advantage, pleasure, good or happiness . . .'.[10] The good, then, for the individual is that action which produces the maximum happiness limited only by the freedom of others to do the same. So the overall principle becomes the well known maxim of 'the greatest happiness of the greatest number'.

The roots of utilitarianism lie further back in the hedonist and liberal theories of Hobbes and Locke in the seventeenth century. Once the Aristotelian teleology of a final end and shared good for all mankind was abandoned, there arose the problem of what to put in its place. In the British tradition, particularly, the most sought after and encompassing value came to be freedom. It was for this reason that Locke laid so much emphasis on the natural right to property: it protected the freedom and self-interest of the organizers of the Whig settlement of 1688. Individual freedom was likewise identified with the right to pursue one's self-interest bounded only by the freedom of others. At the same time, both Hobbes and Locke were hedonists, that is, they identified good and evil with pleasure and pain respectively. In this philosophy of the satisfaction of desires, we can see the root of the subjectivism and the, perhaps unconscious, selfishness of many contemporary moral opinions in the field of sexual and medical ethics—particularly abortion.

Utilitarianism has always been vulnerable to the charge of egoism and selfishness. Bentham hesitated for a lifetime over whether to prefer altruism to selfishness, and Mill countered criticism of Utilitarianism by emphasizing that it wasn't the happiness of the individual but overall happiness that

9. A. MacIntyre, op. cit., p. 52.
10. J. Bentham, *Introduction to the Principles of Morals and Legislation*, ch. 1, sect. 3.

came first. He stressed what he called 'benevolence'. This was justified, however, on the utilitarian principle that one derives pleasure from everybody else's happiness, a principle which leaves the underlying egoism intact. To overcome this same objection, Mill suggested another reason why one's happiness is bound up with the community of man, namely, the 'social feelings of mankind'. In doing this, however, he departed from pure utilitarianism and began to revert to a more common foundation for morals, the nature of man.

The legacy of utilitarianism, for the most part, contradicts the specifically Christian teaching that man's true good consists not in self-interest, but in self-giving and service. As Vatican II puts it, 'man only finds himself by a true gift of himself' (*Gaudium et spes*, 24). It is unsurprising, then, that with such a divergent starting point those who allow themselves to be influenced by utilitarianism, in one form or another, find themselves at odds with the Church's teaching on absolute moral norms in the pro-life domain. The consumer materialism, to which self-interest and technological progress lead, furthers and sustains the anti-life mentality, bringing people to choose material benefits on significant occasions in preference to human life itself.

Secondly, utilitarianism equates goodness with pleasure and evil with pain and so presents us with a hedonistic morality which has fuelled the permissiveness of the latter part of the twentieth century. It was not a new idea, of course, and had been proposed by Epicurus in the ancient world. Many would say that Aristotle had dealt it a mortal blow when he argued that pleasure can never be an adequate or worthy end of an action (let alone a life), but must always accompany, or be a consequence of, the pursuit of some other worthy end. This is shown very decisively by the thought experiment he conducted based on the hypothesis of the experience machine. According to this, one had to imagine being plugged into a machine so that while floating in a tank, one can be given all the pleasures and thrills imaginable. The only condition is that one has to be plugged in for a lifetime, or not at all. How many people would choose it? Very few one suspects. And why? Because man is interested in fulfilment through activity, not simply in the satisfying pleasure of fulfilment.

However, the greatest problem with utilitarianism is that its basic principle—the greatest happiness of the greatest number—is quite impossible to calculate. Indeed, the happiness whether of a group, a lifetime, or an individual action cannot be satisfactorily determined. Bentham stuck to the idea of the quantification of pleasures and believed that in principle, at least, these can be weighed and compared. But Mill faced the facts and admitted there were qualitative differences between pleasures. Hence, pleasure or happiness is not a quantifiable item, and this renders the 'greatest happiness principle' meaningless. How can one compare the pleasure of listening to a symphony with that of giving money to charity? And if this is the case, the standard of comparison has to be something other than pleasure (or happiness) itself, because it is not the pleasure we seek but rather the activity associated with it, which fulfils man and therefore 'pleases' him. Behind this notion is probably an idea of what man ought to be and ought to seek. Mill himself hinted at this point without developing it when he made his famous statement that 'It is better to be a human being dissatisfied than a pig satisfied; better to be Socrates dissatisfied than a fool satisfied.'[11] These criticisms have proved insuperable for utilitarianism over the years, although it has survived in some form to our own day.

CONSEQUENTIALISM AND PROPORTIONALISM

Present-day forms of utilitarianism are often given the names of 'consequentialism' or 'proportionalism' because they endeavour to decide the rightness and goodness of an action by weighing its consequences or determining the proportion of benefit over harm which ensues. A major objection to the consequentialist (and, therefore, also to the utilitarian) method of moral judgement is that it does not allow a statement to the effect that some actions are intrinsically or absolutely good or bad: they are only better or worse than others. We all calculate consequences to see if our actions are going to be worthwhile, of course, but this is to establish the instrumental or useful good of doing them rather than the moral good. Consequentialists tend to rely on this one principle to establish the rightness of actions, and that turns out not to be a moral principle at all.

Within the Catholic Church, particularly in America, a version of utilitarianism has grown up in the last two decades whose authors would normally accept absolute values, but who want to apply a proportionalist criterion in the hard cases and in conflict situations of moral judgement. These situations always involve some evil or suffering which, if physical, is called by them 'pre-moral' or 'non-moral', and the right thing to do (they say) is to chose what they deem to be the 'lesser evil'. So, in situations where the mother's health is considered to be in danger from a further pregnancy, they would allow sterilization, or even abortion. Abortion would also be allowed if the baby were diagnosed as severely handicapped. They

11. J. S. Mill, *Dissertations and Discussions*, I, pp 358-9.

would equally take a permissive stance in other areas such as fornication, *in vitro* fertilization, euthanasia etc., but only as an exception to the general rule, if in a particular case benefit is thought to outweigh harm by doing it.

Before analyzing this position further, it is necessary to define our terms. By moral absolutes we mean 'moral norms identifying certain types of action which are possible objects of human choice, as always morally bad'.[12] They are unconditionally true in every circumstance, always and for always (*semel et pro semper*). Those concrete actions which they condemn, such as abortion, adultery, contraception, euthanasia etc., are referred to as 'intrinsically evil'.

Proportionalist or revisionist theologians strongly deny that they are relativist in morals. While they reject absolute norms in the accepted sense, as explained above, they propose to put another kind of absolute principles in their place. These are what they call 'transcendent principles', which surpass the specific choices of the everyday world. Examples of these are: 'One must always act in conformity with the love of God and neighbour,' or 'One must behave according to right reason' etc.[13] Equally there are (they say) so-called *formal* norms which oblige us to act truthfully, nobly, chastely etc. as an inner disposition. They have, of course, changed the goal-posts considerably and seem to overlook the fact that morals is concerned with specific human acts. They are more preoccupied with the inner moral being of the person. However, once we get away from concrete actions and limit our principles to attitudes of mind, it is doubtful if any coherent meaning can be given to the term 'absolute', particularly since such 'transcendent norms' have been deliberately *designed* to cater for the exceptions of everyday action. The Church's understanding of absolute norms is that they are exceptionless and applicable, always and everywhere.

The fact that revisionists can refer to physical goods and evils before they have been weighed by the proportionalist principle as 'pre-moral' or 'non-moral' is an indication of the dualism which underlies their thinking about the human person. This in itself is contrary to Catholic teaching on the truth and unity of man, as we have seen, and it leads them to say that some physical actions considered evil on account of the object, since apostolic times, may not be so. To this *Veritatis splendor*, 49, responded: 'A doctrine which dissociates the moral act from the bodily dimensions of its exercise is contrary to the teaching of Scripture and Tradition.'

---

12. W. May, *An Introduction to Moral Theology*, Huntingdon, Indiana, 1991, p. 100. This is an excellent exposition and criticism of proportionalism which I rely on in this section.
13. Ibid., pp. 103-4.

In essence, what proportionalists do is to seek to undermine the moral significance of the difference between directly doing evil and indirectly causing it.[14] It is true we cannot be held responsible for all the consequences of our good and well-intentioned actions. But there is all the difference in the world between this and choosing deliberately to do an evil act. Christian tradition allows that, in some cases, if there is a proportionately serious reason, we may carry out an action, as long as it is good in itself and well-intentioned, even if we foresee it will occasion evil consequences (pp. 51f).

However, these cases are completely different from doing evil and desiring it on the assumption, or rather the calculation, that more good will follow from it than harm result. This violates the well known principle of Christian morals deriving from St Paul that 'we must never do evil that good may come of it' (Rom 3:8). Thus, for example, one cannot inflict grievous bodily harm on someone on the unsupported assumption that he might attack you. To deny the difference between a directly willed evil act and one that is indirectly caused amounts to saying that you can sometimes do an act which is intrinsically wrong. This is tantamount to denying moral absolutes. For an evil consequence to be permitted on certain occasions, the conditions of the principle of double effect must be fulfilled. Proportionalists have either chosen to disregard these conditions or have misunderstood their importance.

Even if the revisionist theologians' theory of absolutes were valid, they would still have to answer the objections to the proportionalist/utilitarian principle on which they depend. As we have seen, it is widely recognized today that this method can never be sufficient for any moral system, since no successful and watertight way of calculating benefits over harm has ever been established, or could be. It is particularly inadequate for anyone trying to construct a system based on moral absolutes, and therefore it is rather surprising that any Catholic theologian should ever have espoused it.

THE INEVITABLE CONCLUSION

Given the incommensurability of actions and values, that is to say, the impossibility of weighing, successfully, the moral good or evil by comparing the benefits and harm deriving from them, it is not surprising that

---

14. R. Lawler, J. Boyle & W. May, *Catholic Sexual Ethics*, Huntingdon, Indiana, 1985, pp. 94-5.

G.E. Moore should propose the indefinability of the good. He claims that good is what he calls a non-natural property. This means that while it exists in the natural world in things, it is not like any other natural property, such as red, or humorous, or intelligent etc. Consequently, anybody who equates good with any of the things in which it exists is guilty of the 'naturalistic fallacy'. Good cannot, therefore, be defined in terms of any other property, or set of properties; we can only intuit it. We are able to recognize things that are good, because it is an intrinsic quality in them, but we cannot define it. Moore himself was not prepared to be subjectivist about his ethics, since he believed good was a universal quality everybody recognized in things, but his agnosticism about its true nature and definability made it impossible for him to sustain coherently this objectivity. Thus, it is unsurprising that the following generation of moralists should claim that good, like beauty, is in the eye of the beholder. This theory was held by the emotivist school led by C.L. Stevenson, which maintained that, when you say 'This is good' or "That is bad', you are making statements tantamount to saying 'I approve of this', or 'I disapprove of that'. This school, which was in existence between the wars, made moral judgements completely subjective.

With an intellectual background such as this, it is hardly remarkable that secular contemporary morality is unable to establish *any* absolute moral values, or standards, and seems to assume that every man is his own moral judge, even though this leads to contradictory and confusing conclusions. The uncertainty and relativism of the moral systems we have considered makes the resulting permissiveness of our time all but inevitable. Not even the monumental efforts of Kant and utilitarianism could rescue morality from the downward trend it had earlier assumed, due to inherent intellectual errors, above all epistemological in nature. The story we have traced in outline emphasizes the need to base morality on an adequate understanding of reason, or knowledge, and the full truth about man, if it is to regain the objectivity which it is due.

PART II: FAMILY MORALITY

6

The Sacramentality of Marriage, the Family and Society

Today, we are apt to be told that the traditional nuclear family is dying out and cannot necessarily be considered the norm for living because it is being replaced by other lifestyles. The Christian response is that marriage is divinely instituted from the beginning for the benefit of the person and society, and its break-up cannot but be detrimental to man. The family unit constitutes the most basic communion of persons from which society itself is made up. The latter is an amalgam of families, and therefore the state of whole nations and generations depends directly on family life. The joy, fruitfulness and stability of domestic life should be passed on to society as a whole and to future generations through the children. Thus it contributes to the growth of society and the building up of the Church itself, so that family life is a great treasure and value for both.

The reason for these far-reaching consequences is that man is made for love, and the majority of mankind find and exercise human love in the communion of persons which is the married state. Family life is thus the correspondence of man to his vocation to love both God and others. This love is essentially self-giving and fruitful, and not self-gratifying in the way that it is often understood in modern society. In human beings, it is a reflection of the creative love of God.

Nevertheless, there is a credit and debit side to the way man fulfils his matrimonial vocation. Many aspects of present day society cast a deep shadow over the ideal of family life and morality. These include the continually growing divorce rate, the widespread practice of living together, homosexual activity, evidence of child abuse, pornography and TV programmes which enhance heterodox marital situations. Vatican II said that 'the dignity of marriage is overshadowed by polygamy, the plague of divorce, so called free love and similar blemishes; furthermore, married love is too often dishonoured by selfishness, hedonism and unlawful contraceptive practices' (*Gaudium et spes*, 47).

On the credit side, it may be said that there is a greater appreciation of the dignity of the person in society as a whole and of personal love in marriage, of the equal dignity of spouses and of responsible parenthood. And even the very breakdown of marriage is teaching us again the importance of fidelity and dedication. There can be discerned a search for true and authentic values, the first of which is the genuine nature of love. The Church, illumined by faith in her understanding of human realities, such as marriage and the family, has a particular responsibility to proclaim that knowledge. At a time when the family has been caught up in rapid social changes and changes in mentality, many have lost sight of marriage's original meaning and purpose.

MARRIAGE: ITS SACRAMENTAL ORIGIN

The present state of marriage leads us naturally to go back to its origins, the better to understand its true essence and meaning. Genesis tells us that 'it was not good that man be alone' and so God made 'a helper fit for him' (2:18). This solitude of Adam distinguishes him from animals and plants, emphasizing that only he is a person made in the image and likeness of God. He recognizes that Eve is a gift for him and a person like himself when he says, 'This at last is bone of my bones and flesh of my flesh' (2:23). The text goes on: 'Therefore a man leaves his father and his mother and cleaves to his wife, and they become one flesh, And the man and his wife were both naked and were not ashamed' (2:24–5). Hence, they realise what the Pope has called the nuptial or spousal meaning of the body, that is, the capacity of self-giving of man to woman, and vice versa, which is at the root of conjugal love. The notion of 'one flesh' points to the total nature of this commitment to each other. The lack of shame is due to the fact that they appreciate they are a mutual gift for each other and are without any thought for lust, or selfish possession, or using the other as an object of gratification.

But at the same time God gave our first parents a mission: 'Be fruitful and multiply, and fill the earth and subdue it' (Gen 1:28) The mutual love of spouses was to be productive and outward looking, and the means by which God would populate the earth. Thus, human love was to be creative, or rather *pro*-creative, because it was to be a sharing in the creative love of God. Our call into existence came from the superabundance of God's goodness, that is, from his love. Every human life is, therefore, a gift of the love of God, and human love is necessarily part of it. Spousal love also shares, in its own way, in the Redemption, which equally finds its origin in God's merciful love, so that in family life forgiveness and understanding play a key part.

Some of these characteristics were altered when our first parents committed original sin. The phrase, 'they knew they were naked' (Gen 3:7), indicates the fundamental change in their condition. A further indication is God's warning to Eve that 'your husband . . . shall rule over you' and that childbirth shall henceforth be a painful experience (Gen 3:16). From being in a state of grace and communion with God and of integrity of nature, they lost these gifts and descended into a state of fallen nature, and so they hid from God. In place of the gifts of sanctity and integrity there arises the threefold concupiscence—the lust of the flesh, the lust of the eyes and the pride of life, according to the first letter of St John (cf. 2:17). Consequently, while the meaning of the body and the nature of marriage remain the same they are now perceived more obscurely than hitherto. It is here that we should seek the explanation for the changing face of marriage and the shadows cast over it by divorce, living together, one parent families etc. But as Christ and Genesis make clear, 'at the beginning it was not so' (Mt 19:8) and consequently, according to the truth of man and woman, it is not meant to be so. Unity, indissolubility and fidelity are already written into the truth of marriage at its creation.

The fact that the divine gift of grace is manifested in the era of original innocence in the state of the body and in the conjugal union of the first couple gives marriage a sacramental value from the beginning. Here, the word 'sacrament' is used in a sense which is wider than that in which it is usually applied to the seven sacraments, to mean a reality which makes a mystery of grace visible—an understanding of the term which was some- times given to it by the Fathers. In this sense, it is a primordial sacrament. Although marriage lost the gift of grace after the Fall, it continued to be the *figure* of that sacrament until it was raised up afresh by Christ to the level of its original dignity. It is to the original unity of man and woman in the 'beginning' that we have to look for the *root* of its sacramentality and indissolubility.[1]

PERSONAL LOVE IN MARRIAGE

We read in *Gaudium et spes*, 24, that

> the Lord Jesus when praying to the Father 'that they may all be one . . . even as we are one' (Jn 17:21-22) has opened up new horizons closed

---

1. See Pope John Paul II, *The Theology of Marriage and Celibacy*, Boston, 1986, pp. 240-275.

to human reason by implying that there is a certain parallel between the union existing among the divine persons and the union of the sons of God in truth and love. It follows, then, that if man is the only creature on earth that God has wanted for its own sake, man can fully discover his true self only in a sincere giving of himself.

God himself then is a communion of persons whose mission is the self-giving between the Father, Son and Holy Spirit. St John tells us that 'God is love' and man, who is born in his 'image and likeness', must imitate God, not only in giving love but also in receiving it.

All true love, then, is a share in God's love—that which the Persons of the Trinity have among themselves and that which God has for us. The latter is demonstrated not only in creation but also in Revelation, which is a partnership of love on the part of God with humanity manifested in his Covenant with his chosen people. Marriage is, thus, rightly called a covenant between a man and a woman which has its model in the divine Covenant. Consequently, marriage and fidelity are often used as symbols of the latter and Israel's lack of correspondence is likened to marital infidelity, that is, to adultery and fornication.

Revelation reaches its fulfilment in the Incarnation of our Lord, and particularly in his Sacrifice on the Cross offered for his Body, the Church, to whom he unites himself as head. By so doing he purified it so that it would be holy and spotless. In the same way a man should be united to his wife as to his own flesh, and, in loving his wife, he is but loving his own body. This is why married love, lived in a Christian way, shares in the redemptive and sanctifying love of Christ and why family life is a way of sanctification on earth (cf. Eph 5:22-23). The example of Christ's sacrifice teaches us that love, properly so called, consists in the gift of self and not in self-affirmation or self-gratification which is its contradiction.

Man is called to love in his totality of body and soul. The body, therefore, shares in spiritual love. Hence, sexuality, the way in which man and woman give themselves to one another is not just biological, but deeply personal in that it concerns the inner core of the human being. Consequently sexuality is 'realized in a truly human way only if it is an integral part of the love by which a man and woman commit themselves totally to one another until death. The total physical self-giving would be a lie if it were not the sign and fruit of a total personal self-giving, in which the whole person, including the temporal dimension, is present' (*Familiaris consortio*, 11).

Since true married love is personal, it consists, primarily, in a union of wills and only secondarily in bodily union. The actual covenant, or marriage bond, is based on the mutual consent by which the spouses pledge themselves to a lifelong partnership and gift of themselves as a consequence of which they have exclusive rights over each other, especially sexual rights. The human body is an expression of the person and not the other way round, and that is why bodily union must follow on personal union expressed in an irrevocable decision of the will to self-giving to one another. The widespread practices of pre-marital sex and living together arise out of an inability or an unwillingness to recognize this basic fact, namely, that real love is based on a prior union of wills and exchange of unconditional consent. The result is that the victim is man himself, who suffers in the form of family breakdown, child delinquency, one parent families and so on.

The self-giving of marriage leads spouses not to a selfish possession of the other, but to a partnership and real sharing of life. St Paul says: 'Defer to one another out of reverence for Christ' (Eph 5:12). This requires self-sacrifice and is a point which is well illustrated by a story of the Vienna psychiatrist, Dr Viktor Frankl. He recalls how a widowed doctor, who was a retired general practitioner, came to him for the treatment of depression, brought on by the death of his wife whom he loved dearly. Life was incomplete and unbearable without her, it had lost its meaning, and he wondered why he had been left to carry this burden. Dr Frankl commented that since he loved his wife so much, had he not considered what it would have been like for her if he had died and she had survived. This simple advice encouraging him to put himself in another's shoes gave him a reason for his suffering and solved the problem.[2]

Married love properly understood thus contrasts with love conceived as selfish desire, hedonistic pleasure, or purely natural happiness. In our own time, sensuality and permissiveness have greatly increased family unhappiness and marital breakdown. Fidelity, therefore, cannot be achieved without mastery of self because a degree of selfishness is always present in our fallen nature. This too follows from a proper understanding of the person as one who does not follow every instinct like an animal, but dominates and directs his appetites by means of his intellect and will. He is, thus, able to understand the purpose of his faculties and control their use rationally unlike any other animal. Human sexuality is very different from the sexual instinct of animals. Hence, personal love in marriage is a mixture of self-giving and self-control which requires the virtue of continence and makes conjugal chastity possible.

2. Human Life Congress, Paris, 1986.

UNITY, INDISSOLUBILITY AND FIDELITY

The aim of married life, then, is that spouses achieve an identification with each other rooted in the unity of wills, but including the whole person mind and body. It involves a coming out of oneself, such that husband and wife generously share everything, allowing no unreasonable exceptions, or thinking just of their own interests. One who loves spousally loves not only for what he or she receives but for the spouse's sake, content to be able to enrich the other with the gift of self (cf. *Humanae vitae*, 9). The corollary of this is that spousal love is faithful and exclusive of all other until death. Love for one's wife which was shared with another would not be total. Neither would it be total if it were only for a stipulated part of one's life. We see here the reason why Christian tradition has always insisted on the unity of marriage (one man with one woman) and its indissolubility until death.

Human beings grow through their personal relationships, and this is true in a unique fashion of marriage. What one person alone cannot tackle, two can. And so, in virtue of the mutual aid and support of each other, the two make common cause in confronting the ordinary hardships of life. This unity is, of course, affected by human weakness, although it is equally a remedy for it. Spouses, like violins, occasionally get out of tune although marriage, properly understood, possesses the capacity to regain its harmony. The problems causing the de-tuning of marriage are familiar— unrequited love, disagreements and misunderstandings, pride and selfishness, alcoholism, paranoia, fears etc.—and today we would have to add, increasingly, sensuality and permissiveness. Where, however, love is understood as self-giving and sacrifice, harmony can always be restored, at least in the great majority of cases. The partnership of spouses allows them to grow together not only in spite of, but because of, the difficulties along the way. Love from being partly selfish becomes purified by the sacrifices it faces.

Mutual support in marriage is given not only between the spouses, but also by the parents to the children and ultimately vice versa. Procreation and the upbringing of children is an integral part of marriage and this, in fact, furnishes a further essential reason for its indissolubility. Without the enduring union of parents, this task will not be carried out with the completeness it requires. If we consider the rearing of the child to take twenty years, then parents who have children up to the end of their fertility will be in their late fifties or early sixties by the time this is accomplished. At this time, the other 'meaning' of marriage becomes particularly relevant .

Vatican II speaks as follows: 'Children as living members of the family contribute in their own way to the sanctification of their parents. With sentiments of gratitude, affection and trust, they will repay their parents for the benefits given to them and will come to their assistance as devoted children in times of hardship and in the loneliness of old age' (*Gaudium et spes*, 48). Growing together reaches its climax in the spiritual growth by which husband, wife and family reach God, fulfilling their duties of state and to each other.

To say, however, that all the members of the family are equal in dignity is not to say that they have the same role. Writing to the Ephesians, St Paul sees no contradiction between speaking of marriage as a mutual self-giving of spouses and going on to speak of the husband as the head of the wife. 'Wives be subject to your husbands as to the Lord. For the husband is the head of the wife' (Eph 5:22-23). The Church has always taught that this submission in no way ignores the equal dignity of the two spouses as persons nor does it oblige a wife to yield to the unreasonable demands of her husband. The authority of the husband admits of degrees according to circumstances and, if the husband neglects his duties, the wife must assume command of the family.[3] The reason why the obedience of the wife does not entail inequality is because it occurs in a partnership where the spouses exercise a mutual subjection to one another. Thus, St Paul himself had previously written to the Ephesians before making the above statement: 'be subject to one another out of reverence for Christ' (Eph 5:21).

Though the marriage partnership is likened by the Apostle to Christ and the Church, with the latter being subject to the headship and authority of Christ, in marriage the subjection is mutual unlike in the former case where it is on one side only.[4] That is why husbands are urged to love their wives, that is, to make a sincere gift of themselves. Nevertheless, ultimately there must be an authority which is vested in the husband as the head, while the wife is the heart of the family, so that 'as the first holds the primacy of authority, so the second can and ought to claim the primacy of love'.[5]

Human love, conceived and lived in this way, will lead to fidelity between the spouses, considered by St Augustine and Christian Tradition, together with procreation and the upbringing of children and the sacrament itself to be one of the 'blessings' of marriage. Only a poor concept of marriage considers that the bond between the spouses is threatened when difficulties and incompatibilities arise between the partners with the passing of time. Much modern divorce legislation appears to be based on this premise. On the contrary, if love is considered as an ideal of self-giving and

3. Pius XI, *Casti connubii*, 27-8.   4. John Paul II, *Mulieris dignitatem*, 24.
5. *Casti connubii*, 27.

self-forgetfulness, then such differences will be seen as a means of purifying and strengthening the bond so that it becomes unselfish. Fidelity is the work of a lifetime.

PROCREATION AND PARENTHOOD

As we have seen, marriage has its roots in the mystery of creation and plays a central part in it. This is true, both at the beginning and now, since its role is to prolong God's creation by means of procreation. Today there is much talk about the enriching importance of the love between spouses and of personal development, but we must remember that the same love which makes the couple a communion of persons leads on to that wider communion which is the family. Personal love and family growth are inextricably linked. And personal development is fostered by opening out to others—both to one's spouse and to the possibility of children. Married love is total because spouses give the whole of their lives to each other and because they give all that they are, including their sexuality—namely, the seed of life they carry within them.

This primacy of offspring is evident in various places in Scripture, and indeed in Tradition, as is well summed up by the following passage from *Gaudium et spes*, 50:

> Marriage and married love are by nature ordered to the procreation and education of children. Indeed children are the supreme gift of marriage and greatly contribute to the good of the parents themselves. God himself said: 'It is not good that man should be alone' (Gen 2:18) and 'from the beginning (he) made them male and female' (Mt 19:4). Wishing to associate them in a special way with his own creative work, God blessed man and woman with the words 'Be fruitful and multiply' (Gen 1:28). Without intending to underestimate the other ends of marriage, it must be said that true married love and the whole structure of family life that results from it are directed to disposing the spouses to cooperate valiantly with the love of the Creator and Saviour, who through them will increase and enrich his family from day to day.

The very word matrimony comes from two Latin words *munus matris*, meaning the office of the mother, namely to bear and rear children. Her psychology and physiology are ordered to giving life and bringing it up. The words of Eve ('the mother of all the living') when she says, 'I have brought forth a child with the help of the Lord' (Gen 4:1) are an eloquent testimony to the life-giving role of femininity and marriage.

St Augustine writes concerning the words of St Paul to Timothy: 'The Apostle testifies that procreation is the purpose of matrimony when, having said, "I will that the younger women should marry", he adds immediately, as though he had been asked the reason, "so that they may bear children and become mothers of families".[6] A further proof of the intimate and necessary link between procreation and matrimony is the fact that in heaven there will be no marriage since the need for reproduction will have ceased.

Responsible and prudent parenthood means, first of all, recognizing this moral order and duty. The phrase 'responsible parenthood' has come to mean, on the popular level, family limitation; but though in particular cases it may include this, equally it means the opposite. Paul VI wrote that those spouses exercise 'responsible parenthood who generously decide to have a large family, or who, for serious reasons and with due respect for the moral law, choose to have no more children for the time being or even for an indeterminate period' (*Humanae vitae*, 10).

The notion is perhaps better understood if we call it the 'responsibility of parenthood', underlining thereby the duty as well as the joy that is incumbent on parents. Someone may ask how it is responsible to have a large family? To this it must be said that the value of the bigger family is understated in our time. In general, children in a large family will more easily learn generosity and fraternity, sociability and service towards others. Consequently, it is a greater gift to give children more brothers and sisters than to give them extra material benefits, beyond that which is necessary.[7]

The begetting of children provides a service to society and the Church. In speaking of society in this matter, it is important to note that most countries in Europe at the present time are experiencing a top-heavy, aged population and that young people are society's greatest asset. The future both of society and of the Church is foreshadowed in their young people. If the present trend continues, the population of Europe which in 1960 stood at 25% of the world's population will drop to a level of 5% by the middle of the next century, a fact which prompted some analysts to speak of the 'demographic suicide of Europe'. This is due to an average birth rate in most European countries of just under or over two children per family. The situation has lead some governments, however, to encourage and look positively on childbirth, as in Germany where financial incentives are

6. See *Casti connubii*, 12.   7. Cf. John Paul II, Homily at Mass on Capitol Mall, Washington DC, October 1979.

available and Sweden where one or other spouse is entitled to fifteen months paid leave on the birth of a child.

In a particular case, at a particular time, a couple may decide they cannot cope physically or psychologically with another child at that moment. Also, social conditions such as the size of the house or the state of society (normally this would be outside Europe and the United States) may advise against it. Financial considerations can also come into the judgement as long as material luxuries are not put ahead of a larger family and one is speaking of necessities. If spouses judge that they have *serious* reasons in any of these categories, then they may avail themselves of the infertile period in the cycle. However, these reasons must be assessed in the light of the objective moral order as interpreted by a right conscience and not simply be subjective or matters of convenience. Parents must, therefore, keep in mind their 'duties towards God, themselves, their families and human society' (*Humanae vitae*, 10). Consequently couples are not permitted to act on impulse, or do as they like, in this matter but must ensure that what they do corresponds to the creative will of God.

Responsible parenthood, we may conclude, consists in having as many children as one can reasonably bring up in accord with human dignity. In Victorian England, where fertility control was virtually unknown, many children had to be picked up from wandering in the streets and taken to the workhouse, or the orphanage. A family of ten children where the father was an alcoholic and every child ended up in prison in the next generation was a clear example of parental irresponsibility. But these are exceptional cases, the memory of which has contributed, in the twentieth century, to making the pendulum swing completely in the opposite direction. The anti-life mentality thus created must be superseded by a positive pro-life stance.

What is an anti-life mentality? The present Pope describes it as follows in *Familiaris consortio*, 30:

> Some ask themselves if it is a good thing to be alive or if it would have been better never to have been born; they doubt therefore if it is right to bring others into life when perhaps they will curse their existence in a cruel world with unforeseeable terrors. Others consider themselves to be the only ones for whom the advantages of technology are intended and they exclude others by imposing on them contraceptives or worse means. Still others, imprisoned in a consumer mentality and whose sole concern is to bring about a continual growth of material goods finish by ceasing to understand, and thus by refusing, the spiritual riches of a new human life. The ultimate reason for these

mentalities is the absence in peoples' hearts of God whose love alone is stronger than all the world's fears and can conquer them.

There are, of course, difficult circumstances in life, giving rise to serious reasons for not giving birth at a particular time. And for these cases Providence has placed in the female cycle a time of infertility as well as fertility. Hence John Paul II (as previous Popes since Pius XII) commends efforts to know and educate people more fully in the so-called natural methods of family planning as long as they are not looked at in a purely biological way. They must be seen in a personal and loving way; and in fact modern methods (Billings, Couple to Couple League etc.) require the full cooperation of both spouses. The use of the infertile period is often discounted on grounds of unreliability and in the past received the contemptuous name of 'Vatican roulette', but in fact the modern methods referred to are perfectly effective if there is cooperation and, therefore, mutual self-giving by both parties. Proper use of natural family planning thus presupposes a right intention and a positive, open attitude to life in principle. Like everything else it can be abused if it is applied with a contraceptive mentality, that is to say, if it is used capriciously for family limitation without serious reasons. In such a case, it becomes equivalent to contraception because of a defective intention.

Objectively speaking, there is a great difference between the use of the infertile period and contraception when the former is done with a right intention. The first is cooperating in the creative decisions of God; the second is taking them into one's own hands and, so to speak, usurping them. One is working with nature, the other is obstructing it. Furthermore, natural methods may be said to be fundamentally pro-life, in the sense that the use of them not infrequently leads to a renewed desire for children. They can be, and often are, used to pinpoint infertility and overcome sterility.

THE FAMILY AND THE CHURCH

In the passage from the Letter to the Ephesians in which St Paul compares the love of husband and wife to that between Christ and the Church, he goes on to say: 'This is a great mystery and I mean in reference to Christ and the Church' (Eph 5:32). The great sacrament or mystery (*sacramentum* in Latin, *mysterion* in Greek) spoken of here actually refers, in the first place, to Christ and the Church. It is by this relationship that God carries out the eternal election he made of man before the beginning of the world. But St

Paul's words make clear that just as marriage plays a central part in the 'mystery of creation', so it does also, in a new way, in the 'mystery of redemption'. As Pope John Paul writes: 'The union of Christ and the Church permits us to understand in what way the spousal significance of the body is completed with the redemptive significance.'[8] Marriage thus becomes a way of sanctification and salvation, and a means of leading others along the same path and building up the Body of Christ, and thus intimately participating in the eternal plan of God for mankind.

The Church itself is the 'great sacrament' (or 'mystery')[9] and from the Church marriage and the other six sacraments derive their redemptive power. Christ instituted the sacrament of marriage by his presence at the marriage feast of Cana and by his uncompromising statement in answer to the Jews' question about separation under the Mosaic Law: 'what God has joined together let no man put asunder' (Mt 19:6). There is a divine design about matrimony for everybody, insofar as it is written into the truth of masculinity and femininity and the conjugal meaning of the body and the call to become 'one flesh'. That is why a union between non-Catholic partners who are free to marry is regarded as a valid union and destined to endure for a lifetime. A Catholic, however, is not married in the eyes of God if he or she does not enter a sacramental union blessed by the Church. The purpose of a sacrament is to be an outward sign of inward grace; in this case, it confers the strength to fulfil the duties of the acquired state, namely, those of being a parent and of lifelong commitment and fidelity to one's spouse and family. The sacrament gives the strength and wherewithal to conquer the threefold concupiscence, the work of the devil and the permissiveness of the environment, which are the enemies of marriage.

Parents, therefore, serve the Church by participating in the creative and redemptive love of God through bringing children into the world and initiating them in the journey of faith. They do this when they truly give themselves for spouse and family, as Christ did for the Church, and contribute to building up the Kingdom of God on earth. The family is rightly called the 'domestic church', since parents are the first educators in the faith and piety, guiding their children through the first sacraments—Baptism, Confirmation, Penance and Holy Communion—of the Church. From the Christian family come the vocations, the parents and the majority of the Church's membership of tomorrow.

The fact that Christ was born, lived and worked in the family of Nazareth

8. Pope John Paul II, *The Theology of Marriage and Celibacy*, op. cit., p. 300.
9. *Lumen gentium*, 1.

means that family life is a redeemed and redeeming reality. In imitation of Christ, it thus becomes for Christian families a way of sanctification and a path to holiness on earth. Lived in this spirit it genuinely builds up the Church and gives her new saints. Herein resides the power of Christianity to renew family life and transform society. When the sacrament of marriage is properly received and fully lived, each home becomes another family of Nazareth.

Since Christ raises up marriage to the level of a sacrament, thus conferring grace and strength on the recipients, it is not surprising that he demands perfect fulfilment of the marriage covenant, namely fidelity, indissolubility and parenthood. Such witness Christians continue to be called upon to bear in the face of the winds of permissivism, taking into account that the fundamental principles of marriage belong to the truth about man and woman and, thus, they not only do not change, but are applicable to everybody and are in everyone's best interests. It may be asked why today Catholic marriages break down at a similar rate to the national average. A partial answer is that if the sacrament of matrimony is not received worthily, then the grace of marriage will not become operative until the state of grace is recovered.

Parents, and indeed subsequently the family as a whole, play a full role in the life of the Church, participating in the threefold office of Christ— priestly, prophetical and kingly. As members of the common priesthood, parents sanctify their duties of state, and offer the sacrifices associated with it, by means of the sacraments and a life of piety. They fulfil their kingly office by the authority they exercise over their children and by directing the things of creation to God. These two offices merge into the prophetic or teaching office by which they pass on the Word of God and the doctrine of the Church to the next generation and to those around them. This is the first and most important participation of parents in the apostolic mission of the Church. Family catechesis is particularly important in the face of strong currents of secular and humanist ideas (and therefore unbelief) which are rampant in contemporary society. So necessary is catechesis that a regular period of time must be set aside for it within the routine of the home. The family should be an evangelizing community with its own members and an example and witness of the faith to other families and mankind as a whole.

Thus we read in *Familiaris consortio*, 38:

> So great and splendid is the educational ministry of Christian parents that St Thomas has no hesitation in comparing it with the ministry of priests: 'Some only propagate and guard spiritual life with a spiritual

ministry: this is the role of the sacrament of Orders: others do this for both corporal and spiritual life, and this is brought about by the sacrament of marriage, by which a man and a woman join in order to beget offspring and bring them up to worship God.'

THE FAMILY AND SOCIETY

The family is the most basic communion of persons and hence the first, vital cell of society. It is the first school of values and virtues, and parents are responsible primarily for this education. The quality and stability of a society depend on the standard of family life and parental responsibility. Such conditions, however, are not possible without the unconditional self-giving and commitment brought about by the permanent bond which is established by the institution of marriage. It is the family's task to contribute to the growth of a healthy, balanced and peaceful society, and it is society's task to foster family life. Society needs the family and the family needs society.

The obligation of society is to contribute to the temporal common good, and the family must play its part in that. But, in the last analysis, the family, as society itself, must contribute to the well-being of its members. Thus children have a right to be born into a family and receive an education from their parents which contributes to their religious, moral, intellectual and physical needs and fulfilment. Parents will not ordinarily be competent to deal with all these areas themselves, but they are primarily responsible for making sure competent formation is given in these fields. This role will, therefore, be taken over by the State in a subsidiary way, but it must always allow and cultivate private education so that parents can exercise legitimate freedom as to the way they bring up their children.

The family's task is to contribute to the building of a stable, healthy and neighbourly society through the harmony and self-giving of its members and the balanced education of the children. It should be an oasis of peace and joy to come home to, and of respect and service to others, especially the underprivileged and handicapped, spreading those qualities to the rest of society by the cultivation of bright and cheerful households. It ought to have the right blend of discipline, self-control and compassion that we would expect to find in society as a whole. Parents need to dedicate sufficient time to the education of their children, realizing that the family should not suffer by over-attention to professional work. Special importance should be given to the family spending time together at meals and on outings etc. Such occasions will often provide an opportunity for the transmission of values and criteria to the children. The one-parent family should be the exception rather than the rule, brought about only by undesired and unsolicited circumstances. Children, and indeed the community at large, clearly need fathers and mothers fulfilling a stable role in marriage because they need the authority of the one and the heart of the other.

If society needs healthy families, then the family needs the support of society and the State. It is in the long-term interest of the latter to foster the traditional family unit by such things as child and even housewife benefits and family housing, by ensuring that tax and mortgage allowances favour married people and not those who are co-habiting, by the abolition of free contraceptive advice and suchlike permissive legislation and by the portrayal of stable family life in the mass media, especially on television.

Of course, when the State lays down a particular ideological line on, for example, sex education, it is usurping a primary right of parents. Such education in contemporary society is usually at variance with natural law morality. So, for example, in England over the last two decades a sex education owing more to biology than morality has been put in place in State schools often against the wishes of the parents. Pressure is also exerted by the availability of courses and booklets from family planning associations which are partly government funded. Finally, there was the passing of the National Health (Reorganization) Act, 1973, making free contraceptive advice available to all, including children under sixteen without their parents' consent. Lady Brooks wrote to *The Times* (16 February 1980) expressing a view totally contrary to natural law, and surely to the wishes of the majority of parents, that can only be detrimental to society itself. She said: 'It is now the privilege of the Parental State to take major decisions— objective, unemotional, the State weighs up what is best for the child.'

We should not underestimate these trends. Pressure has been building up for decades from the secular humanist lobby to separate children from the control of their parents, especially in moral and sexual education. For example, Dr Brock Chisholm, the first director of the World Health Organization and afterwards President of the World Federation for Mental Health, claimed that children had to be 'freed' from the religious and cultural prejudices forced upon them by their parents. He saw parents as suppressors of the child's better nature and became an advocate thereby of compulsory sex education in schools.[10]

The renewal of family life and the reaffirmation of parental rights and

10. Brock Chisholm, *Can People Learn to Learn?*, London, 1952.

duties can only come about by parents joining together in family associations in order to exert influence on public policy. Indeed, anti-family trends,
especially since the sixties, have occasioned the growth of many such
associations dedicated to different but related ends, such as the repeal of
permissive legislation, support for large families or ones with handicapped
children, the promotion of pro-life causes etc. While most of these groups
are organized at national level, some work for international cooperation in
this field. In this way, families are rightly assuming their responsibility for
defending their rights and duties and thus transforming society by a reaffirmation of family values. Were they not to take an active stance in fulfilling
this role, families would be 'the first victims of the evils that they have no
more than noted with indifference' (*Familiaris consortio*, 44).

7

Humanae vitae and the Contraceptive Mentality

The contraceptive mentality is not new; it and was known, for example, to the Roman Empire into which Christianity was born. Women resorted to magic and sorcery to avoid having a child, or they used one of the contraceptive drugs known to have been developed at that time. Hence, when the New Testament prohibits 'magic' (*mageia*) and drugs (*pharmakeia*), it seems to be referring to contraceptives (Gal 5:20). We find in the *Didaché*, one of the earliest Christian writings, the following: 'You shall not use magic. You shall not use drugs.'[1]

The Fathers of the Church combat contraception as an evil within marriage. Clement of Alexandria says: 'To indulge in intercourse without intending children is to outrage nature whom we should take as our instructor.'[2] And St Augustine writes: 'Sexual intercourse even with a lawful wife is unlawful and shameful if the conception of offspring is prevented. This is what Onan, the son of Judah, did and on that account God put him to death.'[3]

Onan, the son of Judah, was obliged by the law of the Levirate to marry Tamar, his dead brother's wife. This law, which is found in Deuteronomy 25:5-10, concerned brothers who lived under the same roof. If one of them died childless, his brother was required to marry the widow, and the child born of the widow was recognized as the son of the deceased, so that his stock would not be extinguished and the inheritance kept in the family. Onan did not want to do this and so had sexual intercourse with Tamar but deposited the seed outside her body; by practising withdrawal, he deprived the act of its life-giving purpose. The seriousness of the behaviour can be gauged by the fact that God slew him for it. He was not slain for violating the Levirate, because the punishment for that was to take off his shoes in front of the elders and be spat upon by the aggrieved woman and, further-

---

1. *Didaché*, II, 2.
2. *Paidogogus* II, 9-10, quoted in J. Hardon, *The Catholic Catechism*, p. 368.
3. St Augustine, *De Coniug. Adult.*, quoted in *Casti connubii*, p. 28.

more, his father Judah and brother Shelah also transgressed the same law without dying. Hence, Christian tradition has always maintained that the serious evil committed by Onan was that depriving the sexual act of its life-giving potential (cf. Gen 38:8-10).

The story of Onan is indeed not the only reference in the Old Testament to the wrong use of marriage and sexuality. Tobias was told by the arch-angel Raphael to take the hand of Sarah in marriage, after requesting the permission of her father. Initially he was afraid because he had heard that seven previous husbands had died in the bridal chamber. A devil, he was told, had carried them away, but then the archangel explains that the devil would have no power over him and would flee forever, if he offers the sacrifice that has been indicated to him and prays when he enters the bridal chamber.[4] This is Tobias' prayer: 'And now, O Lord, I am not taking this sister of mine because of lust, but with sincerity. Grant that I may find mercy, and may grow old together with her' (6:16-17; in old versions of the text, this 'sincerity', or upright intention, was identified with the desire to beget children). Both Tradition and Scripture, therefore, clearly identify con-traception as an evil in marriage, that is to say, both the intention and the action of deliberately frustrating the nature of the procreative act. In 1853, for example, the Magisterium condemned onanism and the use of con-doms in marriage as 'intrinsically immoral'.[5]

THE BIRTH CONTROL MOVEMENT

The birth control movement started, in an organized way, at the beginning of the century and was associated with the names of Margaret Sanger in the United States and Marie Stopes in England. Its ostensible motivation was the conquest of poverty and deprivation often found in the big indus-trial cities of Victorian times. Marie Stopes wrote in an article entitled 'Mrs Jones does her worst' in the *Daily Mail* in 1919: 'Are those puny-faced, gaunt, blotchy, ill-balanced, feeble, ungainly, withered children the

4. Tob 6:16-17. In older versions of the Vulgate the following lines appear. The devil only has power over those 'who go about their marrying with all thought of God shut out of their hearts and minds, wholly intent on their lust, as if they were horse or mule, brutes without reason.' Tobias is subsequently told to begin marriage with three nights of continence and prayer so as to proceed thereafter with an upright intention in his dealings with his wife. 'Then when the third night is past, take the maid to thyself with the fear of the Lord upon thee, moved rather by the hope of begetting children than any lust of thine. So in the true line of Abraham, thou shalt have joy of thy fatherhood.'
5. Holy Office, 6 April 1853, Dz. 2795.

young of an imperial race? . . . Mrs Jones is destroying the race.'[6] It fed also on malthusian fears of a population explosion and on eugenic, elitist and even racist ideas of what constituted good breeding.

These ideas were translated into practice by the birth control clinics first set up by Marie Stopes in the 1920s. At the time the movement was opposed to sterilization and abortion, but both were gradually taken on board, the first in the 1940s and the second in the 1960s. From this—a minority idea—family planning quickly took hold of the national (and international) consciousness, until in the present generation it has become part of the conventional wisdom.

This has not happened altogether by accident. The work of the Family Planning Association, in England, and the Planned Parenthood Federation of America was extended throughout the world by the International Planned Parenthood Federation, which was founded by Margaret Sanger in 1952. In the same year, the Population Council was started in New York by John D. Rockefeller, who was prominent in convincing the United Nations of the need to control population.[7] They were ably assisted by some sectors of big business, among other reasons because it was thought small families put more cash into peoples' pockets and so boosted consumer sales. They gradually succeeded in enlisting the support of the medical profession and in influencing governments. The conventional wisdom penetrated the civil service and the public mind, as well as the politicians, to such a degree that, since 1973, family planning advice and contraceptive services are not only available free in Britain on the National Health Service, but financial increment is added to doctors' salaries according to the amount of such service they provide.

In the growth of this mentality, a decision of the Anglican Church was to play its part. Until 1930 the Lambeth Conference, meeting every ten years, consistently and unconditionally rejected contraception. In 1920, for example, it declared that matrimony, apart from making husband and wife one flesh, has the purpose of bringing children into the world. The 1930 conference repeated this statement, but by a majority vote, it gave contraception the green light under certain conditions. If parents considered they ought to limit their families, they should follow Christian principles—the first and most evident of which (it said) is abstention. If such a course should prove inadvisable, then one can use other means but within Christian morals; thus one had to ensure one didn't use contraceptives for

6. See Stephen Trombley, *The Right to Reproduce*, London, 1989.
7. See Valerie Riches, *Sex and Social Engineering*, Milton Keynes, 1986.

reasons of 'selfishness, lust, or mere convenience'. The future history of this subject shows how the Anglicans gradually turned from a negative, grudging acceptance of contraception to a positive espousal of it. This was due to the growth of doubts about complete abstinence and periodic continence, until the Lambeth Conference of 1958 placed the responsibility for deciding the number and frequency of children on the consciences of parents, and introduced for the first time the notion of 'family planning'.

The concession of the Anglicans to contraception occasioned the appearance of Pius XI's encyclical *Casti connubii*, in which he reiterated the primacy of procreation in the marital act and condemned any deliberate impediment to conception. He spoke of the secondary ends of marriage which are subordinated to this primary end: 'For in matrimony, as well as in the use of the matrimonial rights, there are also secondary ends, such as mutual aid, the cultivating of mutual love and the quieting of concupiscence, which husband and wife are not forbidden to consider as long as they are subordinated to the primary end and so long as the intrinsic nature of the act is preserved' (no. 59).

Pius XII reiterated this prohibition of contraception, notably in his Address to Obstetricians on 29 October 1951, when he also confirmed the legitimacy of the use of the so-called 'safe period', or natural infertility, for serious reasons. He also prohibited artificial insemination due to the fact that spouses have inalienable rights to each other's bodies which cannot be ceded, thereby foreshadowing a later judgement on *in vitro* fertilization. He did not, however, rule out the use of artificial means to facilitate the natural act or bring the act to its accomplishment.[8] He later condemned the use of the emerging contraceptive pill on the grounds that it was direct sterilization, which can never be licit. If the intention were to regulate a uterine or organic disorder, even though it was known this would indirectly impede a pregnancy, that is, the so-called therapeutic use, then this could be permitted.[9]

A similar line of argument is used to answer the frequent claim that the pill is just another form of medicine. Why, it is asked, if we can use drugs and perform surgical operations to control nature, can contraceptives not be considered to be in the same category? It must be pointed out here that operations and drugs can only be recurred to if they conduce to the total physical health of the whole person. The contraceptive pill, however, causes direct sterilization, and by it the intrinsic nature of the act is

8. Pius XII, *Address to Physicians*, 29 September 1949.
9. Pius XII, *Allocution to 7th Congress of Hematology*, 9 December 1958.

essentially altered. Consequently, it is not acting like an ordinary medicine, and hence the comparison is ill-conceived. Though in 1960 the oral contraceptive seemed to present a new circumstance, in fact it performs the same function as any other type of contraceptive, and hence the moral judgement is the same. Furthermore, many centuries earlier, in the Decretals of Gregory IX, the Church already had occasion to condemn oral contraceptives, and so the reiterated condemnation was not as new as had been first thought.

When Pope Paul came to make his momentous judgement in 1968 on the now marketed and fully available contraceptive pill, he accepted that circumstances had changed somewhat from the time of his earlier predecessors. There were population issues, a more varied social and professional role of women, and a greater understanding of personal love and its expression in marriage. Unlike the secular world and the Anglican Church, he did not, however, consider these arguments to be overriding of the core doctrine which the Church had traditionally taught, namely, that the unitive and the procreative meanings of the conjugal act cannot be separated.

To the supposed advantages of the pill for modern times the Pope countered with the drawbacks. If it were made licit, it would more easily open up the way to marital infidelity and the general lowering of moral standards. People need incentives for keeping the moral law, not facilities for breaking it. The pill would contribute to man losing respect for woman and considering her as a mere instrument of pleasure. Who can fail to see in the contraceptive mentality one of the sources of the permissive society and the lack of esteem in which the institution of marriage and family life is currently held? The encyclical also pointed out that, if the pill were sanctioned for families, governments could easily impose population control programmes on whole nations. With the benefit of hindsight, we may more easily see why the Church can claim that her teaching upholds true human values.

HUMANAE VITAE

The teaching of Paul VI in *Humanae vitae* is in homogeneous continuity with what went before, although he does not repeat the argument based on the ends of marriage. Rather, the encyclical relies on reasons derived from the truth about the human person and conjugal love. It is these personalist arguments and personal values which we must now examine. The core doctrine of the encyclical, which states that there must be no artificial obstacle placed in the way of procreation, 'is based on the inseparable connection, established by God, which man on his own initiative may not break, between the unitive significance and the procreative significance which are both inherent in the marriage act' (*Humanae vitae*, 13). In other words, conjugal love must not be separated from openness to life. For the marriage act to be an act of love, it must respect the procreative good on each occasion. Pope Paul says the reason is that the *structure of the act* is to be life-giving. Now, what does he mean by this? Why is it not an act of love if it is not also procreative in nature? Why do love and life have to go together in marriage?

The answer lies in the unity of the human person, the importance of which we have been at pains to stress, and the structure of married love as expressed in the conjugal act. The human person is a unity of soul and body, of spirit and matter. Conjugal love is the love of the whole person for the whole of his or her spouse. Indeed it is a spiritual love which is expressed bodily. Consequently, it is a union of minds and wills as well as bodies. It is a personal union and not just a physical one. Contraceptive sex, on the other hand, does not bring about a truly personal union, because the spouses have freely decided to withhold a part of themselves, namely their procreative capacity. Consequently, the fully human and personal nature of married love is damaged, and the dignity of the spouses as whole and unified persons is not respected.

A contemporary writer on marriage, Monsignor Cormac Burke has expressed it in this way:

> Sexual love is a love of the whole male or female person, body and spirit. Love is falsified if body and spirit do not say the same thing. This happens in contraception. The bodily act speaks of a presence of love or a degree of love that is denied by the spirit. The body says, 'I love you totally,' whereas the spirit says, 'I love you reservedly.' The body says, 'I seek you'; the spirit says, 'I will accept you, not all of you.'[10]

The purpose of the conjugal act is to be an expression of the *total* union between the two spouses, that is, of the fact that they are 'one flesh' and a communion of persons. The encyclical says: 'it is a love which is total—

10. 'Marriage and Contraception', *Homiletic and Pastoral Review*, January 1989, p. 14.

that very special form of personal friendship in which husband and wife generously share everything, allowing no unreasonable exceptions and not thinking just of their own interests. Whoever really loves his partner loves not only what he receives, but loves that partner for her own sake, content to be able to enrich the other with the gift of himself' (*Humanae vitae*, 9). Hence, to give oneself without one's procreative capacity, as in contraceptive sex, is not an act of complete self-giving and so is not a true act of conjugal love. This is why John Paul II says that, 'the conjugal act deprived of its interior truth, because artifically deprived of its procreative capacity, ceases also to be an act of love'.[11]

In biblical language, spousal intercourse is often expressed as a man 'knowing' his wife. Thus it can be likened to language—the language of the body—which communicates something reciprocally between the partners. They communicate what they are as persons by means of their sexuality. But, in contraceptive sex, the spouses do not fully 'know' each other, because they have not communicated completely from one to the other. The language, then, is false because it does not communicate the intended meaning properly. The body expresses the person, but here it does not express the fullness of the person in his, or her, masculinity or femininity.

Interestingly enough, some dissenting theologians have criticized *Humanae vitae* for what they call 'biologism' or 'physicalism', meaning that it is based only on the biological structure and consequences of the act and does not allow for what they call higher considerations, such as the overall good of the marriage to direct and override the physical structure. But this accusation, albeit in the name of the whole person, is itself based on a dualist and false understanding of man. The latter is considered as a self-conscious subject, or as a consciousness to which bodiliness is in some way extrinsic, instead of as a unified totality of which the body is an integral part. *Veritatis splendor*, 50, makes its own the definition of man given in *Familiaris consortio*, 11, namely, 'a soul which expresses itself in a body and a body informed by an immortal spirit'. On such an understanding of the human person the objection of biologism fails because all man's actions, if deliberately willed, even though some are expressed bodily, are rational and therefore moral and hence not simply physical.

Since it conditions the fullness of love, over a period of time contraception may well become a destabilising factor in marriage. If one does not give the whole of oneself, there is no way of telling (especially given our fallen nature) that one is not seeking oneself and being selfish in an act

11. John Paul II, General Audience, 22 August 1984.

which is meant to be one of self-giving. There may actually be a predominant search for pleasure, and pleasure is not the meaning of the act, but as
in other activities it only accompanies the right end. In such a case, one
would be contradicting the personalistic norm which prohibits ever using a
human being as an object. Since conjugal love is meant to be self-giving
and creative, if it is selfish and uncreative by design, it is no wonder that
it can lead to frustration and dissatisfaction since fulfilment is the fruit of
self-giving and fruitfulness.

The Church is fully aware that Christian doctrine on procreation is
demanding for couples. But then it also knows that marriage is a vocation
and like any vocation is idealistic. Every Christian vocation demands of
the person that he rise above himself. It is in the effort to transcend
himself with the grace of God that a Christian finds fulfilment. If every
man is called to transcend himself, so is every family. To bring a bigger
family into the world responds to the idealism, and hence the satisfaction,
which is part of the marriage vocation. The welfare state and the consumer
mentality have conspired in our time to offer people the possibility of an
easier life style and eschew the sacrifice and idealism of bringing up a
large family. It is this, perhaps, together with the availability of the pill,
which has made it difficult for many to appreciate the Church's teaching
on marriage.

THE DIFFERENCE BETWEEN PERIODIC CONTINENCE AND CONTRACEPTION

As we have seen, the procreative good is a basic and self-evident human
value which fulfils human beings and must be respected on every occasion. The question then becomes: Why is periodic continence, practised
for serious reasons, acceptable according to the doctrine of the Church and
the use of artificial means of birth prevention is not? Some consider periodic continence to be as contraceptive as the use of artificial means. True,
the intention not to have children is equally present in both actions. However, there is a clear and important difference between them which it is
vital to perceive.

In any action there are three things to take into account regarding its
morality, namely, the intention of the subject, the purpose and structure of
the action (its moral object), and the circumstances, such that all three
must be good if the action is to be morally upright. Now, spouses may
decide for legitimate reasons to carry out the marriage act without intending children, concentrating on the secondary ends only. This may be done

if the circumstances are right, that is to say, if it is an infertile period and there are grave reasons to counsel it. (The circumstances themselves are not a moral determinant of an action except insofar as they change the value of one of the two main intentions). But in addition to the initial intention of the spouses, there is also their further intention to respect, or not, the purpose of the action itself. As free agents, the spouses can override the intrinsic goodness of the act, not simply by the intention not to have children, but by the willingness to change the very structure (that is, the nature) of the act. It is this that may not be done, because if the action is to be good, the intrinsic nature, or finality, of the act must be upheld.[12]

The difference, therefore, hinges on the fact that one can cease to act in favour of a basic good, but one may not directly oppose it. Parallel examples will illustrate this. The truth is not assailed by silence, when there exists a just and serious reason for such silence. No one is bound to reveal everything on all occasions. On the other had, a lie is told whenever the truth is opposed or denied.[13] Similarly, when treating the aged, extraordinary medical procedures may be used or in some cases not used, depending on circumstances. For example, painful and expensive surgical treatment will be more readily offered a younger patient than an older one. What must never be done is to attack the good of life directly (by euthanasia or assisted suicide; cf. pp. 158f).

It will, of course, be objected that the procreative good is not always regarded as a basic and self-evident good by everybody. Here, however, it is necessary to make a distinction. If, at times, procreation is not looked upon positively, it is not usually because of a lack of appreciation of the value of children but because of some particular circumstances which make having children burdensome. Thus, fertility, as such, is almost universally regarded as a blessing, and sterility as a misfortune, whether in the Bible or the common experience of mankind. Human beings even today want fertility, though they often want to keep control of it in their own hands to an illegitimate degree, but they do not want to be without it as the development of *in vitro* fertilization shows. The joy which follows birth is universal even when children are not originally intended.

The principle evoked earlier from Genesis, that while man has the use of his bodily faculties he does not have ownership or unlimited dominion over them, will be recognized by Christians as pertinent here. Man must, therefore, respect the laws the Creator has put into the sexual act and its purpose, especially the procreative one. Paul VI wrote in *Humanae vitae:*

12. Lawler, Boyle and May, *Catholic Sexual Ethics*, Huntington, Indiana, 1985, p. 159.
13. Ibid., p. 160.

'But to experience the gift of married love while respecting the laws of conception is to acknowledge that one is not the master of the sources of life but rather the minister of the design established by the Creator. Just as man does not have unlimited dominion over his body in general, so also, and with more particular reason, he has no such dominion over his specifically sexual faculties, for these are concerned by their very nature with the generation of life, of which God is the source.'[14] It is for this reason that the use of the pill to interfere with the cycle is wholly different from making use of the cycle in the infertile period according to its natural occurrence. Nevertheless, since the intention is one of the ingredients of the act, to use a natural family planning method with a *merely* contraceptive purpose without serious reasons is itself tantamount to contraception.

Christians, then, recognizing the natural law and, therefore, the divine eternal law in the nature of the conjugal act will appreciate that justice to the Creator obliges them to act in accordance with that law. Not to do so would be to set aside the law of God and invent their own, which John Paul II has called setting aside God himself. He writes:

> Therefore, when by contraception the spouses deprive the exercise of marital sexuality of its procreative potential they attribute to themselves a power that belongs to God alone. . . . This viewpoint helps one to understand why contraception has to be judged objectively as so profoundly illicit that it can never for any reason be justified. To think or speak otherwise is equivalent to maintaining that in human life there are situations in which it is allowable not to recognize God as God.[15]

COROLLARIES AND CONSEQUENCES

Up to now, we have concentrated on the explanation of the principle on which *Humanae vitae* and the wrongness of contraception are based, namely, the non-separation of the unitive and procreative significance of marriage. One of the consequences of this principle is the corollary that homosexual relations, fornication, masturbation, etc. are gravely disordered actions. If the pleasure of sex can be separated from responsibility for procreation, then what is to stop people claiming a legitimate place for

14. Cf. *Humanae vitae*, 18.
15. John Paul II, General Audience, 17 September 1984.

these actions? On the other hand, if a sexual act must be truly unitive, and a genuine act of love has to be open to procreation, then it makes nonsense to talk of 'love' between homosexual persons. Fornication is wrong because it is not truly unitive since no lasting consent of the will has been given.

Another corollary of the non-separability of the unitive and procreative aspects of the marital act is that each and every act of contraception is wrong. An argument was put forward in the 1960s to suggest that, in some way, isolated acts of contraception might be merged with normal procreative relations at other times in matrimony so that the marriage viewed as a single entity would be open to life. But Paul VI made quite clear that the non-separability of the unitive and the procreative meaning was an inherent part of the moral order, such that its violation on each occasion was 'intrinsically evil'. He noted that although it is sometimes lawful to tolerate a lesser evil to avoid a greater one, or to promote a higher good, this is only so when it conforms to the conditions which regulate the principle of double effect (the first condition being that the action itself must be good). But since contraception intrinsically contradicts the moral order, this cannot be so. Nor can we do evil that good may come of it. Each and every marriage act must, therefore, be open to life.

The present Pope, as we have seen, has used the expression 'language of the body' to describe the conjugal act, among other reasons because language is susceptible of truth and falsity. If the action is open to procreation the language of the body is being expressed truly. The natural law demands, as stated above, that each basic value must be upheld on each occasion. And so the procreative act must be open to life and truth each time, in the same way as each utterance of speech must be open to truth; otherwise a lie is told. Contraception is thus false language of the body.

The years that have gone by since Paul VI's condemnation of contraception in *Humanae vitae* have confirmed the Church's judgement in many ways. We have already noted his prediction of a wave of permissiveness and marital infidelity. But furthermore, the pill has developed scientifically to the point where most pills now are abortefacient.

In *Evangelium vitae*, 13, the Pope takes up the objection of the secular world that by disallowing contraception the Church actually contributes to there being a greater number of abortions. He says: 'It may be that many people use contraception with a view to excluding the subsequent temptation of abortion. But the negative values inherent in the "contraceptive mentality" . . . are such that they in fact strengthen the temptation when the unwanted life is conceived. Indeed, the pro-abortion culture is especially strong preceisely where the Church's teaching on contraception is rejected.' This was demonstrated in England when Victoria Gillick's appeal not to allow doctors to prescribe contraceptives to under-16-year-old girls without their parent's consent was upheld for close on two years and the number of abortions went down. The encyclical goes on: 'Certainly from the moral point of view contraception and abortion are specifically different evils: the former contradicts the full truth of the sexual act as the proper expression of conjugal love, while the latter destroys the life of a human being; the former is opposed to the virtue of chastity, the latter is opposed to the virtue of justice. . . . But despite their differences of nature and moral gravity, contraception and abortion are often closely connected as fruits of the same tree.' This tree is hedonism, which refuses to accept responsibility in matters of sexuality, and a 'self-centred concept of freedom, which regards procreation as an obstacle to personal fulfilment' (ibid.).

Moreover, since the pill is a kind of poison which kills live and healthy cells, it is not surprising to find it is prejudicial to health in a number of respects. Studies have shown a link between the use of the pill and cervical cancer, pulmonary embolis, gallstones and depression. The growing incidence of depression among adolescents can be linked to the progestogen in the pill. Nevertheless, pharmacologists prefer a progestogen pill with a low dosage of oestrogen because the latter increases the chances of thrombosis. It must be remembered that a thorough knowledge of the exact medical disadvantages of the oral contraceptive is still not available because experiments take decades to conduct and the pill is only a thirty-year phenomenon. Furthermore, the mentality of the times and the massive vested interests of pharmaceutical companies and consumer business in general are against over-publicizing such findings.

Finally, what are we to say to those who, in line with the mentality of the times, are in the habit of using contraceptives and have, so to speak, become hardened to them? They have to try and re-assess their view of marriage which has become incomplete. But in these cases we should proceed according to the 'law of gradualness'. This means step by step advances so that couples can make moral progess within marriage. But the 'law of gradualness' cannot be identified with the 'gradualness of the law', 'as if there were different degrees or forms of precept in God's law for different individuals and situations. In God's plan, *all* husbands and wives are called to holiness in marriage and this lofty vocation is fulfilled to the extent that the human person is able to respond to God's command with serene confidence in God's grace and in his or her own will' (*Familiaris consortio*, 34).

[8]

Uses and Abuses of Human Sexuality and Marriage

Man may be accurately described as an embodied soul, such that personhood resides both in his soul and body and expresses itself in unified actions. His body is thus an integral part of his being, he does not just possess his body. In no sense does Christianity undervalue the human body. Indeed, corporality is the mode of existence proper to the human spirit, and the body 'reveals man' and 'expresses the person'.[1] Nevertheless, if man is to conduct himself according to human dignity, the body must be governed by the higher spiritual powers of intellect and will, according to right reason.

Human love, though in origin spiritual, is expressed bodily in the emotions and by sexuality. The body, insofar as it is sexual, points to the reciprocity and complementarity of man and woman and to the possibility of the mutual gift of self in which love consists. Masculinity and femininity manifest the diversity of the human being, which always exists in equality of nature and of dignity. Sexuality has as one of its constitutive meanings fruitfulness, or participation in the created order, which is part of its intrinsic finality. The body and sexuality call man to an ethical vocation and responsibility and thus to a means of self-fulfilment and human dignity when responded to correctly.

Consequently, sex is an upright and sacred reality provided it is subject to true love, which consists in the mutual self-giving of two spouses, and provided its intrinsic finality is respected. Indeed, all appetites and passions, both concupiscible and irascible, can and should be directed to a noble end by reason. But we cannot forget that man has a fallen nature and is subject to a threefold concupiscence, 'the lust of the flesh, the lust of the eyes and the pride of life' (1 Jn 2:17). He has lost his original innocence and in some cases is only dimly able to glimpse the nuptial meaning of the body and respect it. It is this internal weakness, further undermined by external enemies—the world, the flesh and the devil—which makes impurity of all

---

1. John Paul II, General Audiences, 14 November 1979 and 9 January 1980, respectively.

types a real possibility for man. The Christian virtues of chastity and self-control are directed to overcoming this danger. The consequences of not endeavouring to live in this way for human happiness, the family and the community at large are only too apparent in the permissive society.

Hedonistic permissivism is based on a false notion of the human person, both of his purpose in general, and of the body in particular. The body cannot be used as an object or a machine, but must be considered an integral part of the 'I' of each person. It is part of a person's dignity, and there are ways of acting according to that dignity or against it. To use the body exclusively as an object of sexual pleasure and gratification is not worthy of man or woman, since pleasure must always accompany a worthy action rather than be an end in itself. This is exemplified by the aforesaid consideration that no sane human being would opt for a life of sensual pleasure if this were to exclude him from every other human activity for a whole lifetime. The body, then, should express the wisdom and love with which the human person ought to conduct himself both individually and in his relations with others.

Christians, furthermore, believe that man is made in the image of God and by Baptism becomes a child of God and temple of the Holy Spirit. He must, therefore, live up to being an 'icon of God', as he is sometimes called, or at other times, as 'the sacrament of God's image' in the world. He must act as God acts and express God's love as an embodied soul, and therefore also physically, but according to the plans of God. Men and women live their vocation as the image of God both as single persons and as a 'communion of persons'.

For a Christian, then, sex is something sacred. He knows he must imitate God's love, and God loves by giving, essentially by giving existence or life. God is fullness of being and fullness of life. Life and love in him are the same. Though man expresses love in a bodily way because he is corporeal, like God this love must be self-giving, not self-indulgent, and life-giving at the same time. Here is found part of the basis for the principle of the non-separability between the unitive and procreative meanings of the marriage act.

The other basis of this principle is the unity of man. Human love is not just bodily, but personal, based on the whole person, spirit and matter. Both these dimensions of the person function together in an action if it is human, and they cannot be validly separated. Hence, for an act of love to be human and genuine, it must be a union of wills and not just of bodies. And the act of will must express a permanent and faithful commitment. It is for this reason that fornication and extra-marital sex are morally wrong.

The principles of Catholic sexual morality are drawn from Scripture and the constant teaching of the Magisterium. St Paul speaks about unnatural sexual conduct, which he calls uncleanness or incontinence (*akarthasia*; cf. Rom 1:24); about unlawful sexual intercourse (*porneia*) meaning fornication, incest and prostitution and licentiousness (*alsegeia*; cf. Rom 13:13 and also Gal 5:20); and about adultery (cf. 1 Cor 6:10). He makes clear that each of these actions constitutes grave matter when he says that those who do them will not inherit the Kingdom of Heaven unless they repent and reform.

At times St Paul puts impurity on a par with lying and falsehood, and at other times he likens it to idolatry. These impure sexual practices deny the truth and purpose of the body and its principal faculties. They are false language of the body and to indulge in them is to live a lie (cf. Rom 1:25). To the Romans and the Corinthians he also likens impurity to idolatry, because it refuses to recognize that our bodies belong to God and must be used as he intends, namely, to give him glory and not for our own self-indulgence. A Christian, furthermore, is a member of the Body of Christ and a temple of the Holy Spirit and he, therefore, dishonours Christ and his Body by impurity (cf. 1 Cor 6:9-20).

UNNATURAL ACTS

At the beginning of St Paul's Epistle to the Romans, it is possible to see a rejection of the unnatural acts of masturbation and homosexuality, the latter very explicitly. He speaks of 'practices with which they dishonour their own bodies' (1:24) and of 'women who have turned from natural intercourse to unnatural practices' and goes on to say that their menfolk have given up 'natural intercourse to be consumed with passion for one another' (Rom 1:26 27).

These texts demonstrate that homosexual relations and masturbation have been declared intrinsically wrong and disordered since apostolic times. They are unnatural because they disregard the intrinsic finality of the act. With regard to the former, we must draw a distinction between homosexual inclination and homosexual acts or behaviour. Homosexuals must be treated pastorally with great understanding, and the mere possessing of the inclination is not sinful. They must struggle to live purity and exercise self-control like anybody else, and they must be encouraged and attended to in the hope of overcoming their personal problems.

But no pastoral method can be used to lend moral justification to these acts which are condemned in Scripture as a serious depravity and presented as a sad consequence of rejecting God. All homosexual acts are 'intrinsically disordered' and in no sense can one talk of homosexual 'marriage' since 'homosexual relations are acts which lack an essential and indispensable finality'.[2]

It is the duty of the family, teacher or pastor to endeavour to identify the factors that lead to homosexuality. These could have a physiological or psychological basis or be the result of a false education and lack of normal sexual development, or a contracted habit, or bad example. Other diverse elements should also be investigated such as 'lack of affection, immaturity, obsessive impulses, seduction, social isolation and other types of frustration, depravation in dress, licence in shows and publications'.[3]

Even if masturbation is not mentioned by name in Sacred Scripture the Church teaches that it is condemned there under the name of 'impurity, unchasteness and other vices contrary to chastity and continence'.[4] The constant teaching of the Church is that masturbation is a 'grave moral disorder and an intrinsically and seriously disordered act'.[5] The reason is that the deliberate use of the sexual faculty outside conjugal relations contradicts its purpose. 'For it lacks the sexual relationship called for by the moral order, namely the relationship which realizes "the full sense of mutual self-giving and human procreation in the context of true love".'[6]

Pastorally speaking one must take into account that in certain cases there may be factors, such as adolescence and ignorance, psychological imbalance, or habit, which influence behaviour to the point where there may not always be serious personal fault. But this must not be presumed or made a general rule. In any case, such mitigation could only apply to the subjective conditions, namely, a lack of full knowledge or consent, because the gravity of the act itself cannot be denied.

Sociological surveys are wont to tell us about the frequency and widespread nature of this sin (no doubt exagerrating) especially among the youth, as if this could affect the morality of the phenomenon. What they rather show, insofar as they are objective, is the fallen nature of man as well as the loss of the sense of God, and the permissive and hedonistic nature of much of modern life. In this connection, one may mention 'the commer-

---

2. *Declaration on Sexual Ethics*, Sacred Congregation for the Doctrine of the Faith, 1975, no. 8.
3. Sacred Congregation for Catholic Education, *Educational Guidelines in Human Love*, CTS, London, 1983, no. 102, p. 33.
4. *Declaration on Sexual Ethics*, op. cit., 1975, no. 9.
5. Cf. Pope Leo IX, Letter, *Ad spendidum nitentis*, 1054, Dz. 687-8.
6. *Declaration on Sexual Ethics*, op. cit., no. 9.

cialization of vice, the unrestrained licentiousness of many public entertainments and publications as well as neglect of modesty which is the guardian of chastity'.[7]

The observance of the moral law in sexual matters has been greatly endangered by the tendency to minimize the possibility of grave sin. This is done by arguing that a person only commits mortal sin when he or she adopts a fundamental option against God or people. This happens less easily in sexual matters, the argument goes on, where other factors such as passion and weakness more readily influence the decision. However, mortal sin does not require a direct contempt for God and neighbour but occurs whenever a seriously disordered act is committed freely and consciously, that is to say, when there is grave matter, full consent and full knowledge. Therefore, grave sin can result from a single act carried out through weakness. St Thomas explains that an animal does not want to poison himself, but he does so by eating a delicious fruit which is poisoned. So, in sin there is something the sinner intends directly (sensible delight, or his own self-love) and something he does not intend directly (the corruption of his soul).

In order to attain the standard required by the Christian virtue of purity one must pay attention to the totality of one's behaviour and its habitual pattern. All the traditional means of Christian asceticism, both natural and supernatural, must be availed of to conquer in this virtue. These include: frequenting the sacraments, prayer, humility, guard of the senses, vigilance in entertainments, films and publications, and self-denial in matters of gluttony and self-indulgence. Without an effort in these areas, the sin may very well be voluntary in its cause and, therefore, culpable.

IMPURE THOUGHTS

The ninth commandment teaches us that sexual sins may be committed, even in a grave way, in thought alone. And with our Lord's injunction that 'he who looks at a woman so as to lust after her has already committed adultery in his heart', the prohibition is extended to cover impure looks. Indeed, St Paul also underlines that we must steer clear of impurity both in words and jokes and so on (cf. Eph 5:3-5). Such sins are committed when there is a deliberate intention to derive sexual pleasure or excitement from thoughts or looks of an immoral nature. This may happen by remembering past sinful actions, imagining present ones or desiring future ones. The

7. Ibid.

matter of these sins is grave, and hence they are mortal unless the knowledge and consent are defective. It is also possible that such imaginings may not pass beyond the stage of temptations, since to feel is not the same as to consent. As Blessed Josemaría Escrivá writes in *The Way*: 'Whatever happens, there is no need to worry as long as you don't consent. For only the will can open the door of the heart and let that corruption in.'[8]

The exact degree of culpability is often difficult to gauge. Sexual matters may have to be spoken about and dealt with in a wholly proper way by doctors, parents, moralists and spiritual directors etc. In such circumstances, however, there will not be any arousal of sexual passion or lust, or at least the danger of it will be remote. Should it occur, however, in an indirect and involuntary way as a consequence of carrying out an action which is good or indifferent in itself, then the sinfulness must be judged according to the usual conditions of the indirectly voluntary principle. Sexual matters should be avoided, however, when there is no need, such as listening to gossip, or reading about them in newspapers, magazines etc.

Pope John Paul II has pointed out that, although our Lord's teaching not to look at a woman lustfully is an accusation or a prohibition, it is also, perhaps principally, an appeal.[9] Our Lord is exhorting us to recognize the true beauty of human sexuality and use it for its proper purpose and not in a lustful way. Sex should not be understood in a Manichean or purely negative sense, but the lustful person becomes a slave to passion and is unable to appreciate the positive side of sexuality. In other words, the lesson Christ teaches us (and the Church has constantly repeated) is not to look unnecessarily at immoral pictures or scenes or to dwell on or read things which can lead to the giving of consent and, therefore, to sin. Special care and vigilance have to be exercised over one's thoughts because, although sins of thought are less serious than the corresponding actions, they are less easily adverted to and more easily fallen into. Furthermore, vices usually start in the mind and hence they can lead to more serious sins and actions. One must, therefore, strive to keep custody of one's thoughts, imagination and senses.

EXTRA-MARITAL SEX AND CO-HABITING

Due to the loss of the sense of sin, to the widespread incidence of marriage break-up and to permissive ethics, the phenomena of living together and pre-

8. *The Way*, Dublin, no. 140.
9. See John Paul II, General Audiences, 22 and 29 October and 5 November 1980.

and extra-marital sex have become very common. In a sense, we have come full circle because in apostolic and early Christian times people had to separate from concubines and be faithful to one wife, or celibate, if they wanted to become Christians. The reasons which are usually adduced for extra-marital sex are that it is acceptable if two persons are really in love, that it doesn't do anybody any harm and that, in the case of the pre-marital variety, it is a necessary preparation for marriage.

These arguments have a specious and familiar ring since we have been warned about them from apostolic times, especially in the writings of St Paul. Extra-marital sex is a euphemism for what the timeless language of the Church refers to as fornication or adultery. Here is how St Paul speaks to the Ephesians (5:5-9):

> For you can be quite certain that nobody who actually indulges in fornication or impurity or promiscuity—which is worshipping a false god—can inherit the kingdom of God. Do not let anyone deceive you with empty arguments: it is for this loose living that God's anger comes down on those who rebel against him. Make sure that you are not included with them. You were darkness once, but now you are light in the Lord; be like children of light, for the effects of the light are seen in complete goodness and right living and truth.

Adultery in the Old Testament was considered so serious that its punishment was death by stoning. On the occasion of the encounter with the adulterous woman, Christ compassionately waived the penalty but he upheld the law: 'Go and do not sin again' (Jn 8:11).

In the above passage St Paul makes three points which we will now deal with. He emphasizes the extreme seriousness of fornication and impurity by explaining that it deprives one of entrance into heaven (unless repented of). The arguments used to support it are empty and deceptive. By incurring the anger of God it brings harm on man.

The first point is supported by the constant teaching of the Church. For example, the first Council of Lyons (1245) said: 'Concerning fornication which an unmarried man commits with an unmarried woman, there must not be any doubt at all that it is a mortal sin, since the Apostle declares that "fornicators and adulterers are cast out of the kingdom of God" (1 Cor 6:9).'[10] The Council of Vienne (1311–12) condemned the Beghards and Beguines who supported sexual intercourse outside marriage 'because [they

10. Dz. 835.

said] nature inclines to this'.[11] Later the proposition, 'Fornication involves no malice; it is an evil only because it is forbidden,' was condemned by Pope Innocent XI.[12] This, with the implication that fornication is not wrong if it doesn't harm anybody, and is a mere disregard of the natural law, foreshadows our present time.

What is wrong with fornication—and herein lies the speciousness of arguments in its favour—is that it is a caricature and counterfeit of real love. Spousal love, as we have seen, involves the total and unconditional gift of self to the other, and this is achieved only by the binding and permanent commitment of two wills after consideration by the intellect. Sexual union is a physical expression of this, such that the two become 'one flesh', but if the commitment of wills is absent it is a lie. 'This is why a man must leave father and mother and cling to his wife, and the two become one body. So then, what God has united, man must not divide' (Mt 19:4-6).

Another specious argument is that successful union requires a 'trial marriage'. On the contrary, the Church and the experience of mankind teach that the proper preparation for marriage is virginity and chastity. This is because love requires self-control and such sexual dominion is usually learnt early in life. Previous sexual activity not only remains strong in the memory but leads to incontinence and habits which may well hinder future married life. Wanda Poltawska writes:

> it is well known that pre-marital activity and pre-marital masturbation make future marital intercourse more difficult. . . . Unmarried partners who begin sexual intercourse do not give anything to each other besides the illusory joy of orgasm, and not always even that . . . . Furthermore, by this sin they deprive themselves of contact with God, both in the objective dimension of grace as well as in their subjective feeling. Their experiences are so strong they stay in their memory and cannot be erased from it and from the history of their life. Real deep penance is the only solution. Everybody brings into his marriage the experiences and effects of his pre-marital life.[13]

The *Catechism* (no. 2391) deals with this point in the following way:

> Some today claim a *right to a trial marriage* where there is an intention of getting married later. However firm the purpose of those who engage in premature sexual relations may be, "the fact is that

11. Dz. 897.   12. Dz. 2148.   13. *Position Paper 168*, Dublin, p. 350.

such liaisons can scarcely ensure mutual sincerity and fidelity in a relationship between a man and a woman, nor, especially, can they protect it from inconstancy of desires or whim" (*Persona humana,* 7). Carnal union is morally legitimate only when a definitive community of life between a man and a woman has been established. Human love does not tolerate 'trial marriages'. It demands a total and definitive gift of persons to one another (cf. *Familiaris consortio,* 80).

Permissive sexual morality does potential harm not only to the marriage and the spouses' happiness but also to the children and through the children to society. Since the family is the first cell of society, it has a social significance, and, thus, the marriage bond and commitment must be manifested externally. For a Catholic it must be done before God, and before society, and it must be unconditional. Often in casual liaisons the possibility of children is excluded, which of itself prevents the act being one of true love according to our foregoing arguments. But the children in a family have an inalienable right to be brought into the world in wedlock and enjoy the stable union of their parents for their upbringing. The institution of marriage is essential to society and must always be fostered by it. In England and Wales at present, 25% of children are born outside wedlock and 14% live with one parent.[14] The increasing number of single parent families provides an inadequate backround for children's upbringing and gives rise to many social problems.

DIVORCE

The institutionalized legalization of divorce and the accelerated increase of it over recent decades, with the result that more and more young people are exposed to it, have undoubtedly led to holding marriage in low esteem and to a consequent growth of co-habitation as a way of life. Divorce begets divorce, among other reasons because many people mistakenly think that what is legal is moral. The very possibility of legalized divorce, in fact, means that marriage between two partners becomes not forever but as long as everything goes well. 'Once marriage is seen as a temporary union it loses its meaning.'[15] Hence couples co-habit for as long as things work out without bothering with the formal procedure of marriage.

14. *Social Trends,* HMS, 1990.
15. Mark Hamilton and David Logan, *The Case against Divorce,* Dublin, 1986.

Of course, promiscuity plays its part, but it is a chicken and egg situation because, while permissiveness can be a cause of divorce, it may also be an effect. It leads also to social problems of delinquency and crime, and a significant proportion of the sexual abuse of children has been linked to divorced families. The evil of divorce, therefore, can be gauged from its fruits, but Christ's teaching was clear.

Among the Jews there existed the custom of a man giving a writ of separation to his wife, which allowed both of them to re-marry. There were, however, stricter and laxer interpretations of this dispensation, which is why the Pharisees asked our Lord whether it was lawful for *any* cause to divorce one's wife. Jesus Christ answered that in marriage the two become one flesh and 'what God has joined together let no man put asunder'. When he was further asked why Moses allowed it, he replied that it was to suit the hardness of their hearts and added 'from the beginning it was not so' (Mt 19:8). He, therefore, raised the fidelity required in marriage to its original level and completeness. Divorce is tantamount to issuing a writ to go and commit adultery which, we have seen, is roundly condemned throughout the New Testament.

A further question arises as to why our Lord, both here and in Matthew 5:31-32, includes the words 'except for unchastity'. This phrase should not be taken as indicating an exception to the absolute indissolubility of marriage which our Lord has just rehabilitated. If it were, it would go against the whole Tradition of the Church and, indeed, the parallel reading of Luke 16:18, where this phrase is not mentioned. The explanation, then, is almost certainly that the reference is to unions which were not really or legally marriages either because they were within the forbidden degrees of consanguinity (cf. Lev 8:6-16), or because they were contracted with a Gentile. Hence such persons were never, in fact, joined in true marriage. In our own times, this clause would not refer to those who are truly married, but to divorced and 're-married' persons and, more generally, to those not validly married.

What the Church does allow, where a marriage has irretrievably broken down, is separation without dissolution of the marriage bond, such that neither party may contract a new marriage. This has been the constant teaching of the Church as is borne out by reference to the Magisterium. So the Council of Florence said:

> Three blessings are ascribed to matrimony . . . . The third is the indissolubility of matrimony—indissoluble because it signifies the indivisible union of Christ with the Church. Although a separation

from bed may be permitted by reason of marital infidelity, nevertheless it is not permitted to contract another matrimony since the bond of marriage lawfully contracted is perpetual.[16]

At the Council of Trent it was said that 'If anyone says that the marriage bond can be dissolved by reason of heresy, domestic incompatibility, or wilful desertion by one of the partners: let him be anathema.'[17] Exactly the same is said in more present-day language by Vatican II: 'For the good of the parties, of the children, and of society, this sacred bond no longer depends on human decision alone. For God himself is the author of marriage . . . . The intimate union of marriage, as a mutual giving of two persons, and the good of the children demand total fidelity from the spouses and require an unbreakable unity between them' (*Gaudium et spes*, 48). And the *Catechism of the Catholic Church* (no. 2384) says of divorce that:

> It claims to break the contract, to which the spouses freely consented, to live with each other till death. Divorce does injury to the covenant of salvation, of which sacramental marriage is the sign. Contracting a new union, even if it is recognized by civil law, adds to the gravity of the rupture: the remarried spouse is then in a situation of permanent and public adultery.

Matrimonial consent—the very heart of the marriage bond—demands indissolubility, because it consists in unconditional, mutual self-giving which would not be so if temporal conditions were laid down. Divorce is a falsification of marital consent. It makes nonsense to say, 'I love you as long as we don't become impoverished', or 'as long as you don't lose your good name' or 'provided you don't get in the way of my career'. Hence, also, a naturally childless marriage is indissoluble because of the nature of married fidelity, which is complete and without conditions.

Much confusion is often aroused by the Catholic Church's practice of marriage nullity. It is contended that this is divorce by another name. Here it is important to be precise in our terms. A decree of nullity states that a marriage has not taken place—that the union was not valid in the first place. Hence, we must consider the conditions for a legitimate marriage.

Baptized Catholics who have not formally apostasized can only be validly married in Church in a religious ceremony. Furthermore, they can only

---

16. Council of Florence, *Pro Armeniis*, Dz. 1327.
17. Council of Trent, *De Sac. Matr.*, canon 5, Dz. 1805.

marry other baptized Catholics unless they obtain a dispensation. If they go
through a civil ceremony and separation later follows, a judgement can be
made to the effect that there was no marriage in the first place. Non-
Catholics and non-Christians, however, can contract valid natural marriages
in civil or, indeed, religious ceremonies provided that true and binding
consent is given. Such marriages cannot be dissolved. If, however, somebody marries a divorced person in this way, no marriage would take place,
and a judgement to this effect could be made at a later date leaving the
person still free to marry.

Defects in consent may occur through ignorance or fear. In the case of
ignorance, the error must be more than simple, and it must be such as to
influence the will; purely theoretical error does not invalidate. Thus, even a
simple and theoretical error about the indissolubility of the bond or the
procreative purpose of marriage does not invalidate. However, a *positive*
practical error which was actually stated, regarding the properties of marriage (that is, unity and indissolubility) or the ends (that is, procreation and
the giving of exclusive rights to the other) could invalidate the union. A
positively stated intention *never* to have children or not to contract an
indissoluble union could vitiate the consent. An error about the identity of
the person one was marrying due to impersonation without one's knowledge, could also vitiate the act.

Grave fear at the time of giving consent could also be grounds for a
Church declaration of nullity. We must distinguish here between marrying
with fear and marrying *out of* fear. Only the latter type of fear, when it is
produced externally and is unjust, invalidates the contract.

The inviolability of the marriage bond, once made, cannot be broken by
any human authority. The State does not, therefore, have the right to enact
pro-divorce laws which allow once married partners to 'remarry'. A law
which goes against the natural law is not a law at all; positive law may only
be enacted within the confines of the natural law, based as it is on the eternal
law. Nevertheless, marriage is also a social institution, as well as a divine
one, and therefore the State has the right and the duty to legislate for its civil
effects. Conversely, the State can also allow for the separation of the
spouses for a just cause and determine and lay down the conditions for an
equitable settlement.

As the *Catechism* (no. 2385) says, 'Divorce is immoral because it intro-
duces disorder into the family and into society. This disorder brings grave
harm to the deserted spouse, to children traumatized by the separation of
their parents and often torn between them, and because of its contagious
effect which makes it truly a plague on society.'

It is the duty of the State to uphold standards of human dignity and morality. Experience suggests that once divorce is introduced it becomes more and more liberal. So, for example, in England since 1969, there exists 'no-fault divorce' where the marriage is ended by mutual agreement after a short elapse of time. The reason for this procedure is that apportioning blame causes much bitterness.

Divorce begets divorce. So, second marriages are more likely to end in divorce than first ones. Forty per cent of second marriages end in divorce partly because of the financial burdens imposed by the first divorce. Up to 10% of men in English prisons in the 1970s were there for non-payment of alimony to their partners.[18] Surveys have shown that the majority of divorced people would have preferred to stay with their first spouse. Children of divorced parents are more likely to get divorced themselves, because they have been educated to see divorce as a common remedy for difficulties.[19]

Judith Wallerstein, an American social scientist whose work on divorced families is widely respected, has written: 'the high incidence of divorce has significantly raised levels of anxiety in relationships between men and women, and in many instances between children and their parents; whether or not they come from divorced families.'[20] Studies in the United States have shown that twice as many children from broken homes require psychiatric assistance. According to a study of the University of Michigan, 'children of divorce had a higher rate of anti-social, delinquent problems; specifically drug-taking and sexual behaviour. Additionally it was found that children of divorces are more likely to have overt aggression towards their parents as reason for referral.'[21]

It is sometimes argued that it is uncompassionate and intolerant to oppose divorce because it penalizes those families which have genuinely broken down. This is hardly the case if this apparent unhappiness is weighed against that being caused so widely to spouses and children in Europe and the United States at the moment by marriage break-up and the disastrous permissive and criminal effects on society. Divorce is in a very real sense the enemy within, and the only way to deal with these problems is to go to the root of them. The State has an important part to play here. William

18. *The Case against Divorce*, op. cit., no. 39.
19. Ibid., no. 7.
20. Dr J. Wallerstein, 'Children of Divorce; ten year follow up of young children', *American Journal of Ortho-Psychiatry*, July 1984.
21. Dr Neil Kalter, 'Children of divorce in an outpatient psychiatric population', *American Journal of Ortho-Psychiatry*, January 1977.

Temple, Archbishop of Canterbury, said many years ago: 'You cannot by Act of Parliament make man morally good; but you can by Act of Parliament supply the conditions which facilitate the growth of moral goodness and remove conditions which obstruct it.'[22]

The Church, though opposing divorce, continues to be solicitous for the spiritual welfare and salvation of those of her members, and all souls, whose marriages have broken up. She discerns different situations among the divorced and 'remarried'. There is a difference between those who have sincerely tried to save their first marriage and been abandoned, and those who have broken a valid marriage through their own fault. Still others have entered into a second union for the sake of the children, believing subjectively in conscience that their first marriage had never been valid. To all, though, the Church extends a maternal hand of assistance, inviting them to persevere in their membership of the Church. They are encouraged to attend Mass, listen to the Word of God, persevere in prayer, perform works of charity, educate their children in the faith and do penance so as to implore God's grace of reconciliation when the condition of their life permits it. Until that time, however, they cannot be admitted to Eucharistic Communion since the state of their life objectively contradicts the union of Christ and the Church, which is signified and effected by the Eucharist. Nor can they participate in the sacrament of penance until they are ready to pursue a way of life that does not contradict the indissolubility of marriage (cf. *Familaris consortio*, 84).

CHASTITY AND VIRGINITY

The shadows over sexual and family morality we have been considering point to the vital necessity of re-affirming the Christian virtues of chastity and purity and their related virtues. This, in the end, is a task for the Church, and it is one that she has consistently carried out. Negative prohibitions and strictures are necessary, but chastity and purity must never be considered as negative virtues or a rejection of sexuality. On the contrary, they are a true affirmation of it. The Pope has written in *Familiaris consortio*, 33: 'In the Christian view, chastity by no means signifies rejection of human sexuality or lack of esteem for it: rather it signifies spiritual energy capable of defending love from the perils of selfishness and aggressiveness, and able to advance it towards its full realization.'

22. Quoted in *The Case against Divorce*, op. cit., p. 17.

Purity is a virtue of the human person, who is the only animal able to recognize the truth about himself and his procreative capacity and use it for its true purpose. He also knows his weakness and the tendency to self-indulgence inherent in his fallen passions. Chastity, therefore, consists in recognizing the truth about man and striving to live in conformity with it. Its etymology comes from the word 'chastisement', which implies a certain disciplining of the body and its appetites through the exercise of temperance and self-control with a view to conquering oneself. Scripture presents impurity as sexual falsehood, and hence purity is sexual truth. Consequently, chastity and purity make a man live up to his responsibilities as a human being and, therefore, build up his character and dignity. In so doing they free him from selfishness and enable him the better to love God and others. As Blessed Josemaría Escrivá wrote in *The Way*: 'And so it happens that among the chaste are found the finest men in every way. And among the lustful predominate the timid, the selfish, the treacherous and the cruel—characters of little manliness.'[23]

From a Christian point of view, we can take this further because we realize we do not possess our own bodies or have ownership over them, but rather we enjoy only the use of them. They must be used to honour God and not dishonour him by trying to glorify or ingratiate ourselves. Scripture says that the 'pure of heart' shall see God, and indeed they see the plans and purposes of God in this world as well. They recognize the truth about God because they recognize the truth about themselves and vice versa. They also know they are members of Christ and cannot unite themselves with impurity, by which they would become one with it (cf. 1 Cor 6:15). They would be something defiled in God's sight because untrue to their nature.

Likewise, celibacy as understood in the Christian tradition is, in no sense, a rejection of human sexuality but rather a confirmation of its rightful orientation. We read in *Familiaris consortio*, 16:

> virginity or celibacy for the Kingdom of God not only does not contradict the dignity of marriage but presupposes and confirms it. Marriage and virginity or celibacy are two ways of expressing and living the one mystery of the covenant of God with his people. When marriage is not esteemed, neither can consecrated virginity or celibacy exist. When human sexuality is not regarded as a great value given by the Creator, the renunciation of it for the sake of the Kingdom of Heaven loses its meaning.

23. Op. cit., no. 124.

The self-giving in which marriage consists is, in a sense, confirmed by celibacy, which is a total renunciation of sexual intimacy, for the love of Christ and the Church. It enables one to serve God directly and not via another person and family (cf. 1 Cor 7). We have dwelt on the Apostle's spousal analogy by which he expresses Christ's relationship to the Church; 'Husbands love your wives, as Christ loved the Church, *and gave himself for it*' (Eph 5:25). Celibacy also requires spousal self-giving, but in this case the spouse is Christ. It is lived in imitation of Christ who was celibate and for greater availability to the Church and souls, in order to contribute to the building up of the Church. Having renounced physical paternity or maternity, the celibate person is often blessed with an abundant spiritual fruitfulness. But celibacy also has eschatological significance, because in heaven there will be no giving and taking in marriage and thus it is always a reminder to mankind of the world to come.

Chastity and virginity, which Christians have always borne witness to, are a sign to the world of our times. They serve as a signal and indication of the path humanity and the family must re-learn if they are to solve the problems spoken of in this chapter and if man is to live in accordance with his dignity. As a consequence of fallen nature, the human heart is a battle-field between 'life according to the spirit', in St Paul's phrase, and the threefold concupiscence he carries within him. To the Christian who sincerely undertakes the ascetic struggle, that struggle is the path towards the 'redemption of the body' (Rom 8:23) obtained for us by Christ. The state of historical man is, at the same time, one of fallen but redeemed nature (*status naturae lapsae simul ac redemptae*).

PART III: MEDICAL ETHICS

[9]

Abortion

Legalized abortion, more than any other issue, has become the focal point for those who oppose the permissive legislation of recent decades. The pro-life position maintains that the foetus is a human being from the moment of conception and, as such, enjoys the same rights as any other human person. Indeed, they would say that these rights must be specially defended, in particular those of life and security of person, since they belong to the weakest and most innocent human being. Pope John Paul has not hesitated for this reason to speak of a 'new slaughter of the innocents'. He goes on to compare the Church's defence of the unborn at this time with its role in supporting the liberation of the working classes from the oppression of miserly wages and undignified working conditions in the last century by means of the encyclical *Rerum novarum.*[1]

In Genesis, when the command is issued to 'dominate and subdue the earth', a certain power is conferred over the material universe, but it is not given over human life in the same sense. This is clear when God says to Noah, 'Whoever sheds the blood of man, by man will his blood be shed; for God made man in his own image' (Gen 9:6). Authority over human life belongs in its fullness to God who alone can give it and take it away, and in whose likeness it has been made. Indeed, the very fact that the human being is not capable of creating life at the outset and does not know the secret in which human life consists, means also that he does not have the right to take it away. So, human life must be respected on all occasions; it is sacred and must never be deliberately ended by another individual. The two exceptions where it can be taken away, namely, in war and capital punishment, do not vitiate this principle since only the State can wage war or impose capital punishment (under very stringent conditions: cf. *Evangelium vitae*, 56)[2] and it has authority to do this delegated from God. No individual can ever arrogate this power to himself, and thus the command 'Thou shalt not kill' is always inviolable.

---

1. Pope John Paul II, *The Slaughter of the Innocents*, 19 May 1991.
2. See Charles E. Rice, 'The death penalty', *Position Paper* 265, Dublin, January 1996.

The unique individuality of each human person is clear from the fact that God has knowledge and a plan for each of us before we enter the womb. 'Before I formed you in the womb I knew you, and before you were born I consecrated you; I appointed you a prophet to the nations' (Jer 1:4-5). The fact that God knows us by name points to the individuality and sacredness of the life of each one of us. 'I have called you by your name; you are mine' (Is 43:1). That this knowledge and plan extend to each one of us is clear from what St Paul says to the Ephesians (1:4-5): 'he has chosen us before the foundation of the world . . . and predestined us to adoption as his children through Jesus Christ according to the kind intention of his will.'

It is clear from the Bible that human life is already present in the womb. 'It was you who created my inmost self, and put me together in my mother's womb' (Ps 139:13). It is, furthermore, apparent that Christians have always considered life as beginning at conception from the celebration of the Incarnation of the Divine Word as dating from the Annunciation to the Virgin Mary that she was to be with child by the Holy Spirit. Added to this is Catholic belief in the dogma of the Immaculate Conception of the same Virgin Mary.

Consequently, although there have been disputes about the moment when animation occurs, notably in the Middle Ages, in practice Christianity has always acted on the basis that human life is present from conception and thus opposed abortion from the earliest times. In the *Didaché*, composed before AD 80, we read the well known phrase: 'You shall not procure abortion. You shall not destroy a newborn child.' The *Epistle of Barnabas,* AD 138, says: 'Do not murder a child by abortion, or commit infanticide.' Or again, the *Epistle to Diognetus*, speaking of the similarities and differences of the early Christians to their fellow citizens in the Roman Empire refers to the fact that while Christians married and had children they did not 'throw away the foetus'.

Later writers and Fathers continued to condemn abortion unreservedly as the taking of innocent human life, making no distinction between the formed and the unformed foetus. Tertullian writes: 'Prevention of birth is precipitation of murder: nor doth it matter whether one take away a life when formed, or drive it away while forming. He also is a man who is about to be one.'[3] And St Basil the Great says: 'A woman who destroys a foetus intentionally shall undergo the punishment for murder. We will not go into nice distinctions about a formed and an unformed foetus.'[4]

---

3. Tertullian, *Apogeticus*, ch. 9, quoted in A. Bonnar, *Medicine and Men*, London, 1962, p 35.
4. St Basil the Great, *Opera*, Paris, 1839, vol. III, p. 93; see Bonnar, op. cit., p. 36.

Slightly later on, we know from the Penitential Books of the sixth and seventh centuries that abortion together with adultery, apostasy, murder and idolatry was considered the most serious of all sins. Its gravity may easily be gauged from the penance recommended, namely exile, going on a distant pilgrimage or retreat to a monastery for ten, seven or three years.

A change of emphasis with regard to the canonical penalty for abortion is apparent in the Middle Ages, though not insofar as its condemnation as a grave action is concerned. From the time of the re-discovery of Aristotle in the twelfth century, medieval theologians tended to follow uncritically his doctrine of the delayed formation and animation of the foetus. These views came to be reflected in canon law and, from the time of Pope Innocent III in 1211, less severe penalties than excommunication were given for the destruction of the unformed foetus because it was thought not to have a rational soul. Though not considered as homicide, it was still prohibited as a serious criminal act. This practice continued, with a short break of three years in the pontificate of Sixtus V (1588-91), until Pius IX restored all censures in 1869.

THE HUMANITY OF THE EMBRYO

In the early days of legalized abortion, the majority of pro-abortionists took their stand on the basis that human life is not present at conception or when the abortion is carried out. This group generally favoured viability as the time when a person could be said to be present. Others preferred to say this happened at implantation. Today, however, faced with the increasing evidence of genetics and molecular biology, many of those who support abortion and embryo experimentation accept that the foetus is human but stop short of allowing that it is a human person with rights. Christians, on the other hand, strongly contend that human life is a continuum from conception, or fertilization, and that the dignity and sacredness of the life so conceived confers on it the inalienable rights which are common to every human creature.

From the point of view of dignity and rights, therefore, the really important moment for Christians is, and always has been, conception rather than birth. On the philosophical level, it is true we cannot demonstrate the moment of animation nor will we ever be able to. It has always been assumed for practical purposes that this is conception, and in a matter which is so important, it is surely vital to be on the safe side. Nevertheless, it must be said that progress in science furnishes increasing evidence, and one might say virtually conclusive proof, not just that human life is present in the embryo but that indeed the embryo is a human person. In the well known phrase, it is not a potential human being but a human being with potential.

In the first place, from the moment of conception all the genetic information that goes to make up a unique individual person is present. Secondly, from this time, too, the embryo or zygote is capable of internal growth and development. This is a capability which the separated gametes, that is, sperm and ova, do not possess in the sense that ununited and independent they die in a very short time. Hence, there is a real break with the past at conception after which a completely new reality becomes present. From that moment onwards, not only does the embryo have an independent life and growth of its own, albeit dependent on the environment of its mother's womb, but there is a continuity lasting not only till the birth of the child but also throughout its natural life until the grave. So, on all the available evidence, if the embryo were not human at the time of conception there is no obvious moment later on when it would begin to be so. Hence, it makes little sense to accord rights to it from birth but not from the beginning of its genetic life.

The previously popular argument of secular morality and of the pro-abortion lobby that human life begins at viability, that is, when the foetus is capable of human life outside the womb has been weakened by increased knowledge. The fundamental objection to this postion is that viability varies; it cannot be tied down to a particular time. It was originally thought to be 28 weeks, which is why the abortion law in Britain was first set at that limit, but many premature babies survive at 24 weeks—a fact that has led Parliament to lower the law to this figure. Now, babies born as early as 20 weeks are known to live. Being an indefinite point, then, viability is not a sure basis on which to found personhood.

A stronger argument than viability is implantation, because monozygotic twinning, that is, the generation of identical twins from one fertilized ovum, may occur up to that time. Little or nothing, however, is known about how the latter comes about. It may be that it is genetically determined from fertilization with the identical twin zygote possessing a genetic quality that ordinary zygotes lack. In this case, there would be two individuals present from the start with their own life-plan, destiny and uniqueness.

If identical twinning is not genetically determined, then two hypotheses are put forward to explain it. One sees it occurring in the same way as asexual reproduction where one amoeba gives rise to a second one which splits off from it. In this case one twin would be older than the other, though both would be individual beings from the moment their respective lives begin. The other hypothesis is that the embryo splits into two equal halves at implantation. This would mean that the original embryo ceases to exist and two new ones are formed. In this case, the life-span of the original foetus is very short, but it would still be an individual human being. The lives of the twins would start later than fertilization, namely, at the time of the division. On all these hypotheses there need be no problem about when human life begins, or the necessity of presupposing something less than human prior to it.

Many pro-abortionists acknowledge that the life of the early embryo is human (after all, the genes and chromosomes are human) but deny that a human person with rights is present at this stage. They maintain that personhood requires some exercise of those capacities we observe in grown human beings, such as self-consciousness, will power and rationality, or at least the ability to live viable, independent life, without reliance on the mother's life. But the fact that these capacities are dormant when someone is unconscious or simply sleeping, for example, does not lead us to doubt that a human person is still present. Equally, when the aged lose their human faculties, they continue to be human beings with personal rights, though sadly today some people dispute this.

SLOGANS AND THE CONVENTIONAL WISDOM

A number of standard arguments and slogans are used by the pro-abortion lobby to create the necessary background of conventional wisdom to secure and ensure the continued legalization of their objectives. The unthinking must be wary of these because, together with their undoubted hollowness, it has been revealed that in the initial campaigns to legalize abortion in America and France statistics were manipulated and falsified, and slogans known to be at best half-truths were presented as certainties.[5]

Very widely used in most countries is the slogan that it is a 'woman's right to choose'. We have already seen that the right over our own bodies is limited; it is not absolute. We have the use of them but not the ownership. But in this case from the moment of conception though the baby is joined to the woman's body, it is a separate life and a separate being. The woman, therefore, must choose *before* she becomes pregnant, because afterwards she is carrying another human being with its own rights. Furthermore, it is

5. See B. Nathanson and R. Ostling, *Aborting America*, quoted in John Powell, *Abortion: the Silent Holocaust*, Allen, Texas, 1981, p.83. See also n. 14 below.

an innocent, defenceless human being which we have a duty to defend.

Closely allied to this is the objection put in the form of a rhetorical question: isn't abortion better than having an unwanted child? Whether a child is wanted, or not, does not confer a right to life on it; it has that right by being conceived. It has been said that abortion will get rid of unwanted children, but in fact, child abuse and baby battering have increased since we have had legalized abortion. 'Every child a wanted child' is a very ambiguous phrase and, in truth, planned children are often not wanted with the right type of affection. A study in the United States found that over 90% of battered and abused children were the result of planned pregnancies.[6] The methods used in some abortions are violent, and it is not surprising to find that there is a connection between what we do as a society to a child in the first nine months of its life and what we do to it afterwards.

There are those, of course, who tell us that the law of the land allows abortion, and therefore it must be applied (for example, by a doctor), irrespective of one's personal beliefs. But, as Aquinas teaches, no law which goes against the natural law or the law of God has the force of law.[7] This is the authority on which legislators enact laws, and they cannot go outside its perimeters. If such a law does go onto the statute book, it has no binding force and should be opposed by upholders of the natural law and by all men of goodwill.

A related question is whether Catholics can or should seek to impose their beliefs about abortion on the rest of society. Abortion is a matter of natural law, which is universal and obligatory for the human race and not merely a Catholic issue. Consequently, eliminating abortion is in the interests of the whole society and each of its individuals, and one has every right to put over this point by persuasion, argument etc. On a more practical level, we could ask ourselves to consider the question raised by John Powell in his book *Abortion: The Silent Holocaust*. He asks what the average citizen would do if he had reason to believe the next door neighbours were battering their children. Would he let them get on with it? Or would he ring the police? And if it were the latter, would he consider that he was imposing his beliefs on the rest of society?[8]

Evangelium vitae, 73, develops this theme:

> Abortion and euthanasia are thus crimes which no human law can claim to legitimize. There is no obligation in conscience to obey such

6. Southern California Medical Centre, quoted in J. Powell, op. cit., p. 126.
7. *Summa Theologiae*, I-II, q. 95, a. 2.
8. John Powell, op. cit., p. 111.

laws; instead there is *a grave and clear obligation to oppose them by conscientious objection.* From the very beginnings of the Church, the apostolic preaching reminded Christians of their duty to obey legitimately consititued public authorities (cf. Rom 13:1-7; 1 Pet 2:13-14), but at the same time it firmly warned that 'we must obey God rather than men' (Acts 5:29). In the Old Testament, precisely in regard to threats against life, we find a significant example of resistance to the unjust command of those in authority. After Pharaoh ordered the killing of all newborn males, the Hebrew midwives refused. They did not do as the King of Egypt commanded them but let the male children live (cf. Ex 1:17). But the reason for their action should be noted: 'the midwives feared God' (ibid.). It is precisely from obedience to God— to whom alone is due that fear which is acknowledgment of his absolute sovereignty—that the strength and the courage to resist unjust human laws are born.

HARD CASES

A recurring feature of ethical debate today is the pressure which is exerted from the secular lobby to establish general moral principles concerning marriage, abortion etc. on the basis of the admittedly real, but exceptional, hard cases, as if these were the norm. Since they do, however, produce genuine moral dilemmas we must look at them carefully.

• *Threats to the mother's life and ectopic pregnancy.* The principle of not taking life is inviolable, but the case can arise where the mother's life is endangered during pregnancy, such that two lives are at stake. It may occur that a woman while pregnant has an illness, such as cancer, which is life-threatening and can only be cured by operating on the womb. Such an operation, if essential to save the mother, can be carried out on the principle of double effect as long as the four prerequisite conditions are met. One must, of course, desire the mother's cure and in no way the death of the baby, which comes about indirectly. The direct killing of the baby, because the mother has some other bodily illness unconnected with the womb, such as kidney disease, AIDS, hyper-tension, diabetes etc. is never licit.

Ectopic pregnancy is the name given to those pregnancies which occur outside the womb, usually in the fallopian tube, although in exceptional cases in the ovary. Due to a malformation of the tubes, or disease, the foetus becomes lodged in them, threatening sooner or later to rupture and cause a greater or lesser degree of bleeding with consequent danger for both the mother and child. If a laparoscopy shows that there is little bleeding and the ectopic is not above a certain size, the pregnancy is allowed to continue and the foetus may take up a secondary position, either in the womb or in the abdomen. The child may die at term, but equally a caesarian section may be possible. The ectopic foetus has the same right to life as a uterine foetus, and therefore every effort must be made to save it, such as an operation to transfer it to the uterus if there is a reasonable chance of success.

Once the mother's life is directly and gravely threatened, then the normal medical procedure of excising the tubes, with the consequent loss of the foetus, is licit provided it is done according to the principles of double effect. Hence, the whole process must be directed to curing the illness of the mother once she is in actual danger of death. If the foetus has not died already, it will be an indirect undesired abortion. But to eliminate the baby where there is no grave danger to the mother would be direct abortion and therefore illicit. It should be emphasized that the temptation in extra-uterine pregnancy is impatience, that is, to act before the danger to the mother becomes grave, thus carrying out a preventative direct abortion. When the foetus is at the point of achieving viability, the intervention must be delayed as much as possible, even at the risk of life, because there must be a proportion between the good sought and the evil done.

• *Rape*. It must be said that conception is very rare in cases of unprovoked rape, or incest, among other reasons because of the trauma caused to the victim. In the few cases where conception does occur, however, the rights of the conceived child are paramount and must not be superseded. It is not entirely true to say that the baby in the womb is an alien to the mother conceived by a hostile partner. Even though not willed, the baby is partly hers. The child conceived can very well be loved and cared for by adoptive parents, and then the mother does not have to live with the memory of having terminated a life. It is a sad commentary on the attitudes created by the contemporary anti-life mentality that many pregnant girls consider that, if *they* cannot keep the child themselves, they do not want anybody else to have it either.

• *The handicapped foetus*. In many western countries, a process of screening known as amniocentesis is now carried out on women by extracting fluid from the amniotic sac and testing it for handicapped genes. Ultrasound techniques of radiology may also yield evidence of malformation. These procedures, though not illicit in themselves if done with a right intention, are often carried out to give the option of abortion if a handicap is diagnosed. Such an intention renders them immoral.

As soon as we start talking about quality of life and thinking in terms of 'useless lives' in order to override fundamental rights, we are on the slippery slope. Such phrases are the child of the utilitarian parent principle 'the greatest happiness of the greatest number'. We have found this to be inadequate in all sorts of ways, but it may also be unjust, in that it may be used to discriminate against minorities or weak and defenceless individuals. It is not widely realized that in addition to the Jewish Holocaust, the Nazis put to death some quarter of a million handicapped people in Germany on the grounds that their existence was going to be a burden on the State and the war effort. Hitler signed an order on 1 September 1939 for the details of all patients in State hospitals to be compiled and, later on, a decision was taken as to which ones should die.[9] Lurking behind the abortion for the handicapped position is a version of the hard case argument used so often today to defend divorce and euthanasia as well, and, therefore, to overturn an absolute principle. Every type of human and State assistance should be given to the handicapped and their families, as well as pastoral care, and when this is done it has been amply demonstrated that their lives can be meaningful, happy and worthwhile. So indeed may the lives of those who look after them. Only a thoroughgoing materialistic view of life could oppose this view.

This argument also exhibits one of the great 'heresies' of our time, namely, that pain and suffering are the worst of all evils. This is, of course, a consequence of utilitarianism getting a hold of society as a whole. The greatest of evils is sin, or the offence against God, brought about by infringing the divine or natural law. It is this, in fact, which brings much suffering on the human race. This is not to deny that suffering is an evil or a defect in nature, which we must do our best to conquer, but always in agreement with inviolable moral principles; otherwise the moral evil will occasion yet further physical evil. By the same token, suffering has a positive side in virtue of its role within the redemptive design of God. Very often it brings out the best in people, such as the virtues of solidarity, generosity, fortitude and patience. Herein is the reason why families with handicapped children, provided they have the right values and adopt the proper attitude to the problem, are usually happy and fulfilled in their lives.

9. Ibid., p. 31

SOME CONSEQUENCES OF ABORTION

One can tell a tree by its fruits, and some of the consequences of abortion are particularly disturbing. Given the nature of the case, the decision to have an abortion is often taken hurriedly. Nevertheless, when the woman has had time to reflect on the action, the full impact of it often comes home to her. The resulting guilt gives rise to a phenomenon known as Post-Abortion Syndrome.[10] This consists in the realization that a unique individual who would now be progressing towards adulthood has been deprived of life. Seeing that she has done something irreversible and has cast aside her life-giving capacity, the mother begins to wonder whether her own existence has meaning. This often gives rise to severe depression and not infrequently to psychological problems—a condition well known to priests, doctors and social workers.

For a Christian, this guilt can be enhanced by the knowledge that the child had an immortal soul, and hence its ability to participate fully in eternal happiness is uncertain. An injustice has been done not only to the unborn child but also to God. The guilty one realizes restitution is necessary but feels unable to make it. The irreversibility of the situation means that, even when the woman has received forgiveness, there remains a nagging doubt concerning the destiny of her child and the resulting anxiety associated with this. Those who are so ready to counsel abortion during the pregnancy have no advice to offer in the post-abortion situation. In this connection it must be said that if a recently extracted foetus is found it should be baptized conditionally. Furthermore, moral theologians have always advised parents to make an act of baptism of desire for a child that dies in the womb, for example, as a result of a miscarriage. In the case of abortion, such a desire for baptism will be rare unless there is a last-minute repentance; but it must be said that, in the course of time, grave as the sin is, restitution can be made by prayer and penance and conversion of life.[11]

Some 18% of all conceptions are now terminated in England and Wales.[12] Two doctors must recommend a patient for abortion up to 24 weeks for reasons of the health of the woman or her existing children. In practice most abortions are done for social reasons such as career prospects, the impossibility of keeping up mortgage payments, the necessity of re-decorating the house, going on a foreign holiday or buying a new car. In other words, material values are being put above human life and in reality

10. On this cf. Peter Doherty (ed.), *Post-Abortion Syndrome*, Dublin, 1995.
11. *The Times*, London, Sept. 1988.
12. *Code of Canon Law*, no. 1398.

we have a situation of abortion on demand. Anxiety has been heightened in England by changes to the law in 1990 which, while lowering the limit from 28 to 24 weeks, has actually made the original Act more 'liberal' in other respects and, therefore, more restrictive in the protection it offers to the unborn. Abortion is now allowed at any time prior to birth: (a) where the balance of risk to the mother's health favours termination, (b) to prevent grave permanent injury to the woman's health, (c) in cases of suspected 'serious' foetal handicap. In the opinion of some doctors, serious handicap includes harelip or cleft palate.

The prevailing anti-life mentality which this exhibits has been well described and analysed by the Pope in *Familiaris consortio* (at no. 30). The underlying lack of spiritual values engenders reliance on here-and-now materialism and betrays a deep-seated lack of hope in much of mankind. The demographic crisis which has resulted from contraception and abortion in the industrialized countries of Europe, particularly, could reach catastrophic proportions. The adoption alternative is now practically non-existent.

COOPERATION

It was noted earlier on that from the beginning of Christianity abortion was considered to be one of the gravest of sins. The fact that the procuring of abortion carries with it an automatic excommunication from the Church is an indication that it continues to have that same seriousness.[13] The penalty can usually be lifted in sacramental confession, although in some cases recourse to a higher authority in the Church may be necessary. The *Catechism of the Church* (no. 2272) comments on this point: 'The Church does not thereby intend to restrict the scope of mercy. Rather she makes clear the gravity of the crime committed, the irreparable harm done to the innocent who is put to death, as well as to the parents and the whole of society.'

Abortion is not an action that can be carried out by one person alone; hence, those who cooperate in it, at least formally, directly and immediately, also incur in the sin and censure. Thus, those who advise or pressurize someone to have an abortion, the doctors who sign the forms authorizing it and those helping during the operation, all fall into this category.

Nursing before and after an abortion would be mediate and remote cooperation and could be justified only for the gravest reasons. In normal

13. See ch. 13 for a full discussion of cooperation in evil.

circumstance, it should be avoided, due to the gravity of the sin, and also because, though in itself indirect, it could be the occasion of falling into direct cooperation. Furthermore, in England as in most other countries, the so-called abortion law carries a conscience clause allowing medical staff to opt out on grounds of conscience. This must always be invoked by a Catholic, even though it can bring with it, on occasions, a degree of social ostracization.

Another form of direct cooperation is voting in parliamentary legislatures, or in a referendum, for a law to legalize abortion for the first time, or widen the scope of already existing legislation. Once an abortion law is on the statute book, voting for amendments to it which provide for a reduction in abortions (for example, the time limit), thereby saving lives, is perfectly right and proper and generally to be encouraged. There are those who argue that Christians should fight to stamp out abortion root and branch, but to endeavour to achieve this by a step-by-step process is perfectly moral once the law is in place.

THE SANCTITY OF HUMAN LIFE

Christian morality has always been the upholder of the sanctity of human life from the earliest times under the Roman Empire. This remains equally true today as is evidenced by the teaching of Vatican II: 'the Council lays stress on respect for the human person: everyone should look upon his neighbour (without any exception) as another self, bearing in mind above all his life and the means necessary for living it in a dignified way. . . ' (*Gaudium et spes*, 27). This is particularly true of the innocent and the weak who have equal rights with everybody else, and indeed a civilized society must be specially cognizant of them. British law recognizes the rights of the unborn in some areas, such as the law on the inheritance of legacies, but not in the case of the most fundamental right of all, namely, life itself.

Specious arguments are sometimes used to claim that family planning and even abortion are actually pro-life. The original family planning pioneers, Margaret Sanger and Marie Stopes, whose programmes at the outset were opposed to abortion but eventually espoused it, claimed initially that their reasons were eugenic or the healthy quality of conceived life. The quality of life argument was used by the French abortion campaign for two decades to claim that abortion was pro-life.[14] But Christian teaching points

14. See 'Les étapes maconniques d'une politique de la mort', in *L'Action Familiale et Scolaire*, Paris 1980.

out that this is discriminatory against the weakest and most innocent form of life, the unborn child.

This is why Vatican II (*Gaudium et spes*, 51) states unequivocally that 'God the Lord of life, has entrusted to men the noble mission of safeguarding life, and men must carry it out in a manner worthy of themselves. Life must be protected with the utmost care from the moment of conception: abortion and infanticide are abominable crimes.' Thus, Christianity gradually brought about a civilizing process, virtually stamping out abortion. Such a task awaits it once again, with the proclamation of the absolute inviolability and sanctity of every human life from conception to the grave playing a key role in the process of the re-evangelization of the modern world.

10

Duties to Bodily Life, and Genetic Engineering

Progress in medical technology, particularly in molecular biology and genetics, is increasing by the year rather than by the decade. In the aftermath of the discovery of DNA in 1953, enormous advances have been made in the knowledge of the human genetic system. The diagnosis of inherited diseases and resultant genetic therapy and engineering are at the moment still in their initial stages. The field of medicine as a whole is also marked by technological growth, as is evidenced by transplant and keyhole surgery, equipment to prolong the life of the dying and the 'brain dead', such as respirators, and the ongoing marketing of new drugs.

The Church welcomes these developments as long as they are applied within the moral law, that is to say, for the overall well-being of the individual person and with respect for his or her dignity. The general principle, as Vatican II points out, is that 'the order of things must be subordinate to the order of persons and not the other way round' (*Gaudium et spes*, 26). But if human life is destroyed, endangered or impeded as it is by *in vitro* fertilization and embryo research, or by selective abortion and sterilization of the handicapped, then these methods cannot be countenanced. Negative eugenic thinking often shows itself willing to resort to these techniques today. It is quite insufficient to point to the supposed future benefit to mankind at the price of individual human life.

It is not so much that we need a new 'theology of technology' to deal with these developments as that we need to apply the existing and unchanging moral principles to mutable medical and biological reality. The continuing progress of the latter is exemplified by the *Human Genome Project*, a huge international effort, which aims, over the next two decades, to map out and identify the estimated hundred thousand, or so, genes that make up the human cell. So far two thousand have been discovered and decoded. The successful completion of the project will yield the genetic blueprint of each person, that is, the coded information which gives us all our personal characteristics, like the colour of our eyes, height and susceptibility to certain diseases. The actions which this information could prompt, and who should have control of it, are full of moral implications; hence the need to review the principles which govern human existence and bodily life.

The right to life and the physical integrity of one's bodily members is included under the divine commandment 'Thou shalt not kill.' The taking of innocent life, or homicide, is the crime most universally condemned in all cultures, thereby indicating the force of the natural law relating to the good of life as a fundamental right. In the last analysis all the rights and duties of man rest on this first one—the right to life. It is the basis and condition of all other rights, can never be subordinate to other fundamental values and must be given equal respect.

We have already had occasion to remark several times that human life and, therefore, bodily life, is a gift received of which we are not the owners but only the stewards, and hence we have duties as well as rights to our own human and bodily existence as well as to that of others. It is part of a good and upright love of oneself which leads one to conserve one's physical health and well-being and to take steps to recover it when it is lost. Our bodies are not unconditionally ours to do with as we like. The limits of these rights and duties to oneself must now be discussed as we come to look at the questions of organ donation, transplants, sterilization and genetics.

TRANSPLANT SURGERY

Human existence is emphatically a bodily existence. It is vital to have a balanced view of the two major components of the human person and their relation to each other. Man is an embodied soul or, if you will, a living, animate body. The soul is not imprisoned in the body, nor is the body like a set of clothes an actor puts on. The body is not an instrument or tool; it is rather an integral part of the person; indeed, we may say the body is the person even if it is not the whole of him. If someone is struck on the face, he, and not merely his face, is struck. Equally, while bodily life is present, the person is still there, no matter in how deformed a state. We should, therefore, be careful not to refer to the life of someone with irreversible brain damage living on a lifesupport machine as 'living vegetable life'. The life of a human person is still in existence although not functioning fully and properly.[1]

Consequently, the same duties apply to the body as to life as a whole. Just as man does not have absolute dominion over his life, so neither does he

1. W. May, *Human Existence, Medicine & Ethics*, Chicago,1977, p. 66.

over his bodily members, which must play their role for the good of the whole. An important principle in medical ethics, the principle of totality, lays down that the part must serve the whole, and hence an organ, or part of the body, may be sacrificed to save the whole life of the body. Herein lies the justification for surgical operations; but the mutilation of organs, or parts of the body, for another purpose or for an insufficient reason, is not justified.

In the atmosphere of today's transplant surgery a sufficient reason for parting with a non-vital organ is the overall good of another's bodily life. It is not licit to endanger one's own life, but the donation of an organ that one can live without, such as a kidney, as long as there is no pecuniary advantage, is not only permitted but is often an act of heroic charity. In the words of the *Catechism of the Catholic Church* (no. 2296),

> organ transplants are not morally acceptable if the donor or those who speak for him have not given their informed consent. Organ transplants conform with the moral law and can be meritorious if the physical and psychological dangers and risks incurred by the donor are proportionate to the good sought for the recipient. It is morally inadmissible directly to bring about the disabling mutilation or death of a human being, even in order to delay the death of other persons.

Most transplants, however, are carried out with organs from bodies already dead, with prior permission either from the deceased or from his or her next of kin. One has a legitimate right to dispose of the members of one's own body after death (as do one's nearest of kin) for a purpose such as this, for it shows solidarity and charity with the rest of mankind and bears witness to the fraternal ties which unite us. The *Catechism* (no. 2301) states that 'the free gift of organs after death is legitimate and can be meritorious'. The principle of totality no longer applies, because a corpse is not, strictly speaking, a body but only an amalgam of separate parts and hence is called a body only by equivocal analogy, as St Thomas is quick to point out.[2] Nevertheless, a human cadaver has an important symbolic value having been the seat of the human soul and person and must, therefore, be treated with the corresponding dignity and respect.

Extracting live organs from a dead person for use in transplant surgery has been made possible by modern medicine's ability to keep certain organs alive artificially. This very fact, however, has also made the question of the

2. *Summa Theologiae*, I, q. 78, 2 and 3.

precise moment of death more intricate, and a good deal of debate on this point has arisen over the last two decades. It is a matter which is within the competence of medicine to decide, as Pius XII noted,[3] but since it is an issue which is so closely connected with morality, a few remarks are in order.

In the past a person was 'clinically dead' when the heart was no longer beating, the blood stopped circulating and breathing ceased. But today a stopped heart can be resuscitated, a person can be put on an artificial respirator to continue his vital functions, and an unconscious person may be fed intravenously. All this is usually done in the hope that these functions can eventually be renewed spontaneously. The result is that it is not possible to use the man in the street's concept of death, namely, brain death and a flat electroencephalograph, as the sole criterion, because even then large parts of the body may be kept alive. What the medical profession demands is various complementary tests, as well as the electro-encephalograph to ensure that brain death has actually occurred. For instance, brain death makes spontaneous breathing more difficult, which in turn causes the heart to stop pumping blood. The vital functions of the body are, therefore, integrated, and the cessation of one or two of them points to the cessation of another and vice versa, such that overlapping checks can be made. A flat electro-encephalograph alone does not supply sufficient data to pronounce a person dead. It must be linked to other criteria—to a lack of spontaneous breathing and thus to a non-integrated functioning of heart, lungs and brain. Where all three concur, no amount of artificial means will bring the person back to life. Nevertheless, vital organs may be kept artificially functioning for transplant to another body.

When death occurs, the soul leaves the body, which itself loses its organized unity and becomes an aggregate of parts. As we have seen, a person may include in his will the disposing of his bodily members for medical purposes, but very often for lack of such a will it falls to family members to make such a decision in a short space of time. They may donate organs only when the integrated vital functions have ceased to operate spontaneously and they are advised of the death by the doctor, and not simply informed that the process of dying has become irreversible because one of these functions has ceased. At this point, however, the continued use of a life-support machine is not obligatory because there is no obligation to use extraordinary means to keep someone alive. The definition of 'extraordinary means' varies according to the state of the patient and other factors, but it is relevant to say here that the more certain the fatal outcome is, the

3. Pope Pius XII, *The Prolongation of Life*, 1957, AAS 95, 1027-33.

more extraordinary the means used become. A fuller treatment of this concept in general, and of life-support machines in particular, will be given in the next chapter.

On the part of the recipient in transplant surgery, the general conditions for a surgical operation should be fulfilled. These include a due proportion between the risk and the expectation of a positive outcome. The human person must not be used as an experimental guinea pig for the future benefit of mankind. There must be a good chance of reasonable benefit to the *individual patient* who is operated on. Provided, therefore, the dignity of the human person and his life are respected, and due discretion is exercised, transplant surgery need not present insuperable problems from the moral point of view.

STERILIZATION

Sterilization is a particular form of self-mutilation, and one which in its indirect form can be used for genuinely therapeutic purposes. It is justified by the aforesaid principle of totality, provided one is working on a diseased organ and its extraction or treatment brings with it sterility indirectly, that is, not intended. Direct sterilization is never licit and we shall have to be careful to underline an illicit use of the principle of totality in this respect.

By 'direct sterilization' is understood to mean that action which 'aims, either as a means or as an end in itself, to render child-bearing impossible'.[4] When this is the direct aim, whether it be of the man or of the woman, temporary or permanent, it is totally illicit. The reason is that it is a completely unwarranted mutilation of a part of the body. And since it makes the procreative capacity deliberately infertile, it is intrinsically immoral for the same reason as contraception; but it is all the worse because it is a permanent form of contraception.[5]

The Church, however, allows indirect sterilization when there is a clear therapeutic reason for it, and infertility results as an undesired side-effect, the direct intention being to cure the illness. Thus, Paul VI wrote in *Humanae vitae*: 'But the Church in no way regards as unlawful therapeutic means considered necessary to cure organic diseases even though they also have a contraceptive effect, and this is foreseen—provided that this contraceptive effect is not intended for any motive whatsoever.'[6]

4. Pius XII, *Address to the Italian Association of Midwives*, 1951, no. 27.
5. *Humanae vitae*, 14.
6. Ibid., 15.

This indirect sterilization may be carried out according to the usual conditions of the principle of double effect (the indirectly voluntary). We recall that these conditions were: that the action itself must be good—the first effect must be good, or at least equal first with the evil effect; there must be a proportionate reason for doing the action; and one must desire the good effect but not the evil. This means in sterilization cases that an operation may be carried out on a procreative organ when it is diseased, as in cancer of the womb or testicles, or acute hemorrhaging, to remove the organ, thereby bringing about sterility as a secondary effect. So, a hysterectomy, that is, the removal of a diseased womb from a woman (a not uncommon operation) is fully justified on the above conditions. In all these cases, a diseased part of the body is being sacrificed for the good of the whole.

However, a wrong and wholly inadmissible application of the principle of totality is sometimes used in another kind of case. Often if a woman is weak or infirm in some part of the body, as for example the heart, lungs or kidney, a further pregnancy may be regarded as representing a risk to her life. It is thus argued that she can undergo what is called preventative sterilization in the interests of her total health, or at least so as not to put it at unnecessary risk. But this is an unjustified use of the aforesaid principle. In this case, the procreative organs themselves are in good health; so, to operate on them or mutilate them would be an evil act; and one may never do an evil act so that good may come of it. Paul VI writes in this regard:

> Though it is true that sometimes it is lawful to tolerate a lesser moral evil in order to avoid a greater or in order to promote a greater good, it is never lawful, even for the gravest reasons, to do evil that good may come of it—in other words to intend positively something which intrinsically contradicts the moral order, and which must therefore be judged unworthy of man, even though the intention is to protect or promote the welfare of an individual, of a family, or of society in general.[7]

So, therapeutic sterilization does not extend to protecting a woman from a pregnancy which may be hazardous because of other illnesses she may have. To do so would be to will positively, and carry out, an action which is wrong in itself. Direct sterilization, the tying of the fallopian tubes or vasectomy, is therefore always wrong, even if it has the intention of promoting the overall health of the man or woman.

7. Ibid., 14.

This was stated clearly by Pius XII in a discourse to the Italian Society of Urologists in 1953:

> When gynaecological complications demand surgical intervention, or even when they don't, it is not unusual for healthy fallopian tubes to be extracted, or else to be rendered unable to function, in order to prevent a new pregnancy and the grave dangers which could result from it for the health and even the life of the mother: dangers caused by illness in other organs, such as kidneys, heart and lungs but which are aggravated in the case of pregnancy. To justify the extraction of the fallopian tubes, recourse is had to the principle of totality and it is alleged that it is morally permitted to operate on healthy organs when the good of the whole demands it. Here, however, incorrect use is being made of this principle, because in this case the danger to the mother does not come either directly or indirectly from the presence of, or the normal functioning of the fallopian tubes, or from their influence on the diseased organs, kidneys, lungs or heart. The danger does not occur if it is not occasioned by free sexual activity leading to a pregnancy which could threaten the above-mentioned weak or diseased organs. The conditions which would permit one to operate on the part in favour of the whole in virtue of the principle of totality are lacking. Consequently, it is not morally permitted to operate on healthy fallopian tubes.[8]

GENETIC DISEASE AND THERAPY

Advances in medical science have given us a greater, though by no means complete, knowledge of hereditary and genetic disorders. Furthermore, increased medical treatment now means that individuals carrying such diseases can grow to adulthood and have children of their own (for example, sufferers from diabetes), thereby spreading the risk and incidence of the disease. Hereditary maladies are consequently increasing as the general population increases. This, together with the utilitarian background of our society, explains the increased pressure within the medical profession and in public opinion for eugenic sterilization and foetal screening followed by selective abortion. But, on the other hand, cure is beginning to follow on diagnosis, and genetic therapy holds out hope for the successful treatment

8. Pius XII, *Address to the Italian Society of Urologists*, 1953, AAS 45.

of hitherto incurable and terminal illnesses. The development of genetics looks set to revolutionize medicine.

Increased knowledge brings with it increased moral responsibility, which means that actions must always be governed by the natural law: the mere fact that we can do something does not mean we are justified in doing it. Accordingly, sterilization for eugenic purposes is not an option since it is direct sterilization, and only the indirect falls under the principle of double effect. Besides, from a Christian point of view, disease is not an absolute evil but only a relative one. Our Lord answered the Jews who brought a blind man to him and asked whether he or his parents had sinned, by making no reference to sin but, instead, saying that the reason he was blind was so that the power of God might be made manifest in him. For a Christian, suffering and illness are a share in the Cross and in the co-redemption of the world and, therefore, also have apostolic value. Suffering will always be with us to some degree. We have to do all we can to overcome it but within the moral law.

Medical science is now able to identify many hereditary diseases and in some cases even predict if the baby in the womb has them. Inherited diseases are due to genetic and chromosomal disorders. So, for example, we know which genes produce cystic fibrosis, Huntingdon's chorea, genetic blood disorders, muscular dystrophy, marfan syndrome and Alzheimer's disease. We also know the genetic defect that can lead to high cholesterol levels. Other handicaps, such as Down's syndrome or spina bifida, are not strictly hereditary but are incurred at conception. Down's syndrome, for example, consists in possessing one chromosome too many.

Some hereditary diseases make themselves known only in later life. Huntingdon's chorea is a defect of the brain which manifests itself in late middle age but is due to a faulty gene which is present from the beginning. Once this is known, however, the children of the patient may be subjected to an analysis which will tell them whether they have inherited the disease or not. This is done by extracting the DNA from a blood or tissue sample and exposing it to an enzyme which breaks it into fragments from which the diseased gene may be identified.

Statistical research tells us that a parent with hereditary disease has a 50/50 chance of handing it on to offspring. In turn the child has a 25% chance of passing it on to its own children. Parents with congenital disease, therefore, have an equal chance of having a normal healthy baby. Equally, healthy parents may give birth to handicapped children. Hence, even though a parent may know his or her condition, it doesn't constitute an absolute reason for not procreating. Some conditions, such as cystic fibrosis, require a defective gene from both parents and so, if this were known to be the case beforehand, it might constitute a reason for not marrying, but it cannot take away the right to do so. Nor does it justify contraception, sterilization or much less abortion.

Enforced sterilization, whether it be for the handicapped, for a retarded adult with the mental age of a child, for known carriers of genetic defects, or for population purposes, is a power no State, individual or group possesses. Pius XI wrote as follows: 'Those who act in this way are wrong in losing sight of the fact that the family is more sacred than the State and that men are begotten not for the earth and for time, but for heaven and for eternity. Although often these individuals are to be dissuaded from entering matrimony, certainly it is wrong to brand them with the stigma of crime because they contract marriage, on the ground that, despite the fact that they are in every respect capable of matrimony, they will give birth only to defective children, even though they use all care and diligence.'[9] The right of the individual to procreate is a fundamental one and cannot be taken away from any free innocent citizen, by the State, or anybody else, on any pretext whatsoever.

The Catholic Church applauds the research which is being done with a view to finding cures for treating genetic disorders and endeavouring to eliminate them as far as possible, as long as it is done within the moral order, and the information derived is acted on in the same spirit. Scientists know the four chemicals of which DNA is made up, and in this are contained the genes, or coded information, which give each cell its function. They are thus able to know a good deal about the genetic code, or language, of our bodies and to discover that the lack or deficiency of a particular gene can cause the cell not to produce the enzyme, or protein, necessary for the organism. There are still many conditions, however, where the offending gene has yet to be located. Where it has been, some defects are now rectified by genetic therapy which consists in feeding in the gene to replace the one that is deficient. Operations on genetic disorders which favour the patient, or even baby in the womb, and do no known harm are to be encouraged. But sufficient probability of success must exist. For example, one way of feeding in genes is by non-pathogenic virus carrier particles, but at present sometimes little is known about what effect these viruses can have on the genes as a whole.

Most of the offending genes responsible for the inherited diseases mentioned above have been discovered in the last two decades. In many cases

9. *Casti connubii*, 68-70, quoted in J. Hardon, *The Catholic Catechism*, p. 344.

the therapy for rectifying the defective gene has not yet been developed. Thus, genetics is still very much in its infancy, and there are many imponderables, such as when a gene starts to mutate and become defective. For example, it is known that the defective p53 gene fails to stop cell division and produces cancer, but *when* this mutation begins to occur could only be known by regular screening, and there is no therapy for the condition at the moment. Thus, it is impractical to expect to eliminate hereditary disease to any significant degree in a short time. The genetic discoveries are certainly very encouraging, because they relate to hitherto untreatable diseases. However, given the nature of the case, diagnosis is ahead of cure, and in the meantime it is important for scientists and doctors not to use the information to create social pressure for selective abortion and widespread sterilization.

Some observers point out that environmental causes also play a part in hereditary diseases, such as, for example, diabetes, and so their appearance can be prevented by environmental controls. Also it has been noticed that hereditary diseases associated with racial or social groups differ markedly depending on where they come from. Tay-Sachs disease is found most commonly in Jews from the Baltic Sea area, and sickle cell anemia among blacks from the Lake Victoria area of Africa. As carriers marry more widely outside the area, so the incidence of these maladies can be expected to fall.[10]

The growth in genetic knowledge puts an enormously potent weapon into the hands of mankind. Like all human goods it can be used for good or ill. The ethical debate has already started, though much of it is as yet very hypothetical, since it tends to assume that the Human Genome Project will reach a successful and complete conclusion, that therapy will follow on where diagnosis is achieved, that screening will be widespread, etc.—none of which we are entitled to take for granted at the moment. The Church does not comment morally on hypotheticals until they become a reality, but where negative eugenics, or the elimination of disease is concerned, we have been able to outline the necessary principles. Positive eugenics, or 'enhancement engineering' by which an individual is made more intelligent, beautiful, taller etc. is another matter, as is the dissemination of genetic information. Both these possibilities fill most people with a good deal of alarm and make them realize a boundary must be drawn. These issues must be more fully dealt with when they arise, but it can be said that no one has control over bodily integrity, whether his own or others', unless it be for therapeutic reasons such as we have outlined. As to who should

10. W. May, op. cit., p. 9.

have access to genetic information—the State, employers, insurance companies or the individual—that is a matter of much debate. It is clear, however, that personal freedom and rights demand confidentiality in this matter, as is the case already with medical knowledge. There must, therefore, be a sufficient reason for the holding of such information. One such reason is given by an already enunciated doctrine of the Church which could be used to cover the present case.

Though no individual person and no State has dominion over the life and bodily members of another, an exception is made *with great reserve* in the case of the punishment of criminals. So Pius XI taught that 'public magistrates have no direct power over the bodies of their subjects. Therefore, where no crime has taken place, and there is no cause for grave punishment, they can never directly harm or tamper with the integrity of the body, either for reasons of eugenics or for any other reason.'[11] The reason why the exception is made in the case of punishment is that if the State has power over the life itself of a criminal who is guilty of a corresponding crime, and can resort to capital punishment, then it also has power over the bodily members of its citizens when they are convicted of a proportionate crime. The Church recommends that this power be used very sparingly, if at all. On this basis, genetic information could be used to protect individuals or the common good against criminals.

Once again we cannot fail to remark that the Church's explanation and insistence on the moral law upholds the fundamental rights of the individual and ensures the long-term benefit of humanity. We must not forget that the same argument which is used to justify direct sterilization for the apparently 'upright' reason of preventing people from passing on congenital disease (and we must remember here that the intention alone cannot make an action good) was used by the Nazis ostensibly on eugenic grounds for actions which were in fact racist. Genetic advances have already made people contemplate, albeit with some reserve, the possibility of designer children. We know that the Nazi doctor Mengele conducted such experiments as part of the quest for a pure or super-race, a practice which has been universally condemned. Whether it be a super-race, or a super and élite individual, it is clear that our authority over life and bodily members does not extend that far. The attempt would be fraught with unacceptable dangers of producing either a monster or a handicapped child and would no doubt interfere with the rights and freedom of marriage. It could also have unacceptable social

11. *Casti connubii*, 68-70, quoted in J. Hardon, *The Catholic Catechism*, p. 345.

consequences with regard to the equality of citizens. It would take us a step closer to babies made to order and, if that happens, if they do not measure up to the laboratory's standards, they will in all likelihood be summarily aborted by those who arrogate to themselves the authority to make such experiments in the first place. Scientists must remember that, while in some cases they can mould and improve human life, they have no right to act as lord over it.

11

Euthanasia, the Treatment of Pain
and Drug Abuse

E uthanasia—etymologically 'easy death' or 'good death'—is used to denote the bringing about of death through medical intervention for the purpose of eliminating pain and suffering. Though predominantly referring to the aged who are terminally ill, it also covers the so-called 'mercy killing' of abnormal babies, the handicapped and the mentally retarded.

It is not perhaps surprising that, in a society ingrained with the utilitarian ethic which does not respect innocent life at its beginning, there should be a growing tendency not to respect it at its end either. Hence today some moralities defend euthanasia on the basis that there are values higher than life and that when life has become incapable of achieving them it is useless to prolong it.

In contrast, the Catholic Church holds that no human being is the owner of life, his own or others', but only its steward. Hence euthanasia, like suicide, is a serious attack on the fundamental right and duty to protect human life and the human person. Each person should live their life in accordance with God's plan, respecting his sovereignty over their life and treating life as a good which must bear fruit now, but which only attains its fulfilment after death.[1] Intended and successfully achieved euthanasia, when done intentionally, is therefore as wrong as murder.

Another point to bear in mind is that, for a Christian, pain and suffering are not unmitigated evils but a share in Christ's redemptive Passion, and play their part in the life-plan of the human person, especially *vis-à-vis* eternal life. That is not to say that Christians may not lessen pain whenever medicines are available; although Christ refused a narcotic on the Cross in order to carry out fully the burden of our redemption (cf. Mt 27:34), individuals are never systematically obliged to heroism as a general rule. However, the use of painkillers ought never to contravene the fundamental right and duty to life, the taking away of which ought never to be deliber-

---

1. Sacred Congregation for the Doctrine of the Faith, *Decree on Euthanasia*, 1980.

ately intended. These are the basic principles, but more complex questions arise which can be crystalized into two: (a) to what extent do we have an obligation to treat dying and terminally ill patients? and (b) what is the morality of painkillers especially when they suppress consciousness and hasten death? To answer these questions we will look more closely at some contemporary arguments regarding euthanasia and suffering. But first, since contemporary arguments for euthanasia are usually advanced on the condition that the patient gives his or her consent, some comments must be made about the wider question of suicide.

SUICIDE

As St Augustine points out, the fifth commandment simply says, 'Thou shalt not kill,' not 'Thou shalt not kill thy neighbour.'[2] Suicide is wrong because it violates the fundamental and self-evident good of life, or, to put it another way, it is an injustice towards God who is the sole owner and arbiter of each human life. It is also an injustice towards the community of man in that it deprives mankind of a human life and its accompanying talents.

Traditionally, morality distinguishes between direct and indirect suicide. In the first case, one freely makes an attempt on one's own life, while in the second, one puts one's life in mortal danger without directly seeking death. Indirect suicide is licit only if there is a proportionately grave reason. It must be done in agreement with the principle of double effect, and hence there should be a proportion between the good desired and the evil tolerated. An indifferent or frivolous end, such as Russian roulette or the vanity of seeking publicity, is altogether insufficient. Among the reasons that justify indirect suicide are the public good, such as the defence of one's country, fire fighting, or the spiritual good of souls, as when a priest attends the dying during a national disaster, even at the risk of his own life. It is also justified for reasons of heroic virtue, or charity, as when doctors treat patients who have contagious illnesses. It can also be licit in order to avoid a certain and more painful death, as when someone jumps out of the window of a burning building, especially if there is some chance of thereby saving himself.

When the danger of death is more remote, the risk may be more readily assumed for a less serious reason. Hence it is permitted to work in mines, or chemical industries, knowing the dangers of silicosis, for example, as long as one takes reasonable precautions.

2. St Augustine, *The City of God*, Bk. 1, ch. 20.

May a woman allow herself to die rather than be raped, to defend her virtue? Certainly, direct suicide is not permitted in this case, although indirectly she may put her life in danger, for instance, by jumping from a window. Nevertheless, a woman does not have a duty to desire death rather than be raped. Thus, material cooperation with the sin in order to save her life is licit. The conduct of St Maria Goretti, who died rather than suffer this treatment, is a case of the *heroic* practice of a virtue rather than a norm of conduct to be followed.

TAKING A LIFE AND ALLOWING THE DYING TO DIE

We cannot, however, make a corresponding distinction between direct and indirect euthanasia as we have done with suicide. Most moralists who attempt such justification do so implicitly when they speak of active and passive euthanasia. The latter would be to allow a dying person to die by giving pain-killing drugs which hasten death or by withdrawing preventative treatment. As we shall see in the next section, these actions can be done on certain conditions but never in such a way as to desire or cause death, but only to relieve pain and not prolong death unnecessarily. This cannot be called euthanasia, passive or otherwise. There is a difference between taking a life and allowing those dying to continue the process of death when it would be unreasonable to extend it. But the proponents of mercy killing, failing to make this distinction, go on to say that if passive euthanasia is allowed, then there is what they call a 'right to die', and hence on some occasions, at least, active euthanasia must also be permitted.

The next step is taken on proportionalist grounds. When there is no proportionate reason for a severely ill person to go on living, the taking of life can be justified (it is alleged). This step involves putting certain human goods above the value of life. So, for example, the proportionalist, Richard McCormick, argues that if a human being is no longer capable of human relationships, of exercising the human values of friendship and justice, then there is no proportionately good reason for him to be kept alive.

The first thing to notice about these positions is that their justification depends upon accepting the argument that 'the end justifies the means'. That is to say, the alleviation of suffering, falling below a minimum level of quality of life, and relieving society of a burden are all ends which justify taking away life, or confer a 'right to die' and absolute disposability over one's own life. We have already had occasion to remark that the end cannot justify the means, because any element of the action that is evil makes the whole action evil. As St Thomas said, 'bonum ex integra causa, malum ex quoque defectu' (good requires a completely good cause, evil proceeds from any defect in the action). Now, to take away innocent life is to contravene a fundamental good and can never be justified, no matter how good the intention, since a good intention is simply not enough to justify an action.

From a certain point of view, the good of life is the most fundamental of all. Certainly, like other basic goods, it is incommensurable and cannot be compared or made subject to any other ones. Hence, as we have seen, there is no such thing as a right to die or an absolute and unlimited self-determination over one's own life. As a gift held on trust, life is an intrinsic good which is sacred and inviolable, but it is being treated here as a relative good which may be bartered away under certain conditions. It is regarded as expendable in some circumstances.

Thus *Evangelium vitae*, 72:

> Consequently, laws which legitimize the direct killing of innocent human beings through abortion and euthanasia are in complete opposition to the inviolable right to life proper to every individual; they thus deny the equality of everyone before the law. It might be objected that such is not the case in euthanasia, when it is requested with full awareness by the person involved. But any State which made such a request legitimate and authorized it to be carried out would be legalizing a case of suicide-murder, contrary to the fundamental principles of absolute respect for life and of the protection of every innocent life. In this way the State contributes to lessening respect for life and opens the door to ways of acting which are destructive of trust in relations between people. Laws which authorize and promote abortion and euthanasia are therefore radically opposed not only to the good of the individual but also to the common good; as such they are completely lacking in authentic juridical validity.

Once the principle of the inviolability of human life is breached, the floodgates are opened. Most of those who argue for euthanasia, under certain conditions, might not want to eliminate the handicapped and mentally retarded. But on their principles, there is nothing to stop someone doing this. Of course, proportionalists will argue that the consent of the patient must be obtained. But such consent may be given in a moment of weakness, or extreme pain, and not represent the true intention of the patient. In the case of the mentally retarded it will be said they are unable to give informed consent, and we already have judges making major ethical decisions on their behalf, for example regarding sterilization. It is known that under the Nazis, thousands of handicapped and infirm persons were exterminated because they were considered a burden on the State.[3] In the light of this, the Holy See was asked: 'Is it permissible, upon the mandate of public authority, directly to kill those who, although they have committed no crime deserving of death, are yet, because of psychic or physical defects, unable to be useful to the nation, but rather are considered a burden to its vigour and strength?' The answer was: 'No, because it is contrary to the natural and divine positive law.'[4] Most people would readily concur and yet, what is the logical difference between this and the taking of innocent life in abortion and deliberately ending it prematurely in terminal illness.

Furthermore, given the value of human suffering from a Christian point of view, how can anybody declare another human life in whatever circumstances to be useless? Very often suffering strengthens the character and prepares one for death as its natural conclusion. Moreover, the handicapped (at least the physically handicapped) can be very fulfilled people. On the other hand, suffering may break a person or lead him to be unfulfilled. Nevertheless, it is part of the challenge of existence and thus an integral part of human life. Hence we have no reason for calling any human life 'useless', least of all on the grounds of suffering. The euthanasia syndrome is another example of modern ethics' inability to declare any human good, including life itself, to be an absolute value of intrinsic worth and hence inviolable on all occasions.

CARE OF THE DYING

Having safeguarded the principle of the inviolability of human life, we may now turn to the question of the care of the dying and how far we have to go in keeping people alive who are in the final stages of life. That is to say, to what extent are we obliged to use life-sustaining medicine and technology for those in an advanced stage of terminal illness or for the aged who suffer from a combination of the loss of vital functions, of liver and heart, for example? It is important that the dying die with human dignity and care and hence that their dying be not unnecessarily prolonged if there is not a sufficiently proportionate reason for doing so, as Pius XII noted.[5] The

3. See John Powell, *Abortion: The Silent Holocaust*, Allen, Texas, 1981, p. 24ff.
4. Decree of Holy Office, 2 December 1940.
5. Pius XII, Allocution, 24 February 1957, in *The Relief of Pain*, CTS, London, pt. III.

proportionate benefits of applying life-saving methods have to be weighed against the disadvantages to the patient. A calculation of consequences does enter into moral decisions such as this; but it must never be the master category or principal determinant of morality.

It should be noted immediately that this action is totally different, as we have seen, from what some authors (mistakenly) call passive or indirect euthanasia. In both active and passive euthanasia the intention or end of both the act and the agent is to bring about death, that is to say, to kill either by commission (for example, lethal injection) or by omission (for example, withdrawal of nourishment). If, however, one decides that to give life support measures to a dying person will prolong his agony unnecessarily and unreasonably, one is not killing him by the deed, but letting him die the death he is already dying. 'It is morally decisive that the patient dies not from the act but from the underlying disease or injury.'[6]

The guiding principle for deciding when one may or may not allow a dying person to continue the dying process has traditionally been given to us in the distinction between ordinary and extraordinary means. One is always obliged to use ordinary means to keep a person alive, but one is not always under an obligation to use extraordinary means. The decision as to whether a course of action is extraordinary is not simply to be made on the basis of whether those means are in short supply in the area, whether they are expensive etc., but also in relation to the patient receiving them. A respirator may be ordinary means for a young victim of a car accident but extraordinary for an 85-year-old patient with heart and renal failure who has cancer. To prolong the life of the latter is not to cure him but simply to prolong the dying process.

It is for this reason that the Church now uses the terms 'proportionate' and 'disproportionate' reasons to help us decide when medical intervention is ordinary or extraordinary. To make the decision, one has to take into account the following elements: 'the type of treatment to be used, its degree of complexity or risk, its cost and the possibilities of using it, and comparing these elements with the result that can be expected, taking into account the state of the sick person and his or her physical and moral resources.'[7]

Consequently, the same decree of the Congregation for the Doctrine of the Faith on euthanasia goes on:

6. J. Russell Elkington, quoted in W. May, *Human Existence, Medicine & Ethics*, Chicago, p. 145.
7. SCDF, *Decree on Euthanasia*, op. cit., 1980, p. 10.

> When inevitable death is imminent in spite of the means used, it is
> permitted in conscience to refuse forms of treatment that would only
> secure a precarious and burdensome prolongation of life, so long as
> the normal care due to the sick person in similar circumstances is not
> interrupted. In such cases the doctor has no reason to reproach himself
> with failing to help the person in danger.[8]

In the immediate aftermath of accident or illness, the life-support
machine may often be an ordinary means functioning as transitory treatment to restore the patient to spontaneous breathing. But if the condition is
considered irreversible and this stage cannot be reached, then there is no
obligation to continue with the use of the respirator. To decide this, the all-
round condition of the patient should be taken into account. If, as in the
Karen Quinlan case in the United States, spontaneous breathing follows on
the switching off of the ventilator, then intravenous feeding should be
carried on as ordinary treatment. It is important to remember that patients in
such a state are not 'vegetables' but are still alive as human persons, even
though in the process of dying, and must be treated with the dignity and care
to which every human being has a right.

With medical progress and treatment advancing year by year, another
corollary of the ordinary/extraordinary means distinction concerns the
question of whether a person with a mortal illness can, or should, use new
techniques, or drugs, which still carry certain risk factors. When no other
adequate remedies are available and given all the usual conditions of the
indirectly voluntary, particularly that there is a proportionate reason between the seriousness of the illness and the risk involved, the patient *may*
have recourse to them even if the methods are still at the experimental stage.
By accepting them, the patient is also serving the cause of humanity. He
must, however, always be given sufficient information so as to be capable
of giving informed consent and be allowed to terminate the treatment at any
point. Doctors in their turn must decide whether the cost of the new
treatment is warranted, taking into account the foreseen benefits. The fact
remains, however, that no one is obliged to recur to extraordinary means
and is perfectly at liberty to pursue only normal treatment. There is nothing
untoward about this, nor is it bordering on suicide; on the contrary, it is an
acceptance of the human condition and a desire not to cause undue effort
and expense to the family and community.

---

8. Ibid., p. 11. See also *Catechism of the Catholic Church*, no. 2301.

THE USE OF PAINKILLING DRUGS

A certain amount of pain and suffering is necessary and inevitable in life. It is necessary to the extent that it is needed for man to impose control on his unruly passions and obtain mastery of himself and his fallen nature. Pain is also necessary to tell us we are being injured or need treatment. The value the suffering can have is to be gauged from the Passion of Christ, who took it voluntarily upon himself and even maximized it. Although Christians are encouraged to practise voluntary mortification and self-denial, the better to dominate the passions and contribute to interior purification, there is no obligation to accept pain which can be be suppressed by drugs. The voluntary acceptance of such pain is heroic, and heroism is never imposed as a general moral obligation.

Here is how Pius XII stated the point:

> the Christian is bound to mortify his flesh and to seek to effect his interior purification, because it is impossible in the long run, to avoid sin and to acquit oneself faithfully of all one's duties, if one refuses to make this effort at purification and mortification. To the extent that mastership of oneself and of one's unruly tendencies is impossible to achieve without the help of physical pain, to that extent it is necessary and one must accept it; but insofar as it is not required to that end, it cannot be asserted that its acceptance is a strict duty. The Christian is, then, not obliged to wish it for its own sake; he considers it as a means, more or less adapted to the end he is pursuing.[9]

Consequently, to use drugs to suppress pain and control suffering, when there is a sufficient reason to do so, and in due proportion to need, is perfectly in line with the natural moral law and the Gospel. Given, however, that a number of drugs have unwelcome and even dangerous side effects, the beneficial consequences must be weighed against the harmful ones and a due proportion of good over bad maintained throughout. This question becomes most acute when administering painkillers to the terminally ill.

It is clear that one must never administer a lethal dosage of pain-relieving drugs to a terminally ill patient for any reason whatsoever. No matter how good the intention, it can never justify an action which is wrong in itself, such as taking the life of a person into one's own hands. Nevertheless, the

9. Pius XII, Allocution, 24 February 1957, collected in *The Relief of Pain*, op. cit., no. 15.

problem arises from the fact that, because the human body becomes habituated to drugs, increased dosages are required to achieve the same result. Can one then continue this treatment knowing that it is going to bring forward the moment of death? To this question Pius XII answered, 'Yes, given certain conditions.'

He was asked: 'Is the suppression of pain and consciousness by means of narcotics (when it is demanded by a medical indication) permitted, by religion and morality, to the patient and doctor (even at the approach of death and when one foresees that the administration of narcotics will shorten life)? One must reply, if there exist no other means and if, in the given circumstances, it does not prevent the fulfilment of other religious and moral duties—Yes.'[10]

The conditions, therefore, are that a dying person must be given the opportunity to fulfil his religious and moral duties, such as to be reconciled with God (confession), to make his last will, etc. No one has authority to take away consciousness before such duties have been discharged. One would need to know whether the effects of drugs will be of brief or prolonged duration and whether the use of the higher faculties will return at some point. It would be false charity on the part of relatives to put a patient out of his agony so that he suffer and die unconsciously when he will normally want to say a final prayer, have the assistance of a priest and be surrounded by family and friends. If, however, the dying person has fulfilled his grave religious and moral duties, and there is a serious medical reason for it, drugs not exceeding the necessary quantity may be given even if they lead to unconsciousness. If the patient himself insists on narcotics after having been reminded of his duties, the doctor may administer them without formal cooperation in the fault committed.

DRUG ABUSE

Man is under an obligation to preserve his physical health and well-being, and avoid anything that may endanger it. It is also wrong for him to take alcohol in volumes which affect his rightful use of reason and his consciousness, as is testified to by moral tradition and the Scriptures (for example, 1 Cor 6:10 ; Gal 5:21). A similar judgement must apply to drugs. Although alcohol is perfectly acceptable in moderate quantities, the same cannot be said of addictive drugs taken simply to produce pleasant sensa-

10. Ibid., no. 42.

tions and, therefore, without sufficient reason, principally because of the dependency they create but also for other reasons.

Pius XII expressed himself as follows:

> It follows that one may not alter consciousness or suppress it for the sole reason that one wants to provoke for oneself agreeable sensations, by becoming drunk or by taking poisons designed to procure that state, even if one seeks only a certain euphoria. Beyond a certain dosage, these poisons more or less markedly affect consciousness or even produce a complete "black-out". The facts demonstrate that the abuse of stupefacient drugs leads to the complete forgetting of the most fundamental requirements of personal and family life. It is not, then, without reason that the civil authorities intervene by regulating the sale and use of these drugs, in order to protect society from grave physical and moral damage.[11]

By drugs we understand natural or synthetic substances which, by acting on the central nervous system, modify sensations and affect behaviour. More specifically, they produce pleasant and agreeable feelings which incline the person to repeated doses so that what begins as free and voluntary use soon becomes addictive. A distinction can theoretically be made between sporadic use and habitual use of drugs, just as another distinction is made between so-called 'soft' and 'hard' drugs. Some moralists maintain that the sporadic use of 'soft' drugs is morally equivalent to the moderate use of alcohol.

These distinctions, however, are more theoretical than real. The implication is that 'soft' drugs are innocuous when there is increasing evidence that they produce dependence and open the door to an addictive use of 'hard' drugs. Hence John Paul II has spoken of 'those drugs which are erroneously called "soft".[12] While the sporadic use of marijuana, for example, does not cause serious physiological effects, recent research shows it can lead to grave psychological disturbances, such as apathy, depression, obsessions and fixed ideas, and, in extreme cases, suicidal tendencies. These symptoms disappear when the drug ceases to be used, but the recuperation period can be long when the drug has been taken over a number of years.

While the habitual use of 'hard' drugs is clearly gravely immoral and sinful, the same must also be said even of the sporadic use of so-called 'soft' drugs. They endanger one's psychological and perhaps physical health,

11. Ibid., no. 29.   12. Pope John Paul II, Homily, 9 August 1980.

expose one more easily to serious sins against chastity and are a proximate occasion of becoming habitually addicted and starting on the road to a life of vice. To expose oneself to such dangers, without any reason or necessity for doing so, is itself a serious matter. The gravity of such sins may be increased by particular circumstances if, for example, the purpose for taking them is a sort of existential escapism from the meaning and duties of life, or if by taking them one encourages others to do so and contributes to trafficking in drugs.

Apart from being an offence against the individual human person, drug addiction is also a destabilizing factor in society as a whole. The relationship between rising crime and drug abuse is evident. For that reason, the State has a duty, in the interests of the common good, to make all forms of drug-taking illegal, not to speak of trafficking in them. It would abdicate responsibility if it permissively tolerated any form of so-called 'soft' drugs.

Drug abuse is a clear indication of moral vacuum in the consumer society and a sign in itself that man desires to transcend that society. It can, in a sense, be seen as a warped search for that true happiness for which man is made but which he can only find in spiritual, not material, values.[13] It is a demonstration of the way modern culture and laws have undermined the moral conscience of youth, the indispensable value of family life and parental control, and the moral and religious values which should be at the heart of personal and civil life.

13. Cardinal J. Ratzinger, Fisher Lecture at Cambridge University, 25 January 1988 on 'Consumer Materialism and Christian Hope'.

[12]

Human Life and the New Reproductive Technology

In 1978 a momentous step was taken by medical science when the first test-tube baby, Louise Brown, was born in Oldham, England, to be followed by many thousands of others around the world in the succeeding years. It was the scientifically successful result of years of experiments to bring about the union of the gametes (sperm and ova) *in vitro* (literally 'in a dish') and then implanting the embryo in the mother's womb for the continuation of the pregnancy.

The technique was developed to overcome infertility, most commonly in females, where the fallopian tubes are blocked, but also some forms of male infertility. The embryo is placed directly in the uterus with the intention of implanting. Since only between 6% and 15% of embryos (according to different claims) implanted in this way are successful, it is usual to create and transfer more than one embryo. Often more embryos may be created than it is appropriate to transfer to the mother's womb. With regard to the resulting superfluous embryos, one is left with the choice either of freezing or of destroying them.

This procedure has, consequently, given man an enormous power of scientific and technological control over the beginnings of life. But, of course, such power should not be exercised without ethical guidelines and limitations, as is generally agreed; where there is not general agreement is on what the ethical guidelines should be. The spectre of a society where procreation is detached from marriage, where 'love is free' and babies are made to order, was raised in *Brave New World* by Aldous Huxley in 1932. This very influential work foresees a society that is less than human because it sets aside the inalienable rights of marriage and of children to be born of the personal union of their parents. In this way the human being becomes a subject of technology rather than a master of it.

Catholicism teaches that technological progress must, above all, respect the moral imperatives of human life and dignity. Human life can never be taken away or endangered. The human person can never be used as a means to justify an end. As St Paul says, 'you cannot do evil that good may come of it' (Rom 3:8). Technology must, therefore, serve man and not man technology.

These principles, however, are being set aside by the practice of *in vitro* fertilization. The superfluous embryos, which are not implanted, are usually destroyed. Indeed, the Warnock Report in Britain on the subject of embryology recommended that such embryos be destroyed after 14 days and that has now been passed into law. It has been said that this is the first time English law has actually ordered rather than permitted the taking of life. The Catholic Church maintains, on the contrary, that the life of every individual, especially the most innocent, must be protected from conception to the grave. Human dignity gives every individual without exception a right to such protection.

On the hypothesis that there could be a simple case of *in vitro* fertilization whereby only one embryo is fertilized and implanted, hence avoiding any wastage, Catholic teaching would still oppose the procedure. The reasons, in summary form, are that it goes against the dignity of marriage and the rights of the individual conceived. It also separates the unitive significance of the matrimonial act from the procreative significance which, as we have seen in relation to contraception, may not be done. Conception should be the result of a personal act.

Before developing these reasons as they are taught by the Church's Magisterium, we may anticipate an objection of the advocates of test-tube technology. They will argue that Catholicism is here opposing a scientific breakthrough which brings happiness to countless childless couples. This is a natural reaction, but we must ask those who justify the technique to consider very seriously the many possible consequences of legally and morally permitting procreation to be separated from the marriage act. A number of them are nothing short of alarming.

The *in vitro* technique puts an extremely potent weapon into the hands of mankind which can easily be used by the unscrupulous for evil and undesirable purposes. It already involves egg donation from one woman to another, embryo donation and the surrogate carrying of an embryo by a woman who is not the biological mother or intended parent. It also puts within man's grasp the following possibilities:

- cloning, or the splitting of the embryo to make twins;
- the freezing of embryos or sperm for later use;
- the sex determination of the child;
- trans-species fertilization with the possibility of producing a hybrid.

- Finally, it greatly facilitates negative eugenics, or the elimination of handicapped and defective foetuses.

From this it will be agreed that careful ethical limitations and guidelines must be put in place on the matter, and they must be set down early enough in the process before the practice gets out of hand. From this vantage point one may begin to understand the Church's position that the manipulation of life by human beings in this way is in itself wrong. The full array of reasons for this is what we must now examine.

REASONS AGAINST *IN VITRO* FERTILIZATION

The first argument concerns the right which an individual human being enjoys from the moment of conception. If medical intervention is genuinely to serve the good and the health of the individual patient—if that is what is meant by therapeutic—then it can be done. But if it endangers life, or takes it away, or otherwise does harm, then it is not licit. *In vitro* fertilization involves super-ovulation and the fertilization of ova which are not implanted, and hence the human being is regarded as expendable.

Secondly, the rights of the human person also extend to that of being born *within* the marriage of his or her parents. This demand of the dignity of the individual is the same argument the Church has used against cases of AID (artificial insemination by donor) and AIH (by husband). Hence: 'the child has the right to be conceived, carried in the womb, brought into the world and brought up within marriage: it is through the secure and recognized relationship to his own parents that the child can discover his own identity and achieve his own proper development'.[1] If the child were to be born as a result of biological techniques it would be equivalent to reducing a human being to an object of scientific technology. It is, moreover, a requirement not only of the individual, but of society, that children begin life within marriage. The 'vitality and stability of society require that children come into the world within a family and that the family be firmly based on marriage'.[2]

Thirdly, the dignity of marriage itself is offended against in an unwarranted fashion by the new *in vitro* techniques. The fidelity of the spouses in the unity of marriage involves the reciprocal respect of their right to become a father or a mother only *through* each other. The intrusion of a third party,

1. SCDF, *Donum vitae*, 22 February 1987, II, 1.   2. Ibid.

in any way whatsoever, is opposed to the exclusive fidelity between the spouses that is demanded by the marriage bond.

If homologous artificial fertilization (that is, where the donor is the husband) is excluded on the grounds that the child has the right to be conceived in the womb and not in a laboratory, then with much more reason is heterologous artificial fertilization to be opposed (where the donor is a third party). This not only goes against the right of the child, but also undermines the respect that is due to the unity of the marriage. It thus threatens the family and the stability of society, opening the way to promiscuity.

Surrogate motherhood is wrong for the same reasons: the child has the right to be carried in the womb of its own mother. Surrogacy of this type goes against the obligations of maternal love, conjugal fidelity, and responsible motherhood.

Finally, and decisively, the *in vitro* technique falls foul of the Church's doctrine already enunciated in *Humanae vitae*, concerning the inseparability of the unitive and procreative aspects of the marriage act. This principle is based on the fact that the human being is a union of spirit and matter. The marriage act is not just a biological union, but also a spiritual and personal one. That is to say, if the act is not open to procreation it will not be a loving and unitive act either, as we have seen. Just as these two aspects cannot be separated to inhibit a pregnancy, neither can they be separated to facilitate it. The Church is rigorously and logically consistent here.

Homologous *in vitro* fertilization and embryo transfer is brought about outside the bodies of the couple through the actions of third parties—technicians in a word—whose competence and technical activity determine the success of the procedure. Such fertilization entrusts the life and identity of the embryo to the hands of doctors and biologists and establishes the domination of technology over the origin and destiny of the human person. Such a relationship of domination is contrary to the dignity and equality which both parents and children should enjoy. Man must dominate technology, not technology man.

At this point a further consideration is in order. A medical intervention respects the dignity of persons when it seeks to *assist* the conjugal act, to facilitate its performance or to enable it to achieve its objective once it has been normally performed. If such a technique could be developed, it would be morally valid. It sometimes happens, however, that a medical procedure technologically replaces the conjugal act in order to obtain a conception which is neither its result nor its fruit. In such a case, the medical act is not at the service of conjugal union, but rather it appropriates to itself the procreative function and thus contradicts the dignity and the inalienable rights of parents and children.

The question as to whether the well known technique of GIFT, or gamete-inter-fallopian-transfer, assists or substitutes the procreative act has not been finally decided by the Church. The method involves the collection of the husband's sperm after a natural sexual act, and if necessary treating it, together with the acquisition of an ovum and the placement of both in the fallopian tubes or uterus of the woman where (it is hoped) fertilization will take place. We should bear in mind the principle that conception must be the result and fruit of a conjugal act in which the spouses can become 'cooperators with God for giving life to a new person'.[3] The parents must, therefore, be the principal cause of the new life, not just the biological cause, and there should be a unity between the conjugal act and the procreative process. It seems that in this case the principal role in the fertilization is taken over by the scientists and that their intervention interrupts the unity of the generative action. If this is judged to be the case, then GIFT is not ethically permissible, for human life is being instrumentalized rather than assisted, and this goes against the dignity of the human person.

RESEARCH AND EXPERIMENTATION

In vitro fertilization technique is the result of much research by molecular biologists. Its success has led to scientific demands to continue with that research on the embryo. In England legal authorization has been given for up to 14 days. It is argued that research on embryos is necessary to develop infertility treatment. It should also yield, so it is claimed, further knowledge about factors leading to congenital disease and the detecting of gene and chromosomal abnormalities from implantation, as well as improve contraception and over-all scientific knowledge.

There is, however, a great difference between research on the separate gametes and that done on the embryo. Christians have always acted on the assumption of the presumed existence of a human being from conception. Therefore, the same rules concerning medical intervention and experimentation apply to the embryo as to any other human being. Unless the experiment gives the moral certainty of not harming the child and is therapeutic for the individual concerned, and not just for society in general, it should not be done. Parents must also give their consent. 'Bio-medical research,

---

3. Cf. *Donum vitae*, II, 5.

too, a field which promises great benefits for humanity, must always reject experimentation, research or applications which disregard the inviolable dignity of the human being, and thus cease to be at the service of people and become instead means which, under the guise of helping people, actually harm them' (*Evangelium vitae*, 89).

Certainly the 14-day rule for experimentation is gratuitous and arbitrary because there is no scientific or logical reason for stipulating 14 days. It has been suggested that no worthwhile research on hereditary diseases could be done in that time and so it is just the 'the thin edge of the wedge'. The noted French geneticist Jerome Lejeune, who discovered the chromosome responsible for Down's syndrome, maintained that no experimental knowledge of any significance can, or has been discovered, from research on the embryo which cannot be obtained from that done on the separate gametes before fertilization. The successful diagnosis of a genetic disorder, for example, has been achieved by examining the DNA which was removed from the polar body of a human egg.[4] After all, we are talking about genetic and chromosomal research, and there is no reason why this should not be done prior to the embryo stage.

It is a tenet of the advocates of embryo experimentation that life is a continuous process and that in reality we are unable to pinpoint its beginning or moment of conception. This flies in the face of the biological facts about fertilization. From its first moment, the embryo possesses its own life and genetic information which will grow in continuity of development into foetus, child, adult etc. In normal conditions it will live for 70 years whereas, even if you do all you can to save the gametes, they will die within 24 hours. This is not to say that the embryo does not need special conditions in which to survive; it is just to make the point that its life is autonomous and not dependent on another.

The pro-experimentation lobby maintains that life is a continuous process, whereas, in fact, it is a continuous process *after fertilization*, which has historically always been considered the moment of conception. No moment before or after is as significant as this one. The organized unity of the 46 chromosomes and their genes, which is to be the individual human person, is already there. Although at fertilization the embryo may be as small as a period, this does not prevent all the genetic information from being present, even though the cells still have to develop as they do rapidly from this moment on. Just as the size of the micro-chip is no barrier to the storage of a

4. *The Lancet*, 28 April 1990. This research was carried out by the Medical Research Council Mammalian Development Unit. See also *New Scientist*, 25 November 1989.

great quantity of information, neither is the size of the human embryo.

Many consider the most important moment in the life of the embryo to be viability. In their view, the foetus does not enjoy independent life until this time, but is considered to be part of the mother. The way in which it has its own independent life, though requiring the environment of the mother's womb to develop, may best be shown by the example used by William May of the deep-sea diver. 'He is viable so long as his lifeline is functioning properly, and his individual identity is obviously independent from those who monitor this equipment. If they choose to sever his lifeline, or inject saline solution into it, he will obviously die, as will a foetus in similar circumstances. But neither the foetus nor the diver is nonliving; each is living and viable, that is, capable of staying alive, so long as each is provided with the environment necessary for sustaining life.'[5]

What the Church does not oppose is pre-natal diagnosis of the human embryo or therapeutic intervention when that genuinely benefits the individual and does not involve disproportionate risks. Thus, it is now possible, by the process called amniocentesis, to draw fluid from the amniotic sac and test for malformations in the foetus. If this process is carried out to safeguard life and anticipate genuine therapeutic procedures which might be necessary, then it is to be commended. In practice, however, very often the aim is to test for a handicap with the intention of carrying out an abortion if an abnormality is found. Such a manner of acting is a grave offence against the moral law. Specialists who carry out screening with a view to an abortion and advise it when malformations are detected, and hence establish a link between the procedure and abortion, are guilty of collaboration in the act.

Equally, medical experimentation carried out on embryos in the womb which is genuinely therapeutic and does not involve disproportionate risks to the individual, for example, locating chromosomal defects with a view to their treatment, must be considered licit and desirable. Pope John Paul II has written: 'A strictly therapeutic intervention whose explicit objective is the healing of various maladies such as those stemming from chromosomal defects will, in principle, be considered desirable, provided it is directed to the true promotion of the personal well-being of the individual without doing harm to his integrity, or worsening his conditions of life. Such an intervention would indeed fall within the logic of the Christian moral tradition.'[6]

5. William E. May, *Human Existence, Medicine and Ethics,* Chicago, 1977, p. 96.
6. Allocation of Pope John Paul II to World Medical Association, 29 October 1983, quoted in *Donum vitae,* p. 15.

IS THE CHURCH ANTI-PROGRESS?

The Church has to face the objection that here once again she is anti-progress and is needlessly opposing technological advance. Will the scientists not do it anyway and look back on the Church's stance as obscurantist? It will further be alleged that, apart from holding up medical research, she is heartlessly depriving infertile couples of the possibility of having their own children.

The Church, however, is completely logical and consistent in believing in the human status of the zygote, or embryo, and hence that a human person can never be a means of benefit to others at the expense of his or her own life. This conforms to the principle that the end does not justify the means. Evil may not be done that good may come of it (as in this case). Evil may be tolerated as an undesired consequence of an otherwise good action, according to the conditions mentioned earlier. The Church holds that the transgression of the fundamental moral principles can never be in the interests of man and hence is not true progress. It is worth noting that infertility research does not depend on *in vitro* fertilization and does not, in fact, cure infertility. Furthermore, such research is costly and in many respects degrading.

It has been noted that, in Genesis, man was given the command to dominate and subdue the earth but that this dominion was over the animal world and material environment. We are not given the same dominion over human life, which is a gift of God, to be administered by man but not under his ownership. It is due to this Christian and human tradition emanating from ancient times that Britain, together with many other nations, signed the 1948 Geneva Convention which affirmed the Hippocratic principle in medical matters, 'Do no harm, do not take life.' Then, barely 20 years later it was cast aside and abortion was countenanced. And in 1990, the British Parliament actually legalized the taking of the life of the human embryo up to 14 days.

The Jewish-Catholic philosopher and saint, Edith Stein, has noted a threefold urge in man, namely: (1) to subdue the world by knowledge; (2) to possess it with all the enjoyments it offers; (3) to make it his own creation by forming it. In other words, man wants to pass from knowledge, to possession, to the creation of things. But if he does this outside the moral law, thus usurping God's rights, he is falling into the temptation, 'you will be like God.' The fact is that man does not create but can fool himself into thinking he does. Behind the protestations of helping the infertile and conquering genetic disease there lurks, perhaps unconsciously, man's pride in his own scientific achievements. It is not that man should not seek cures for inherited disease, but he must do it by fair means and not foul. He must not seek to do it by moral short cuts.

Man's pride tends to blind him to the danger of paying more attention to progress in technology than to his own dignity and personal morality. The Church presents and guarantees a total and correct vision of man, soul and body. However, in many of these experiments he is being treated as an object of biology and laboratory experiments, something more akin to a thing than a human being.

There are limits to man's sovereignty over his actions and self-determination in the same way as there is a true and false autonomy of human affairs. Temporal matters have their own causes and reasons, but they are secondary causes, ultimately dependent on the universal causality of God. 'The Church is charged to show forth the mystery of God and man's last end', says Vatican II (in *Gaudium et spes*, 41), and therefore neither from a Christian nor from a logical point of view can she stand by and allow man to proceed in these matters concerning human life as if God did not exist.

The Church sympathizes profoundly with those who do not have children, but sees here the hand and will of God and looks on all children as a blessing from him. The fact that human life is a gift from God which he reserves to himself alone means that spouses do not *have a right* to a child. They have very legitimate aspirations to be parents and a right to conjugal intercourse as a means to parenthood, but not to the gift of a child. In this respect the Christian says with Job: 'The Lord has given and the Lord has taken away; blessed be the name of the Lord' (Job 1:21). The *Catechism of the Catholic Church* (no. 2378) says:

> A child is not something *owed* to one but is a *gift*. The 'supreme gift of marriage' is a human person. A child may not be considered a piece of property, an idea to which an alleged 'right to a child' would lead. In this area, only the child possesses genuine rights: the right 'to be the fruit of the specific act of the conjugal love of his parents', and 'the right to be respected as a person from the moment of his conception' (*Donum vitae* II, 8).

The real progress of man will always go hand in hand with the power and glory of God, as Vatican II pointed out. 'Far from considering the conquests of man's genius and courage as opposed to God's power as if he set himself up as rival to the creator, Christians ought to be convinced that the achievements of the human race are a sign of God's greatness and the fulfilment of his mysterious design' (*Gaudium et spes*, 34). But it goes on to warn: 'With an increase in human power comes a broadening of responsibility on the part of individuals and communities . . .' (ibid.). That responsibility consists in pursuing human progress according to God's plan for the human race and in agreement with his Commandments.

THE CHURCH: AN UPHOLDER OF CIVILIZED VALUES

If *in vitro* fertilization is to be outlawed, then other techniques flowing from it, facilitating it, or associated with it are equally to be declared illicit. Hence some of the more alarming and difficult problems arising from it such as sperm banks, the freezing of embryos, surrogacy and eugenic manipulation are eliminated at source.

The Warnock Report recommended that a voluntary licensing authority be set up to control *in vitro* fertilization and associated practices within certain competent limits. The Church goes further and says it must be a matter of civil law. This reflects the different underlying premises of Warnock and the Catholic Church: namely, for the former, that moral questions are matters of personal opinion and 'strong sentiments', whereas for the latter, they concern absolute principles and fundamental rights, both of which are involved in the *in vitro* fertilization debate.

The inviolable right of every innocent human individual, the rights of the family and the institution of marriage are fundamental values derived from the human person. They are also the constitutive elements of the right order of society. Since reproductive issues have a social dimension affecting the common good of society, the State has a duty to legislate on them. They cannot be left to the self-regulation of each human conscience. Legislation has the added advantage of protecting the individual from himself, since in matters of the human body he is a steward rather than an owner. Furthermore, if the legislature does not take the initiative and act in the public interest, man could find himself surrendering his prerogatives to researchers who claim to govern humanity in the name of biological discoveries and the improvement of mankind.[7]

Difficult cases have arisen over, for example, surrogacy and embryo freezing. The former, especially, is open to commercial exploitation. A further problem arises if the surrogate mother does not want to give up the baby at the end of her term, as occurred in the so-called baby M case in New

7. Cf. *Donum vitae*, III.

Jersey in the United States. And if the parents of a frozen embryo die unexpectedly, or divorce and differ over its future, what is to be done with it? With the growth of such things as sperm banks, the possibility of eugenic manipulation greatly increases.

Legislation must be inspired and guided by the moral law although civil law need not be commensurate with it. Sometimes the latter must tolerate what is morally wrong when it cannot forbid it without greater evil resulting. Hence, not everything that is not legally penalized is moral. But there are limits to toleration, and the Church maintains that the inalienable rights of the person must be defended by civil law. Among these rights are (a) every human being's right to life and physical integrity from conception to death; (b) the rights of the family and marriage as an institution; and (c) the child's right to be conceived, brought into the world and brought up by his parents.

In many States, protection under the law is denied to the weakest sector of the population—the unborn. If governments give legal approval to *in vitro* fertilization they will widen the breach opened up by abortion. The law must also forbid the use of the human embryo as an object of experimentation and also the practice which permits its destruction with the excuse that it is superfluous, or incapable of developing normally. Penal sanctions must be introduced to enforce this protection for the unborn. Failure to implement such protection will undermine the rule of law—or the very basis on which the State is founded.

Furthermore, governments are also under an obligation to guarantee the family the legal protection to which it has a right. Consequently, civil law should not approve techniques done with the intervention of third parties or for the benefit of third parties. This is contrary to the rights of spouses inherent in marriage and contrary to their privacy. It follows, therefore, that the State should not legalize the donation of gametes to those who are not legitimately joined in marriage. Legislation must also prohibit embryo banks, post-mortem insemination and surrogate motherhood, by virtue of the support which is due to the family.[8]

In sum, the Church bases her stance on the transcendent value of man over technology, and the transcendence of the moral law over man. Man is not the arbiter, much less the creator, of the moral law, and he must ever be guided by it if true progress is to be made. The Church claims to interpret that moral law both for individuals and States. It lays down that procreation must not be separated from the personal act of love within marriage. Nor

8. Ibid.

may sex be used freely and promiscuously or independently of marriage. In cutting across *Brave New World* forms of artificial fertilization, the Church's interpretation of natural law safeguards marriage and the rights of children to be conceived and born in a family and with it the stability of society and the humanity of earthly existence.

[13]

The Drama of Moral Decisions: Cooperation in Evil

Man has a duty, not only to know moral principles, but above all, to put them into practice. He is obliged to seek the truth and to practise goodness. But, bearing in mind that he is a social being, this obligation extends to spreading good to the society and environment around him. As Donne's well known words remind us, 'No man is an island alone of himself, each one is part of the whole.' He must, therefore, cooperate and work for the common good of society and the spreading of the truth by upholding the moral law. Though this is true for all men, it holds especially for the Christian who is exhorted to be the 'salt of the earth' and 'the light of the world'; 'a city cannot be hidden if it is built on a mountain top' (Mt 5:13-14).

One cooperates in good both by fulfilling one's own personal responsibilities, particularly to one's family and at work, and by public activity and witness, when this is called for. Laws must be guided by morals and man has a duty to promote laws which are in keeping with the natural law and oppose and strive to repeal those that go against it. Such action is in the long term interest of mankind. An example of this is the existence today of pro-life groups in nearly every western country, whose purpose is to promote the natural law in family and sexual morality and medical ethics, by education, formation of attitudes, parliamentary lobbying, demonstrations etc.

The first principle of the moral law requires us to do good and avoid evil, but in the complex circumstances of today, one must be vigilant to avoid cooperating in the evil of others. Such is the case of medical personnel with abortion, sterilization, euthanasia, *in vitro* fertilization etc., of judges and lawyers with divorce cases, of shop assistants selling articles designed for immoral purposes, of journalists and advertisers cooperating with immoral publications, and actors and actresses collaborating in dubious plays and entertainment etc. Legislators can foster evil if they do not vote in line with natural law, and even in marriage one partner may not maintain the minimum standards of natural morality.

Just as one can be an accomplice in a crime without actually carrying out the action, so one can share the guilt of another by willing or condoning his or her evil. One cooperates with evil also by advising, encouraging, commanding, or voting in favour of it, or by being instrumental in any other way in bringing it about. In principle, then, one is obliged to oppose actions against the moral law or, at least, avoid being associated with them.

Evangelium vitae raises the question of the sacrifices that have to be made by those working in such fields as health care and the law where unjust laws are in force, so as not to cooperate, but also do what they can to mitigate the effects of such legislation. It says (at no. 135):

> The passing of unjust laws often raises difficult problems of conscience for morally upright people with regard to the issue of cooperation, since they have a right to demand not to be forced to take part in morally evil actions. Sometimes the choices that have to be made are difficult; they may require the sacrifice of prestigious professional positions or the relinquishing of reasonable hopes of career advancement. In other cases, it can happen that carrying out certain actions, which are provided for by legislation that overall is unjust, but which in themselves are indifferent, or even positive, can serve to protect human lives under threat.

The Pope is thinking here, for example, of abortion legislation in some countries which requires the woman to undergo counselling before going ahead with the action. Pro-life counsellors in this situation may well save some lives, but all counsellors are obliged to sign a form saying the candidate has been counselled and thereby they become a material participant in the process. Hence, the encyclical goes on,

> There may be reason to fear, however, that willingness to carry out such actions will not only cause scandal and weaken the necessary oppositon to attacks on life, but will gradually lead to further capitulation to a mentality of permissiveness.

Such situations call for recourse to the principles governing cooperation in evil actions. The encyclical goes on (in no. 136) to emphasize that all formal cooperation, which it defines, is wrong:

> Christians, like all people of goodwill, are called upon under grave obligation of conscience not to cooperate formally in practices which, even if permitted by civil legislation, are contrary to God's law. Indeed, from the moral standpoint, it is never licit to cooperate

formally in evil. Such cooperation occurs when an action, either by its very nature or by the form it takes in a concrete situation, can be defined as a direct participation in an act against innocent human life or a sharing in the immoral intention of the person committing it. This cooperation can never be justified either by invoking respect for the freedom of others or by appealing to the fact that civil law permits it or requires it. Each individual in fact has moral responsibility for the acts which he personally performs; no one can be exempted from this responsibility, and on the basis of it everyone will be judged by God himself (cf. Rom 2:6; 14:12).

Nevertheless, there are cases where more evil may be caused by opposition or avoidance, and good is not furthered. The Church says that 'Charity which obliges one to avoid participating in the sin of another does not oblige where serious harm can result.'[1] So there are times when a form of cooperation in evil, known as material cooperation, can be countenanced, though subject to various conditions. This is not an exception to the general rule that one must do good but rather a form of actually cooperating and furthering good.

It is never legitimate to do or desire evil even though good may come of it; but when there is no other alternative one may perform a good or indifferent action knowing that there will be evil consequences. That action must, therefore, be in some way necessary, because if the evil can be avoided in another way, then that course of action should be followed. Most importantly, the cooperation can be material, but never formal. Formal cooperation is when the accomplice wills the evil and consents to it, whereas material cooperation has regard to the physical action only, without wanting the evil itself. Cooperation which is simply material, as a general rule, is also illicit, because charity obliges one not only to refrain from helping someone commit sin but also to prevent him from doing so, as far as possible. Nevertheless, under certain circumstances it may be licit to cooperate materially in the sin of another, in order to obtain a necessary good or avoid grievous harm.

Such material cooperation may be carried out on the usual conditions of the indirectly voluntary which has previously been referred to. It will be remembered that the third condition required a just and proportionate cause between the good achieved and the evil occasioned. In order to assess this, the following moral principles should be used:

1. Reply of Sacred Penitentiary, 3 April 1916.

- The cause or motive that justifies material cooperation must be all the more important, the more serious the sin of the other is.

- The cause must be all the more important, the more probable it is that the other's sin would not be committed without that cooperation, or the more certain the effect of the sin is.

- The cause has to be all the more serious, the more proximate the cooperator's action is to the sinner's action.

- The cause has to be all the more important, the lesser the right of the cooperator to perform the action whereby he cooperates.[2]

These principles will become clearer in the light of what is said below. For there to be licit cooperation in evil, all the conditions must be fulfilled. Hence, even though cooperation may be the only possible means to obtain a given good, it does not follow that it is permissible to do it. Equally, the argument that if one does not collaborate in a bad action, someone else will and it will be done anyway, does not justify cooperation.

Two further qualifications must also be made. (a) Scandal to others must be avoided. An action is scandalous when it leads another into sin or to underestimate the seriousness of an action. Many people, especially the simple or less well educated, easily look upon cooperation in the sin of another as approval of that sin. Hence, 'in applying the principle of material cooperation, in those cases in which it applies, great care must be taken to avoid scandal and the danger of doctrinal confusion.'[3] (b) Proximate occasions of sin have to be avoided. Cooperation in the sins of others often entails the danger of eventually consenting to those sins. Consequently, all necessary precautions should be taken.

Two other types of cooperation must be added to those we have already seen. Firstly, cooperation may be direct or indirect. It is direct when one takes part in, or shares in, the sinful action itself of the person who sins; for example, helping the thief to carry stolen goods. Cooperation is indirect when someone supplies or provides an instrument which the other person will use in order to commit the evil, but which in itself is not necessarily connected with the evil; for example, selling a weapon which another person will use to commit a murder. Secondly, cooperation can also be divided into proximate and remote, depending on how closely—physically

2. See St Alphonsus Liguori, *Theologia moralis*, Bk. III, no. 89.
3. SCDF, *Quaecumque sterilizatio*, 13 March 1975.

or morally—the cooperating action and the sins of the other person are associated.

It is obvious that all direct cooperation is also proximate but not all indirect cooperation is remote. For example, by placing money in a bank a person cooperates in an indirect and *remote* manner in the sin of a person who uses a loan from that bank to finance an immoral or unjust enterprise. On the other hand, the representative of the bank who authorizes the loan cooperates in the same sin in an indirect and *proximate* way.

THE CASE OF ABORTION AND STERILIZATION

Naturally, in dealing with any sort of association with abortion, one is talking about an extremely grave sin and injustice, because an innocent third party is being deprived of life. Consequently, in ordinary circumstances no sort of cooperation is permissible, for nothing could be grave enough to match the injustice perpetrated. Whether in very exceptional circumstances some degree of remote material cooperation can be justified is one of the questions we must ask and answer.

Primarily, we must assess the proximity of the cooperator's action to the act of abortion itself. We have seen that the more proximate the action is, the more severe must the cause be for the cooperation to be licit. We are speaking here both of physical and moral proximity. This would include, therefore, both the actions performed in the operating room and those others which are uniquely directed to abortion and make it possible, for example, administering anaesthetics prior to the operation, issuing a medical certificate authorizing it, encouraging a wife, partner, relation, friend etc. to have one.

All these are cases of direct or immediate material cooperation which in the case of abortion is never licit given its gravity. The Italian Episcopal Conference stated in July 1978 that (a) 'Direct abortion is never licit,' and (b) 'Proximate cooperation, such as that required of the operating team in the operating room, is never licit.'[4]

All cooperation with patients undergoing abortion, both before and after the operation, such as nursing them, should be avoided. This is normally possible given the conscience clause written into most abortion laws. In cases where conscientious objection is not recognized, or where it is theoretically recognized but in practice serious harm results from a refusal to

4. *Osservatore Romano*, 17 December 1978.

cooperate, indirect material cooperation may be licit. This refers to something like pre- and post-operative nursing, but never purposive collaboration. It may only be done when the harm resulting is so grave as to be
proportionate to the gravity of abortion, that is to say, it presupposes that
one cannot change employment without serious inconvenience and harm to
oneself and one's family. A statement from the Vicariate of Rome in June 1978
said: 'Indirect material cooperation in the preparation and execution of
abortion is only allowed if its refusal would cause health personnel, who have
appealed to conscientious objection (doctors, para-medics, and all who work in
the health field) harm proportionate to the assistance required of them.'[5]

Similar considerations apply to *in vitro* fertilization, embryo research
and sterilization. Direct and proximate cooperation is never licit. The first
two are specialized fields and employment in them depends on personal
choice, and hence it is difficult to imagine harm resulting for anybody
refusing to be associated with them. Sterilization is a different case and is more
generally practised in health services, and there is often no conscience clause
attached to it as there is to abortion. Grave harm and inconvenience may,
therefore, result, especially for junior staff, if they refuse indirect and
remote material cooperation. But they may go no further than this, and it
should be done only when all other alternatives have been exhausted.

COOPERATION IN THE SALE AND DISPENSATION OF CONTRACEPTIVES

It is generally agreed that there are moral implications in the sale of drugs
and that where their use is going to be harmful to the person, it is wrong to
deal in them. Only if they have a therapeutic purpose may their sale be
justified. This responds to the general moral principle that 'it is wrong to
sell objects which of their very nature do not have any use other than an evil
one'.[6] The pharmacist must make moral and professional judgements in his
or her sale of such articles.

The same principles apply to the more specific case of contraceptives. If
there are pharmaceutical products with a real, and not just theoretical,
therapeutic effect but which are also contraceptive, then they may be sold.
If, however, this cannot be said in good conscience, which is so in the
majority of cases, or it is difficult in practice to sell them for this purpose,
then it is wrong to dispense these products since that amounts to cooperation in evil. In doing so, a pharmacist would be cooperating in the sale of

5. Ibid., 7 June 1978.   6. Prummer, *Theologia Moralis*, I, n.623.

something that is 'intrinsically evil'. The fact that today most contraceptives are abortifacients increases the gravity of this cooperation.

Pope Pius XII had already laid down this criterion authoritatively in 1950 when speaking to an international congress of pharmacists: 'Sometimes you must oppose the pressure and the petitions from clients who come to you in order to make you accomplices in their criminal intentions. You know that when a product, by its very nature and by the intention of the client, is undoubtedly destined towards a criminal end you may under no pretext or pressure concede to take part in those crimes against life, against the integrity of the individual, or against the propagation of the mental and bodily health of humanity.'[7]

It is true one must bear in mind that people can participate in selling in different degrees and with different intentions, thus giving rise to degrees of moral responsibility. The morality of selling varies according to whether the seller is the owner of the object, an intermediary, or a salaried employee. In this latter case, he does not sell in the strict sense of the word, because the object sold is not his nor is the money received. Rather, he cooperates with the seller, who is the real owner, usually only materially; indeed, traditionally in morality the cooperation of employees is considered as material cooperation.[8]

This criterion is today complicated by two factors. Firstly, contraceptives now all have an abortifacient effect in that if they fail to stop ovulation they impede implantation of the fertilized ovum in the womb. Secondly, in the UK for example, a qualified pharmacist, even if he is not the owner of the pharmacy, is expected to make his own independent professional judgements without outside pressures, and his right to do so is upheld by his own professional body. Now because of the abortifacient effect the same criterion must be applied regarding the morality of cooperation in dispensing abortifacients as is applied for cooperation in abortion itself, namely that there should be none at all because of the seriousness of the matter. Since the cooperation of the pharmacist would be proximate in that he is a necessary link in a chain that leads to a possible abortion it is illicit for any Catholic. Consequently, a proprietor, or manager with full authority in a pharmacy, or any qualified pharmacist should never dispense contraceptives. Since it is important that Catholics remain in the profession, they need to find work where they are not alone in a pharmacy and arrange with their colleagues to be exempted from any requirement to dispense contraceptives/abortifacients.

The earlier consideration which classified selling by those who are not

7. Address, 2 September 1950.   8. Prummer, op. cit., I, n.621.

owners as indirect material cooperation would, in the case of pharmaceutical products, apply at most to shop assistants who are merely passing the prescription from customer to pharmacist; it would not apply to the pharmacist himself. But even in the case of the assistants, now that contraceptives have an abortifacient effect they should avoid participation, since as we said above no cooperation should ever be tolerated in the case of abortion, because of its gravity. The same criterion would apply as for abortion itself, namely indirect material cooperation could only be considered if it caused harm to the assistant proportionate to that of the participation required (which is highly unlikely in a country like England at present). They, therefore, should and normally could, find employment in pharmacies which do not stock such products, or in alternative types of retailing.

In the particular case of England, contraceptives are provided by the State through the National Health Service, for which most doctors work. It is not, however, part of their contract to dispense contraceptives, or at least it is up to their clinical judgement and they are, therefore, at liberty to refuse to do so. Indeed, only when a sufficient number of doctors refuse to prescribe them and explain their reasons, thus giving Christian witness, will an awareness of the harmful effects and immorality of contraceptives increase. In particular cases, however, Catholic doctors who refuse to prescribe can be discriminated against in job interviews. There has indeed been a procedure set in place to require of candidates for one-handed practices (that is, practices with a single doctor) that they prescribe contraceptives; but this has never been legally enforced.

VOTING DUTIES WITH RESPECT TO IMMORAL LAWS AND TOLERANCE

It is never permissible for a Catholic to vote either in a legislative body, or a referendum, for a law that is contrary to the natural law, even to avoid a worse one, since evil may not be done that good may come. Hence, one may not vote for, nor abstain from voting against laws, relating to divorce, abortion, *in vitro* fertilization and free contraceptive advice. Once such a law has been passed, one may and should vote on amendments to mitigate its force and endeavour to contribute to its disappearance.

It is not possible to apply the principle of tolerance to laws opposed to the natural law and so attempt to justify such legislation. It is true there is a legitimate principle of tolerance which allows one not to repress a certain evil in the interests of a greater good, but the evil can never be positively authorized. Pius XII explaining the right interpretation of this principle, said:

First, anything which is not in accord with truth and the moral norm does not possess any right to exist, or be disseminated, or to be acted upon. Second, the failure to impede it by means of civil laws and sanctions may be justified in the interests of a superior, broader good. Whether this condition is verified in a given case—this is a question of fact—or not, is a matter which has to be judged in the first instance by the Catholic statesman. In making his decision he must be guided by the harmful consequences which would derive from tolerance as compared to the harmful consequences to the community which are avoided by pursuing the course of tolerance.[9]

Thus it may very well happen that, as a matter of fact, it would be inopportune to repress adultery, since among other things repression may actually undermine family life. However, adultery must never be positively authorized. Legislators must ensure that it, and parallel states of affairs, such as 'living together', are not favoured by laws on taxation, mortgages etc. Indeed, they must do all they can to promote family life and the right of children to a stable family.

The principle of tolerance must be used sparingly with regard to the civil law, because one of the factors legislators must consider in deciding whether to criminalize a course of action is the educative role of the law. It is common knowledge that many people incorrectly identify what is legal with what is moral or ethically legitimate. Pope John Paul II has said:

> the law should not be a mere recording of what is happening, but a model and stimulus for what must be done . . . .One thing is certain: there is a Christian consistency in public life; a Christian must always be a Christian, at all levels, without wavering, without giving way; in deeds and not just in name.[10]

One may neither vote, nor encourage, nor speak in favour of laws that go against natural law and are intrinsically evil. One must always foster the good that they oppose. This is often not done in a pluralist society by people who, in the name of freedom, claim to be pro-choice, but it should be clear that to go against the moral law, far from furthering freedom, sooner or later restricts it.

9. Pius XII, *Address to Italian Union of Catholic Jurists*, 1953.
10. John Paul II, *Address to Italian Women's Centre*, December 1979.

JUDGES, LAWYERS AND IMMORAL LAWS

With the growth of legislation opposed to natural law and Christian morals, difficulties are placed in the way not only of those who practice medicine, but also of those who are members of the legal profession. Like doctors, judges and lawyers may take not a passive stand on unjust laws, casting all blame on the legislators. The latter carry the principal responsibility, but those who apply or defend such laws take part in the injustice by their cooperation.

A judge may never oblige anybody to commit an intrinsically immoral act, that is, one opposed to natural law. Further, he may never expressly recognize and approve of an unjust law and, therefore, cannot pronounce a sentence which would be tantamount to such an approval. He must also avoid public scandal, that is to say, the danger of leading a significant number of people to think that a particular law, for example, pro-divorce legislation, is no longer unjust. Hence Pius XII said:

> In particular cases the Catholic judge may not pronounce, unless for motives of great moment, a sentence of civil divorce for a marriage which is valid before God and the Church. He must not forget that such a sentence, in practice, does not have civil effects only, but in reality leads rather to an erroneous belief that the present bond is broken and the new one valid and binding.[11]

However, why is it possible at all to pronounce a sentence of divorce 'for motives of great moment', and what are these motives? In answer to the first, it must be remembered that judges do not make the law but exercise an interpretative role, by applying the law to concrete cases. If grave harm were to ensue from a judge's refusal to hear a divorce case, and he could take his place on the bench, fulfilling the conditions mentioned in the preceding paragraph, then he may do so. He may issue a divorce, for example, so that the civil effects of separation be granted to the parties. He must, however, make clear that his judicial decree has no effect whatever with regard to the religious marriage, which is always unique and indissoluble.

If it is taken in this sense (as applying only to the civil effects), the decree is not intrinsically evil. However, it does render possible a subsequent civil marriage, and the judge becomes a proximate material cooperator in another's evil. It also leads to the error in the common mind of thinking that the marriage bond itself has been severed, as we noted. There must, therefore,

---

11. Pius XII, *Address to 1st National Congress of Italian Jurists*, 6 November 1949.

be a very serious reason for issuing the decree—one which is proportionate to the harm produced. Naturally, the mere fact that a judge would earn less money for refusing to handle such cases or that he would suffer detriment to his professional standing would not be a sufficient reason.

The 'motives of great moment' which might render material cooperation in divorce cases permissible include the grave common harm that could befall Catholics, or the Church in general, if Catholic judges refused to take part in the application of such legislation. They also include the danger of removal from the judges' bench and a consequent allowing the administration of justice to fall into the hands of persons of lower moral standards who might cause grave harm to society. It might be argued that the scandal which arises from judges taking part in this work is less in societies where divorce has long been legal (as in England). Nevertheless, in that country, judges may work in three separate divisions, namely, Queen's Bench, Chancery, and Family Division. Since there is freedom to choose, there would *normally* seem to be no good reason for participating in the third one.

A similar assessment applies to lawyers (solicitors and barristers) in the application of divorce legislation. Since he has freedom to accept or reject cases, a lawyer should not accept a divorce case except for grave motives, even if he is certain that, once divorced, the parties will not attempt a new marriage. It is not merely the avoidance of future possible evils which is at stake, but material cooperation in the application of an intrinsically evil law opposed to the natural law. A lawyer could not justify cooperation on the grounds of loss of earnings or of future clients. The only exception to this is where there is no possibility of legal separation and unless a divorce is obtained grave harm could result to the parties. In general, however, as with the judge, the lawyer is at liberty to exercise his profession in other areas where his conscience will not be compromised.

Work is an activity and a right which points to and increases man's dignity. But he begins to lose that dignity if his activity is carried out in opposition to the moral law and moral truth. The moral obligations of professional life are in some areas especially demanding and difficult for a Christian today. But he is asked to put his light on a lampstand and not hide it under a bed (cf. Lk 8:16). In other words, he cannot compromise his moral and Catholic principles without doing grave harm in those areas we have been examining. One wonders if society has not become as secular and non-Christian as it has because too many Christians have compromised the moral principles that flow from their faith. If a re-conversion is to take place, and the tide of secularism is to be turned, then Christians have no

alternative but to stand up and be counted, and live up to the full consequences of their beliefs, sometimes to a heroic degree, in all the professions
so as to 'restore all things in Christ' (Eph 1:10).

PART IV: ECOLOGY

Man and the Environment:
The Moral Basis of Ecology

Material and technological progress, together with man's lifestyle, have occasioned the most recent moral problem we have become aware of, namely, the erosion of the natural environment.[1] This in itself can be seen as an indication that man is not living altogether in the way he ought to. Selfish materialism, indiscriminate use of natural resources and disposal of waste are probably creating more problems than they are solving and they are damaging the world we live in, particularly for future generations. What are the Christian and moral implications of all this?

The Old Testament, and particularly Genesis, explains clearly, if in general terms, man's role in creation and why the world is in its present state; the New Testament spells out what is going to happen to the earth. The Church, however, has had little to say on the subject in modern times before this pontificate, and, in a sense, the arrival of Green issues has brought about a new awareness of the Christian principles at the root of this matter. In fact, John Paul II points out that it is a moral issue since it has to do with man's cooperation, or otherwise, with the plan of God for creation. He writes:

> The commitment of believers to a healthy environment for everyone stems directly from their belief in God the Creator, from their recognition of the effects of original and personal sin, and from the certainty of having been redeemed by Christ. Respect for life and for the dignity of the human person extends also to the rest of creation, which is called to join man in praising God (cf. Ps 148:96).[2]

Though it is a subject of common interest for Christians and non-Christians alike, the Green Movement, for the most part, cannot be said to be Christian-inspired and, although we coincide in calling the environment

1. For this topic see *Catechism of the Catholic Church*, nos. 2415-8.
2. Pope John Paul II, *New Year Message of Peace for 1990*, no. 16.

a moral problem, what the Greens mean by morality is rather different from what orthodox Christians mean by it. The result is that, while many share the Greens' concern for greater responsibility towards the environment, they find it impossible to go along with some of the more outlandish so-called 'moral' demands it makes. One thinks of their call for accepting a zero or negative growth rate, their support for 'animal rights' and prohibition on buying even secondhand fur coats etc. There seems to be no end to the 'Green' commandments!

Recent writers, including the British Government's White Paper on the Environment, see the antecedents which have given rise to the Green reaction in the Enlightenment of the seventeenth century.[3] It will be helpful to analyse this background to see why it is not Christian in origin. When Enlightenment figures spoke of 'nature' and 'the universe', they had in mind the system of the cosmos which can be progressively known, measured, calculated and, therefore, dominated by science. The cosmos has a harmony and rationality which can be better and better understood and possessed by man, thereby giving rise to constant progress. Many Enlightenment thinkers accepted Deism—a natural or rationalist religion according to which God was the Creator or Architect of the world but after creating took no interest in it, leaving its development in the hands of man and the laws of nature.

This view neglects the evidence of Christian Revelation according to which God cares for creation and conserves it in existence, leading it to its end by his Providence. To this extent, though transcendent to creation, God enters into it. What is missing in the purely secular outlook is the realization that we are secondary causes, free and responsible, acting under the universal causality of God. The rest of creation is subject to the laws of nature, which in turn participate in the eternal law.

There is another flaw in the Enlightenment concept of nature, at least as it was expressed by a writer like Rousseau. With his romanticism he tended to see creation as primitive nature (hence his idea of the noble savage) which in its pristine state was entirely good. It was progress and society, he believed, which generated evil. Sin was located primarily in society, not in man or nature. This was the meaning of his famous expression, 'Man is born free, but he is everywhere in chains.'

Rousseau lacks the notion of original sin and the harm which this sin does, not only to man but also to the natural world. The Enlightenment also produced a false view of what man is and of his difference from the non-rational animal world. It is a view whose influence is still felt today.

3. *The Common Inheritance*, HMSO, London, September 1990.

Science's view of the human being tends to make him a machine or assimilate him to the rest of nature from whom, in the eyes of many, he is indistinguishable.

GENUINE CHRISTIAN ECOLOGY

We are told in Genesis concerning each step in God's creation that it was 'good'. When he created man and woman, the refrain changes to 'God saw everything that he had made and behold it was *very* good' (Gen 1:31). Adam and Eve were given dominion over the material creation but not over human life. They were to share in God's plan by subduing their environment and developing it. Hence, we can say that the material world is for man but man is for God. There is a harmony and order in the universe; but man destroyed this harmony to some extent, by deliberately going against God's plan through sin. Apart from the death, suffering and fratricide this brought upon him, it also resulted in the earth's 'rebellion' against him and in the disharmony of nature.

Genesis goes on: 'cursed is the ground because of you . . . thorns and thistles it shall bring forth to you' (3:17-18). Hence the perfection of the world has been attenuated by man's sin. 'If man is not at peace with God, then earth itself cannot be at peace', says the Pope and he quotes the prophet Hosea: 'Therefore the land mourns and all who dwell in it languish, and also the beasts of the field and the birds of the air and even the fish of the sea are taken away' (4:3). This is the background to St Paul's teaching that the earth is groaning in travail, subject to futility and waiting to be set free in the glorious liberty of the children of God (cf. Rom 8:20-21).

God created the world with just the right balance for human life to live on it; with an ozone layer to filter the ultra-violet rays of the sun and an atmosphere to keep in sufficient of the earth's natural heat to make human life bearable, creating a natural greenhouse effect; with trees to turn the carbon dioxide back into oxygen; and fertile topsoil for the earth to give nourishment etc. Ecclesiastes speaks of the harmony of creation when it says: 'Into the sea all rivers flow, and yet the sea is never filled, and still to their goal the rivers go' (1:7). Here is a hint of what science was later to discover—that the sea vapourizes, giving rise to rain, which in turn fills the rivers again. But this balance, in its perfection, was upset by original sin and continues to be disturbed by our personal sins. It is important to understand how.

Original sin is, of course, primarily a moral evil, an offence not only against the divine law but against God himself. But it brings physical evil, death and suffering to man and, as we have seen, an adverse effect on the earth itself. Christ's Redemption reconciled mankind to the Father, who was pleased, St Paul tells us, as a consequence also 'to reconcile to himself *all things*, whether on earth or in heaven, making peace by the blood of his [Christ's] cross' (Col 1:19-20). This plan of God to unite all things in himself will take place in the fullness of time (cf. Eph 1:9-10) and bring about 'a new heaven and a new earth' (Apoc 21:1) which will consist in the transformation of the present world. The prophet Isaiah already spoke about this when he said: 'The wolf shall dwell with the lamb, and the leopard shall lie down with the kid, and the calf and the lion and the fatling together, and a little child shall lead them' (11:6-7). This suggests that the hostility within the animal kingdom and towards man is an imperfection which will be overcome and that the superiority of man will be reasserted.

THE MORAL PROBLEM

It is because of its origin in, and relationship with, sin, the struggle with it and the victory over it, that the ecological problem is a *moral* one. Sin introduced disharmony into all human relationships, namely, man with God, man with man, and man with the environment. We have learnt, in recent times, that we cannot implement advances in science and technology indiscriminately; we should not do all that we can do. Nor must we use the earth for selfish and hedonistic purposes by putting material consumerism above other more important considerations. We should be wise stewards of creation, using it to serve the Creator and all men as a whole, to whom it belongs before it belongs to any particular man, or group of men. Hence, control must be applied so that the consequences of an activity in one part of the earth's surface do not damage it in another. That is to say, we must regulate the emission of gases and industrial waste which deplete the ozone layer and contribute to the greenhouse effect, perhaps leading to the flooding of land masses, destruction of life and other types of devastation. For similar reasons, we must pay attention to the preservation of forests and wildlife species.

It is not the Church's job to give specific solutions but simply to point to general moral guidelines. The former is a task for governmental bodies, experts and the international community. Most of the decisions are not absolutes and like all temporal matters, notably politics and economics, thus fall within the sphere of the free and responsible decisions of mankind. The

Church is only interested in stating the theological basis of the problem and the moral boundaries of it. An outline of the Church's theology of the environment was contained in John Paul II's first encyclical when he said it consisted in 'the priority of ethics over technology, in the primacy of the person over things, and in the superiority of spirit over matter'. (*Redemptoris hominis*, 16).

We have spoken of the theological basis of ecology. We have seen that the world is already in an imperfect state and that, just by living in it, man destroys it to some extent. Progress means raising dust, but that does not mean for a moment that we should not seek to progress or, as many Greens want, that we should aim at zero growth rate. Indeed, the signal to progress was contained in the Genesis command. If man's stewardship is carried out wisely, we know the earth has the capacity to replenish itself. Rivers will flow into the sea and the sea eventually back into rivers, without flooding the land, provided we do not melt the ice caps. The world is like the wheat field in the gospel parable. We do not cease to grow wheat simply because weeds grow with it. Similarly, the Church is not against technological progress *per se*, which brings many benefits to mankind, such as, for example, the positive effect which the invention of underground sewers had in stamping out cholera and plagues. New drugs combat disease more effectively and X-rays diagnose it, but both of them can have serious side effects. So it is with the environment: we have to make responsible and informed choices, not extreme ones.

Christianity teaches us that man's mastery over the planet must not be motivated by a thirst for power, profit or domination but by a desire to serve. Some Green solutions are delightfully quaint, not to say hilarious, such as the decision of a well known architect to build his house in the Hebrides completely underground, since the islands are so beautiful, it is preferable that the hand of man not be seen! Others are downright dangerous, such as those who want to turn the earth into some primitive earthly paradise, *à la Rousseau*, because this implicitly, at least, denies original sin and blames all evils on 'society'. Others are prepared to put animal life and the environment above human life and are even ready to declare man and human life to be the earth's enemy.

What, then, are the moral boundaries? It must always be borne in mind that man as the image of God is at the apex of creation, and God himself transcends it. Respect for human life directed towards its last end in God is, as we have pointed out, the guiding norm of morality. There is an absolute prohibition on the deliberate destruction of human life through embryo research and genetic manipulation, and its well-being must always be the major factor in environmental decisions. Man may not use the earth for his own schemes of power, grandeur, selfishness, enrichment or any sort of unscrupulous exploitation, nor must he treat the world as an end in itself. He must treat it responsibly, with wisdom and love.

Pope John Paul II has spoken in this vein:

> Modern society will find no solution to the ecological problem unless it takes a serious look at its life style. In many parts of the world society is given to instant gratification and consumerism while remaining indifferent to the damage which these cause. As I have already stated, the seriousness of the ecological issue lays bare the depth of man's moral crisis. If an appreciation of the value of the human person and of human life is lacking, we will also lose interest in others and in the earth itself. Simplicity, moderation and discipline, as well as a spirit of sacrifice, must become a part of everyday life, lest all suffer the negative consequences of the careless habits of a few.[4]

This leads us to ask what man's mastery of the earth consists in—more specifically and positively. If the earth is for man and man is for God, then man must contribute to ordering the world around him to God. The Church teaches that he has this 'kingly' power and authority over the material world, but authority for a Christian is exercised as service. He must, therefore, serve creation according to God's plan for it and for himself. It is work which shows man's dominion over the created world and which in the new economy of the Redemption becomes a redeemed and redeeming reality, and a means of sanctification for man when it is ordered to God, as Blessed Josemariá Escrivá tirelessly taught.[5] Cain and Abel brought to God an offering of their work. One was accepted and the other rejected. There is, therefore, a right and a wrong way of working. Work done properly is a participation in the creation and, for a Christian, in the Redemption; hence it contributes to the renewal of the earth. This includes, in addition to what we have already said, concern for the beauty of the natural world and rational town planning so that we create surroundings for man to live in which are worthy of human dignity.

By his work being done in a moral and spiritual way, man contributes to 'restoring all things in Christ' (Eph 1:10). However, although man plays his part in contributing to the renewal of the world, this will only come about in

4. John Paul II, *New Year Message of Peace for 1990*, no.13.
5. *Christ Is Passing By*, Dublin, 1973, no. 47.

a proper sense at the Parousia, or Second Coming of Christ. At the same time, man's quest for Christian perfection inevitably improves human life, because it harmonizes with the true good of the human person.

It is clear from the New Testament references to the end of the world and its renewal that this will involve the destruction, to a great extent, of the present world although, at the same time, this is to be the basis of the 'new heaven and the new earth'.[6] As *Gaudium et spes*, 39, explains:

> We do not know the time of the consummation of the earth and of humanity, nor do we know how the universe will be transformed. The figure of this world, deformed by sin, is passing away . . . . [But] all the good fruits of our nature and our effort (after we have spread them on earth in the Spirit of the Lord and according to his command) we will find again . . . transfigured when Christ hands over to the Father the kingdom . . . of truth and life . . . now on this earth present in mystery, and to be consummated when the Lord comes.

St Augustine liked to repeat:

> I think about the earth and I see that it was created. Its beauty is great but it had a Creator. I look at the vastness of the sea surrounding us, it amazes me and I admire it, but I seek out its Creator. I raise my eyes to heaven, I admire the beauty of the stars and the sun's splendour; I see the moon; they are marvellous all of them: I admire them, I exalt in them, but I thirst for the One who created them.[7]

The Pope went on to comment: 'God is the maker of all things. It is he whom we seek also when we make efforts to construct a more beautiful world: he is the changeless Truth and Being without defect. The visible world, changeable and limited, cannot totally fulfil the expectations of the human mind and heart.'[8]

Only through man's reconciliation with God can harmony be restored to the universe, and only through Christ can man be reconciled to God. When final union with God is achieved, the integrity of man's being and the balance of nature will return to the order they enjoyed at the time of creation. Thus, the ecological problem is intimately connected with man and his transcendent vocation and, therefore, moral life. As de Lubac put it,

6. See Mt 24, Lk 21, Rom 8:23, 1 Cor 15, Apoc 21.
7. St Augustine, *Commentary on Ps 41*.
8. *Osservatore Romano*, 8 October 1990.

'The truth of his [man's] being transcends his being itself.'[9] A human life is made up of many mediate and intermediate ends, but there can only be one final end. Man is called to keep this end in view and conquer the threefold lust so as to enjoy the 'glorious freedom of the sons of God' (Rom 8:21). Sin and concupiscence will only be finally overcome by the 'redemption of the body' (Rom 8:22) and of the whole material world. The ultimate goal of the universe will be attained when each person receives his or her spiritualized body from the One who says, 'Behold I make all things new' (Apoc 21:5).

9. H. de Lubac, *Catholicism*, London, 1961, p. 202.

Sources

Dates etc. of some official Catholic Church documents
mentioned in the text

Second Vatican Council
Dignitatis humanae, Declaration on Religious Liberty, 7 December 1965
Gaudium et spes, Pastoral Constitution on the Church in the Modern World,
7 December 1965
Optatam totius, Decree on the Training of Priests, 28 October 1965

Paul VI
Humanae vitae, Encyclical Letter, 25 July 1968

John Paul II
Christifideles laici, Post-Synodal Apostolic Exhortation, 20 December
1988
Evangelium vitae, Encyclical Letter on the Value and Inviolability of
Human Life, 25 March 1995
Familiaris consortio, Apostolic Exhortation on the Role of the Christian
Family in the Modern World, 22 November 1981
Veritatis splendor, Encyclical Letter on Fundamental Questions of the
Church's Moral Teaching, 6 August 1993

Sacred Congregation for the Doctrine of the Faith
Donum vitae, Instruction on Respect for Human Life in its Origin and on
the Dignity of Procreation, 22 February 1987

and
Catechism of the Catholic Church, Rome, 1992; first English language
edition, 1994

Index

twinning, monozygotic, 134

ultimate good, 34
unity of life, 33
   of man, 32-4
usury, 49
Utilitarianism, 15, 17, 19, 20, 22, 76-8,
   78, 81, 138, 156

ventilator, see life-support machine
Veritatis splendor, 33, 37-8n, 39, 40-1n,
   49, 58, 59, 60, 79, 107

viability of embryo, 133-5
Vienne, Council of, 119
violence to children, 136
voting on moral issues, 186-7

Wallerstein, J., 125
Warnock Report on embryology, 18,
   168, 176
World Health Organization, 99
World Medical Association, 18

zygote, 134, 174

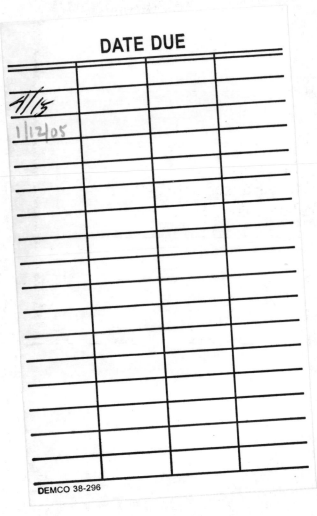